ideals
Christmas Cookbook Treasury

From the kitchens of IDEALS, we bring
you the three following best selling cookbooks
combined in one single volume for your
holiday enjoyment:

Book I   Christmas Cookbook

Book II   Gourmet Christmas Cookbook
          by Naomi Arbit and June Turner

Book III Christmas Kitchen Cookbook

Bonanza Books
New York, N.Y.

CONTENTS

Book I Christmas Cookbook

Book II Gourmet Christmas Cookbook

Book III Christmas Kitchen Cookbook

ISBN: 0-517-329131
THE IDEALS CHRISTMAS COOKBOOK
Copyright © IDEALS PUBLISHING CORPORATION MCMLXXV
CHRISTMAS GIFTS FROM THE KITCHEN
Copyright © IDEALS PUBLISHING CORPORATION MCMLXXVI
HAVE A GOURMET CHRISTMAS!
Copyright © NAOMI ARBIT AND JUNE TURNER MCMLXXVIII
ALL RIGHTS RESERVED.

THIS EDITION IS PUBLISHED BY BONANZA BOOKS,
A DIVISION OF CROWN PUBLISHERS, INC.,
BY ARRANGEMENT WITH IDEALS PUBLISHING CORPORATION.
a b c d e f g h
BONANZA 1980 EDITION

MANUFACTURED IN THE UNITED STATES OF AMERICA

Book I

Christmas
COOKBOOK

Appetizers

Sandwich Wreath

20 party rye slices
20 party pumpernickel slices
  Butter or margarine, softened

Spread bread with butter. Spread 10 slices of rye bread with Deviled Ham Spread; the remaining 10 slices with Chicken Salad Spread. Top sandwiches with the pumpernickel slices. To form wreath, arrange sandwiches around rim of a round plate. Decorate with a velvet or satin bow.

Deviled Ham Spread

1 4½-ounce can deviled ham
¼ cup chopped celery
½ teaspoon Worcestershire sauce

Combine all ingredients.

Chicken Salad Spread

1 4¾-ounce can chicken spread
¼ cup chopped apples
1 tablespoon sour cream

Combine all ingredients.

Glazed Meatballs

Makes 5 dozen meatballs.

1 pound lean ground beef
½ cup dry bread crumbs
⅓ cup minced onion
¼ cup milk
1 egg
1 tablespoon snipped parsley
1 teaspoon salt
⅛ teaspoon black pepper
½ teaspoon Worcestershire sauce
¼ cup shortening
1 12-ounce bottle chili sauce
1 10-ounce jar grape jelly

Mix beef, crumbs, onion, milk, egg, and next 4 seasonings. Gently shape into 1-inch balls. Melt shortening in a large skillet; brown meatballs. Remove meatballs from skillet; drain off fat. Heat chili sauce and jelly in skillet until jelly is melted, stirring constantly. Add meatballs and stir until coated. Simmer 30 minutes. Serve hot in a chafing dish.

Note: Put toothpicks in a few of the meatballs and place a dish of toothpicks beside chafing dish.

Creamy Cheese Ball

1 8-ounce package cream cheese, softened
2 cups (8 ounces) crumbled blue cheese
⅓ cup flaked coconut
1 teaspoon finely grated onion
1 teaspoon Worcestershire sauce
¼ cup flaked coconut
¼ cup chopped pecans
¼ cup minced parsley

Combine cheeses; cream well. Blend in the ⅓ cup coconut, onion, and Worcestershire sauce. Cover and chill at least 6 hours. Before serving time, combine remaining ingredients on piece of waxed paper. Form cheese mixture into a ball and roll in the coconut, pecan, parsley mixture until completely covered. Place on a platter. Serve with crackers.

Basic Fondue

½ pound American cheese, cubed
½ pound Colby cheese, cubed
1 cup milk (or ¾ cup milk and ¼ cup white wine)

Combine all ingredients and simmer, stirring often. Add milk or wine mixture to thin as necessary. For dipping, use cubed French bread, ham cubes, small meatballs, mushrooms, tiny onions, cauliflowerets, large shell macaroni, and wiener puffs.

Note: To make wiener puffs, cut wieners into ¾-inch pieces. Bring to a boil in a little water. This will cause them to puff up.

Party Wieners

Makes ¾ cup sauce.

Frankfurters, Vienna sausages or cocktail wieners
⅓ cup prepared mustard
½ cup currant jelly

Cut meat into bite-size pieces. Mix mustard and jelly in a 1-quart saucepan. Add meat. Cover and simmer for 10 minutes. Serve on toothpicks with crackers.

Cheese Buds

Makes 60 cheese buds.

2 cups flour
½ pound butter or margarine, softened
½ pound grated cheese, room temperature
Salt and ground red pepper to taste
Pecan halves

Blend flour, butter, cheese, and seasonings. Pinch off small bits the size of a half dollar and place on a cookie sheet. Top with a pecan half. Bake at 400° for 15 minutes or until brown. Cool.

Chicken Livers in Sherry

½ cup butter
2 pounds chicken livers, halved
1½ teaspoons salt, divided
¼ cup minced onion
¼ cup sherry or white wine
½ teaspoon Tabasco sauce

Heat butter in a large skillet. Add half of the liver; sprinkle with ¾ teaspoon salt. Brown quickly on both sides. Place in a chafing dish. Add remaining liver to skillet and sprinkle with remaining ¾ teaspoon salt. Brown and place in chafing dish. Add onion to skillet; cook until tender but not brown. Stir in sherry and Tabasco sauce; heat, stirring occasionally, until all drippings are loosened from the pan. Pour into chafing dish. Heat, stirring frequently, 10 minutes or until livers are done. Serve with cocktail picks.

Appetizer Cheese Tray

A simple cheese tray is one of the easiest of appetizers to create. Begin with a centerpiece of club cheese in its attractive brown crock. Surround with slices of tangy blue or smoky provolone. Add cubes of brick, Monterey Jack or Muenster cheese. Slices or wedges of Cheddar and Colby cheese, along with Swiss, add to an interesting selection. Garnish with crisp vegetables such as radishes, cucumber slices, celery, and carrot sticks and olives. Crackers and sesame sticks add contrast. For special occasions, make balls of Edam and serve in the cheese's own bright red shell.

Tomato Teaser

1 pint cherry tomatoes
½ pound bacon, cooked and crumbled
¼ teaspoon Tabasco sauce

Cut small hole in the top of each tomato. Combine bacon and Tabasco sauce. Spoon mixture into tomatoes. Serve on toothpicks.

Shrimp Mold

1 10¾-ounce can tomato soup
1 8-ounce package cream cheese
2 envelopes unflavored gelatin, softened in ½ cup cold water
½ cup minced onion
½ cup chopped celery
½ cup chopped green pepper
1 cup mayonnaise
3 cans small shrimp

Combine soup and cream cheese in top of double boiler; heat until blended. Add remaining ingredients; mix well. Pour into a greased mold. Chill 24 hours. Unmold and serve with crackers or rye bread rounds.

Beverages

Hot Apricot Grog

Makes 7½ cups.

    1 46-ounce can apricot nectar
    2 tablespoons lemon juice
 1½ cups brandy
       Lemon slices
       Whole cloves

Pour apricot nectar, lemon juice, and brandy into a large saucepan. Bring to a simmer. Ladle into mugs or punch cups. Garnish each serving with a lemon slice studded with a clove.

Cranberry Punch

Makes 30 servings.

    4 cups cranberry juice
 1½ cups sugar
    4 cups pineapple juice
    1 tablespoon almond extract
    2 quarts ginger ale

Combine first 4 ingredients. Stir until sugar is dissolved; chill. Add ginger ale just before serving.

Christmas Cider

Makes 16 servings.

    2 quarts apple cider
    1 cup brown sugar
    3 3-inch sticks cinnamon
    1 teaspoon whole cloves
    1 teaspoon salt

Heat cider to boiling. Lower heat; add remaining ingredients. Simmer 15 minutes. Strain and serve.

Festive Punch

    1 package fruit-flavored Kool-Aid
 1½ cups sugar
    1 6-ounce can unsweetened frozen orange juice
    1 6-ounce can frozen pink lemonade

Add all ingredients, one at a time, to a gallon jar; add water to make 1 gallon. Stir until dissolved.

Traditional Eggnog

Makes 25 to 30 servings.

  12 eggs, separated
    1 cup sugar
    1 quart milk
    2 cups bourbon
    1 cup Jamaica rum
    1 quart whipping cream, whipped
       Nutmeg

Beat egg yolks slightly. Gradually add sugar; beat until smooth. Pour in milk, bourbon, and rum; stir until well mixed. Beat egg whites until they form stiff peaks; fold egg whites and whipped cream into yolk mixture, gently but thoroughly. Serve cold with freshly grated nutmeg on top.

Punch Cubes

       Juice of 2 lemons
       Juice of 2 oranges
    2 bananas, mashed
    1 cup canned crushed pineapple and juice
  ¾ cup sugar
    1 cup water

Combine all ingredients; blend well. Pour into ice cube trays and freeze. To serve, place 3 or 4 cubes in a glass and pour chilled ginger ale over cubes. Garnish with a maraschino cherry or mint leaves, if desired.

Wassail

Makes 1 quart.

 1½ cups sugar
    4 cups boiling water
    3 whole allspice
    6 whole cloves
    1 tablespoon ground ginger
    1 1-inch stick cinnamon
 1⅓ cups orange juice
  ⅔ cup lemon juice

Combine sugar and 2 cups of the boiling water; boil 5 minutes. Add spices, cover and let stand 1 hour. Add remaining water and fruit juices; mix well. Strain. Heat to boiling. Serve immediately.

Soups

Cream of Potato Soup

 5 large potatoes, pared and sliced
½ cup sliced carrots
 6 slices bacon, cooked and crumbled, drain reserving 2 tablespoons fat
 1 cup chopped onion
 1 cup sliced celery
1½ teaspoons salt
¼ teaspoon white pepper
 2 cups milk
 2 cups light cream or evaporated milk
   Cheddar cheese, shredded
   Parsley

Cook potatoes and carrots in boiling water until tender. Drain. Sauté onion and celery in the 2 tablespoons bacon fat. Combine all ingredients except cheese and parsley. Simmer 30 minutes. Garnish each serving with Cheddar cheese and parsley.

Pimiento Bisque

2½ tablespoons butter or margarine
2½ tablespoons flour
 5 cups milk
½ teaspoon grated onion
¾ cup chopped pimiento
   Salt and pepper to taste

Melt butter in a saucepan; add flour and mix well. Add milk. Cook until thick, stirring constantly. Add onion, pimiento, salt and pepper. Heat, stirring occasionally. Do not boil.

Ham Bone Soup

 1 trimmed ham bone
 6 quarts water
 1 medium can tomatoes
 1 teaspoon dried parsley
 2 ribs celery, sliced
 3 peppercorns
 2 tablespoons barley
 3 carrots, sliced
   Salt
½ head cabbage, cut up
 2 large potatoes, diced

Place ham bone in a two-gallon kettle; add water, tomatoes, parsley, celery, peppercorns, barley, carrots, and salt to taste. Boil for 2 hours. Add cabbage and potatoes; cook 30 minutes.

Note: More carrots, cabbage, and a little catsup can be used to improve the flavor. The ham bone does not need to be trimmed too much, as all parts of ham add to the flavor.

Beef Tingler

Makes 5½ cups.

 2 10¾-ounce cans condensed beef broth
 2 10¾-ounce soup cans water
¼ cup brandy
¼ cup whipping cream
⅛ teaspoon vanilla extract
   Dash nutmeg
⅛ teaspoon grated orange rind

Combine soup, water, and brandy in a saucepan. Heat, stirring occasionally. In a separate bowl, combine cream, vanilla, and nutmeg; beat until cream just mounds. Fold in orange rind. Serve on soup.

Oyster Bisque

 1 dozen large raw oysters, shucked, diced, drained, reserve 1 cup liquor
 3 cups milk
 1 cup heavy cream
 1 slice onion
 2 ribs celery
 1 sprig parsley
 1 bay leaf
⅓ cup butter or margarine, melted
⅓ cup flour
1¾ teaspoons salt
½ teaspoon Tabasco sauce
   Chopped chives

Place oysters and liquor in a saucepan. Bring to a boil over low heat. Pour into a bowl and set aside. In the saucepan scald milk and cream with onion, celery, parsley, and bay leaf. Strain. Blend butter, flour, salt, and Tabasco sauce. Slowly stir in scalded milk. Stir over low heat until thick. Add oysters and liquor. Heat and serve with chopped chives.

Tossed Mushroom Salad

Makes 12 servings.

    1 head romaine lettuce
    ¼ pound mushrooms, sliced
    ¼ cup lemon juice
    1 quart chicory, cut into bite-size pieces
    1 quart escarole, cut into bite-size pieces
    2 to 3 heads endive, cut into bite-size pieces

Arrange romaine leaves with ends up around the sides of a large salad bowl; set aside. Place mushrooms in a separate bowl; sprinkle with lemon juice. Drain. Combine chicory, escarole, and endive with mushrooms. Shake Dressing and pour over salad greens and mushrooms; toss. Place in salad bowl.

Dressing

    ⅔ cup salad oil
    ½ cup tarragon vinegar
    2 tablespoons sugar
    2 teaspoons garlic salt
    1 teaspoon seasoned salt
    ¼ teaspoon pepper

Combine all ingredients in a covered jar; shake to mix. Refrigerate 30 minutes before using.

Yuletide Salad

    2½ cups crushed pineapple, drained, reserve juice
    1 3-ounce package lemon-flavored gelatin
    1 3-ounce package pineapple-flavored gelatin
    ½ pound miniature marshmallows
    1 8-ounce package cream cheese, softened
    1 cup mayonnaise
    1 4-ounce jar maraschino cherries, minced
    1 cup whipping cream, whipped
    1 3-ounce package strawberry-flavored gelatin

Add hot water to pineapple juice to make 4 cups. Stir in lemon and pineapple gelatins until dissolved. Stir in marshmallows; cool. Add cream cheese, mayonnaise, pineapple, and cherries to the whipped cream. Combine with cooled gelatin. Pour into mold; chill until set. Prepare strawberry gelatin according to package directions. Cool and spoon onto lemon-pineapple salad. Chill until firm.

Shrimp Salad Louis

Makes 4 servings.

    1 cup mayonnaise
    ¼ cup French dressing
    ¼ cup catsup
    1 teaspoon horseradish
    ½ teaspoon salt
    1 teaspoon Worcestershire sauce
    ½ teaspoon Tabasco sauce
    1 pound shrimp, cleaned and cooked
      Shredded lettuce

Combine mayonnaise, French dressing, catsup, horseradish, salt, Worcestershire sauce, and Tabasco sauce. Add shrimp; mix well. Serve on shredded lettuce.

Note: 1 7½-ounce can crabmeat may be added to shrimp in salad.

Christmas Ribbon Salad

First Layer

    2 3-ounce packages lime-flavored gelatin
    2½ cups hot water

Combine gelatin and hot water; stir until gelatin dissolves. Pour into a 9 x 13-inch pan. Chill until firm.

Second Layer

    ½ cup pineapple juice
    20 large marshmallows, cut up
    1 3-ounce package lemon-flavored gelatin
    1½ cups hot water
    1 8-ounce package cream cheese, softened

Combine pineapple juice and marshmallows in a saucepan. Heat until the marshmallows melt. Dissolve the gelatin in hot water. Combine the hot marshmallow mixture, gelatin, and cream cheese; mix well. Cool and pour over the first layer. Chill until firm.

Third Layer

    1 3-ounce package cherry-flavored gelatin
    1 3-ounce package red raspberry-flavored gelatin
    2½ cups hot water

Combine all ingredients; mix until gelatin dissolves. Cool and pour over the second layer. Chill until firm. Cut in 2- or 3-inch squares to serve.

Gelatin Christmas Trees

    1 3-ounce package lime-flavored gelatin
    1 cup boiling water
    1 envelope unflavored gelatin
    ½ cup cold water
    1 16-ounce can fruit cocktail and juice
    9 pointed paper cups

Dissolve lime gelatin in the boiling water. Soften unflavored gelatin in the cold water; add to first mixture and stir well. Add fruit cocktail and juice; stir. Cool at room temperature. Rinse the paper cups with water and stand in glasses, pointed side down. Pour cool gelatin mixture into cups. Chill until firm. To serve carefully unwrap the paper cup. Place gelatin tree on salad plate. Surround with cottage cheese or sour cream.

Note: Trees may be decorated with sour cream or whipped cream in a decorating tube, if desired.

Jellied Tomato Salad

Makes 6 servings.

    1 tablespoon unflavored gelatin
    ¼ cup cold water
    2½ cups fresh or canned tomatoes
    1 tablespoon minced onion
    ½ small bay leaf
    ½ teaspoon sugar
    ½ teaspoon salt
       Pepper to taste
    1 tablespoon lemon juice
    ½ cup minced cucumber
    ½ cup minced celery
       Lettuce or salad greens

Soften gelatin in cold water. Cook tomatoes, onion, and bay leaf (about 20 minutes for fresh tomatoes, 10 minutes for canned) in a saucepan. Press tomatoes through a sieve. Measure 1¾ cups, adding boiling water, if needed to fill measure. Add hot, sieved tomatoes to gelatin; stir until gelatin dissolves. Stir in sugar, salt, pepper, and lemon juice. Chill. When slightly thickened, add cucumber and celery; mix well. Pour into a mold rinsed in cold water. Chill until firm. Unmold onto a bed of lettuce.

Eggnog Holiday Salad

    2 envelopes unflavored gelatin
    1 16-ounce can fruit cocktail, drained, reserve juice
    1 11-ounce can mandarin oranges, cut in half
    1 cup flaked coconut
    2½ cups dairy eggnog
       Dash nutmeg
       Maraschino cherries, halved, optional

Soften gelatin in fruit cocktail juice and melt over hot water. Combine with rest of ingredients. Place in a 5-cup mold; refrigerate until firm.

Creamy Fruit Salad

    1 8-ounce package cream cheese, softened
    ½ cup mayonnaise
    1 small can crushed pineapple, drained
    1 4-ounce jar green cherries, drained
    1 4-ounce jar red cherries, drained
    2 cups miniature marshmallows
    1 cup chopped walnuts
    1 cup whipping cream, whipped

Blend cream cheese and mayonnaise. Add fruit, marshmallows, and nuts. Fold in whipped cream. Chill before serving.

Noel Apple Salad

    6 apples
    ⅛ cup lemon juice
    1½ cups chopped dates
    1 4-ounce jar green maraschino cherries, drained and chopped
    1 4-ounce jar red maraschino cherries, drained and chopped
    ¾ cup chopped walnuts
       Granulated sugar
    1 cup sour cream

Partially peel apples, leaving some skin on for color; quarter and coarsely chop. Sprinkle lemon juice on apples to prevent discoloring; toss thoroughly. In another bowl combine the dates, cherries, and nuts. Sprinkle apples with sugar. Refrigerate both bowls of fruit. Just before serving, mix all together, adding as much sour cream as desired for dressing.

Poinsettia Salad

Place a slice of pineapple on a lettuce leaf. Arrange a few strips of pimiento on pineapple. Place a marshmallow in the center; top with a nut. Serve with salad dressing.

Purple Lady Salad

    2 3-ounce packages strawberry-flavored gelatin
    1 cup boiling water
    1 small can crushed pineapple, undrained
    1 can blueberries in heavy syrup, undrained
    1 banana, chopped, optional
    1 cup prepared whipped topping
    ½ cup chopped nuts

Dissolve gelatin in boiling water. Add pineapple and blueberries with syrup, and banana. Refrigerate until thick. Fold in whipped topping and nuts.

Christmas Wreath

    1 3-ounce package lime-flavored gelatin
    1 cup boiling water
    1 20-ounce can sliced pineapple, drained, reserve syrup
       Maraschino cherries
    1 3-ounce package red, fruit-flavored gelatin
    1½ cups boiling water
    1 16-ounce can whole cranberry sauce
    1 cup whipping cream, whipped
    1 cup salad dressing

Dissolve lime gelatin in the 1 cup boiling water; add pineapple syrup. Pour into a 6-cup ring mold. Place pineapple slices in mold, slightly overlapping; place a cherry in the center of each slice. Chill until almost set. Dissolve red gelatin in the 1½ cups boiling water and chill until partially set. Add cranberry sauce. Spoon over green layer. Chill until firm. Combine whipped cream and salad dressing. Unmold gelatin ring onto a serving platter. Place dressing in center of mold.

Cranberry Whipped Cream Salad

Makes 8 to 10 servings.

    1 8¼-ounce can crushed pineapple, drained, reserve syrup
    1 3-ounce package raspberry-flavored gelatin
    1 16-ounce can whole cranberry sauce
    1 teaspoon grated orange peel
    1 11-ounce can mandarin orange sections, drained
    1 cup whipping cream, whipped

Add enough water to pineapple syrup to make 1 cup. Heat syrup in a saucepan. Dissolve gelatin in hot syrup. Stir in cranberry sauce and orange peel. Chill until partially set. Fold in mandarin oranges and pineapple. Fold in whipped cream. Pour into a 6-cup mold. Chill until firm. Unmold.

Note: May be garnished with green grapes and cranberries rolled in egg white and lime- and raspberry-flavored gelatin.

Fruit Salad Dressing

    1 can sweetened condensed milk
    2 eggs
    ½ teaspoon dry mustard
    ½ teaspoon salt
    ¾ cup vinegar

Pour milk in a mixing bowl. Add eggs, mustard, and salt; beat slightly. Add vinegar and beat well. Store in refrigerator.

Cauliflower Salad

Makes 8 servings.

    1 medium cauliflower, broken into flowerets
    ½ cup French dressing
    1 small avocado, diced
    ½ cup sliced stuffed green olives
    3 tomatoes, cut in eighths
    ½ cup crumbled Roquefort cheese
       Crisp salad greens

Cover cauliflowerets with ice water; chill 1 hour. Drain. Add dressing and let stand 2 hours. Just before serving, add avocado, olives, tomatoes, and cheese. Toss lightly. Serve on crisp greens.

Herbed Cucumbers

Makes 4 servings.

- 2 tablespoons salad oil
- 1 teaspoon salt
- 2 cucumbers, thinly sliced
- 1 small onion, sliced
- 2 tablespoons water
- ½ teaspoon Tabasco sauce
- 2 tablespoons chopped fresh thyme

Heat oil with salt in a skillet. Add cucumbers and onion. Cook over medium heat, stirring constantly, about 3 minutes. Add water, Tabasco sauce, and thyme. Cover. Cook, shaking skillet occasionally, about 2 minutes or until tender-crisp.

Minted Peas

- 1 20-ounce can peas, drained, reserve liquid
- ½ teaspoon salt
- ¼ teaspoon pepper
- 1 tablespoon margarine
- ⅓ cup mint jelly

Cook liquid from peas until ¼ cup remains. Add remaining ingredients. Simmer and serve.

Cottage Cheese-Asparagus Mousse

Makes 6 to 8 servings.

- 1 envelope unflavored gelatin
- ¼ cup water
- 1 15-ounce can cut green asparagus spears, drained, reserve liquid
- 1½ cups cottage cheese, sieved
- 2 tablespoons lemon juice
- ½ teaspoon prepared mustard
- ½ teaspoon salt
- 1 cup chopped blanched almonds

Sprinkle gelatin over water to soften. Add enough water to asparagus liquid to make 1 cup. In a 1-quart saucepan, heat liquid to boiling. Stir in softened gelatin until dissolved; cool slightly. In a bowl combine cottage cheese, lemon juice, mustard, salt, almonds, and asparagus. Add gelatin mixture. Pour into a 4-cup salad mold. Chill until firm. Unmold on salad greens.

Creamed Celery with Almonds

- 4 cups sliced celery
- 1 10¾-ounce can cream of celery soup
- ½ cup milk
- 1 teaspoon instant minced onion
- 1 tablespoon minced parsley or chives
- 1 tablespoon minced pimiento
- ½ cup toasted diced almonds

Cook celery in boiling salted water for 5 minutes. Drain. Combine next 5 ingredients; add to celery. Pour into a 1½-quart casserole. Sprinkle almonds over top. Bake at 350° for 20 minutes or until heated and lightly browned.

Delicious Potatoes

- ½ cup butter or margarine
- 1½ cups milk
- 6 medium-size potatoes, grated
- ¼ green pepper, grated
- ¼ sweet red pepper, grated (or ¼ cup chopped pimiento)
- 5 green onions with tops, chopped
- 1 teaspoon salt

Preheat oven to 250°. Heat butter and milk in a small saucepan until butter melts. Do not boil. Combine grated potatoes, peppers, onions, and salt in a 1½-quart casserole. Pour on milk. Bake 4 hours, adding more milk if necessary.

Note: Leftover portion may be pan fried for breakfast.

Candied Sweet Potatoes

- 1 cup orange juice
- 2 tablespoons butter, melted
- ½ cup white sugar
- ½ cup brown sugar
- 1 tablespoon cornstarch
- 2 1-pound cans sweet potatoes, halved or quartered

Combine all ingredients except the potatoes; mix well. Place potatoes in a greased casserole. Pour mixture over potatoes. Bake at 325° for 1 hour.

Note: To cook on top of stove prepare syrup, add potatoes and heat to serving temperature.

Glazed Carrots

⅓ cup sugar
1 tablespoon flour
2 teaspoons grated orange rind
¾ cup orange juice
3 cups cooked carrots

Combine sugar, flour, orange rind, and orange juice in a small saucepan. Cook and stir over low heat until thick. Pour over carrots.

Sweet Potato Balls

Makes 12 balls.

6 medium sweet potatoes, cooked, peeled and mashed
½ cup margarine
1 cup brown sugar
1 cup chopped pecans or walnuts
12 large marshmallows
2 cups crushed cornflakes

Mix sweet potatoes with margarine, sugar, and nuts. Form a ball around 1 marshmallow; roll in crushed cornflakes. Just before serving, warm balls in a 350° oven 15 minutes, or until marshmallow has softened or melted.

Note: Balls may be made ahead of time and refrigerated or frozen for later use.

Broccoli with Stuffing

2 eggs, beaten
1 onion, minced
1 10¾-ounce can mushroom soup
½ cup mayonnaise
2 10-ounce packages frozen broccoli, cooked and drained
1 cup grated Cheddar cheese
1 package herbed stuffing mix, prepared
¼ cup butter or margarine, melted

Combine eggs, onion, soup, and mayonnaise. Place a layer of broccoli in a 2-quart casserole. Add a layer of cheese. Pour a small amount of sauce over top. Repeat layers until all ingredients are used. Top with stuffing mix. Sprinkle butter over top. Bake at 350° for 30 minutes.

Squash Puffs

Makes 6 servings.

1 quart frozen yellow squash
½ cup water
½ teaspoon salt
¼ cup milk
3 tablespoons flour
1 tablespoon light brown sugar
½ teaspoon ground nutmeg
⅛ teaspoon ground black peppr
2 large eggs, beaten

Place squash in a saucepan with water and salt; cook until tender. Combine squash with remaining ingredients and mix well. Place into a buttered 1-quart casserole. Bake at 350° for 35 minutes.

Beets Russe

2 cups hot cubed beets
½ cup French dressing
1 cup sour cream, whipped
½ cup minced green onion

Mix beets with dressing. Place in a serving dish. Top with sour cream; sprinkle with minced onion.

Fruited Rice

Makes 6 servings.

1 cup sliced carrots
3 tablespoons vegetable oil
1 cup sliced green onions
2 cups unpeeled apple slices
3 cups cooked brown rice
1 teaspoon salt
½ cup seedless raisins
1 tablespoon sesame seed

Sauté carrots in the oil about 10 minutes. Add onions and apples. Cook 10 minutes. Stir in rice, salt, and raisins. Cook, stirring constantly, until rice is heated through. Add sesame seed and toss lightly.

Casseroles

Corn Bake

Makes 7 servings.

- 3 1-pound cans whole kernel corn, drained
- 1 cup milk
- 2 eggs
- ½ cup ground ham
- ¼ cup grated cheese
- 1 slice bread, ground
- 2 tablespoons minced onion, optional
  - Salt and pepper to taste
- 1½ cups bread cubes
- 2 to 3 tablespoons butter, melted
- 1 tablespoon grated Parmesan cheese

Combine first 8 ingredients; pour into a greased 10 x 6-inch baking pan. Mix bread cubes with melted butter and place over top. Sprinkle with grated Parmesan cheese. Place pan on a baking sheet and bake at 350° for 25 minutes.

Note: Chopped peppers may also be used for added color and flavor, if desired.

Sweet Potato Casserole

Makes 6 to 8 servings.

- 3 medium sweet potatoes
- ½ cup margarine
- 1 cup brown sugar
  - Milk
- ⅛ teaspoon ground cinnamon
- ⅛ teaspoon ground nutmeg
- 1 teaspoon salt
- ½ cup toasted, salted pecans

Cook potatoes until tender. Drain and mash. Add margarine, brown sugar, and enough milk to make soupy. Add cinnamon, nutmeg, and salt. Mix and place in a casserole. Pour Topping over potatoes. Sprinkle with nuts. Bake at 400° until bubbly.

Topping

- 2 tablespoons margarine
- ½ cup sugar
- ⅛ cup milk
- 1 teaspoon vanilla extract

Melt margarine in a small saucepan. Add sugar and milk. Cook until thick and bubbly; cool. Add vanilla and beat well.

Yuletide Scalloped Onions

Makes 8 servings.

- 2 pounds small white onions
- ¼ cup butter or margarine
- ¼ cup flour
- 2 cups milk
- ½ teaspoon salt
- ¼ teaspoon pepper
- 1 cup grated sharp cheese
- ¼ cup chopped pimiento
- ¼ cup chopped parsley
- ½ cup bread crumbs
- 1 tablespoon butter, softened

Peel onions and cook in salted water 15 minutes until just tender; drain. Place in a baking dish. Melt ¼ cup butter; add flour and blend until smooth, cooking 3 minutes. Heat milk and slowly stir into flour mixture. Bring just to a boil and cook 5 minutes, stirring constantly with wire whip. Add salt and pepper. Stir in cheese until melted; add pimiento and parsley. Pour over onions. Mix crumbs with softened butter. Sprinkle on top around edges. Bake at 375° for 15 minutes or until brown.

English Pea and Chestnut Casserole

- ½ cup butter
- 1 small onion, minced
- 2 tablespoons chopped green pepper
- 1 cup sliced celery
- 2 cans peas, drained
- 1 can sliced water chestnuts, drained
- 2 pimientos, diced
- 1 10¾-ounce can cream of mushroom soup, undiluted
  - Buttered cracker crumbs

Melt butter in a heavy skillet. Add onion, green pepper, and celery; sauté over medium heat, stirring often until soft. Remove from heat; add peas and chestnuts. Fold in pimientos. Arrange ½ of the vegetable mixture in the bottom of a 2-quart buttered casserole; top with ½ of the soup. Repeat layers. Sprinkle with buttered cracker crumbs. Bake at 350° for 30 minutes.

Chicken and Sweet Potato Bake

    3 chicken breasts, split or 1 fryer, cut up
 ¼ cup flour
 ¼ teaspoon salt
 ¼ teaspoon paprika
    Dash pepper
 ¼ cup oil
 ½ cup chopped celery and leaves
    1 green pepper, sliced
    1 medium clove garlic or garlic salt
 ⅛ teaspoon thyme
    1 bay leaf
    Dash rosemary
    1 10¾-ounce can mushroom soup
 ½ cup liquid (wine, broth, or water)
    1 can whole white onions, drained
    1 can sweet potatoes or 6 medium sweet potatoes,
      cooked

Dust chicken with flour, salt, paprika, and pepper. Sauté lightly in oil; arrange in a large casserole or pan. Add celery, green pepper, garlic, thyme, bay leaf, and rosemary to drippings. Cook 5 minutes; stir in remaining seasoned flour and gradually blend in soup and liquid. Arrange onions and sweet potatoes around chicken in casserole. Pour seasoned soup over all. Bake, covered, at 375° for 30 minutes; uncover and bake 30 minutes or until chicken is tender.

Flemish Beef Casserole

Makes 2 2-quart casseroles.

1½ pounds onion, thinly sliced
    2 cloves garlic, minced
 ¾ cup vegetable oil, divided
    4 pounds round steak, fat trimmed and cubed
 ¼ cup flour
    Salt and pepper to taste
    4 sprigs parsley, minced
 ½ teaspoon ground nutmeg
 ½ teaspoon leaf thyme
    2 bay leaves
    2 12-ounce cans beer

Sauté onion and garlic in ¼ cup oil until transparent. Remove from pan. Dredge meat in flour mixed with salt and pepper. Add remaining oil to pan and brown meat well on all sides. Line 2 2-quart casseroles with heavy-duty aluminum foil. Divide ingredients between the 2 casseroles. Place meat on bottom, spread with onion and sprinkle parsley over top. Add remaining herbs. Top with beer and an additional ½ teaspoon salt over each casserole. Cover casseroles with aluminum foil. Bake at 325° for 2 hours, or until meat is tender. Serve 1 casserole; cool and freeze the other.

Asparagus Almondine

    1 10¾-ounce can cream of chicken soup
 ¼ cup milk
    3 hard-cooked eggs, sliced
    1 cup cubed American cheese
    1 10-ounce package frozen cut asparagus,
      cooked and drained
    1 cup sliced almonds
 ½ cup bread crumbs
    2 tablespoons butter

Combine soup and milk. Stir in eggs, cheese, and asparagus. Spoon mixture into a buttered casserole. Sprinkle almonds and crumbs over top. Dot with butter. Bake at 350° for 30 to 40 minutes, until bubbly and slightly brown on top.

String Bean Casserole

    2 medium cans whole green beans, drained
    1 medium can Chinese vegetables, drained
    1 10¾-ounce can cream of mushroom soup
      Salt and pepper to taste
    1 medium can French fried onion rings
    1 cup grated Cheddar cheese

Combine beans, vegetables, soup, salt and pepper in a casserole. Top with onion rings. Bake at 325° for 25 minutes. Sprinkle cheese over top and bake an additional 5 minutes.

Meats

Walnut-Stuffed Beef Rolls

Makes 6 servings.

      2 1-pound top round steaks, ½ inch thick
     ¼ cup flour
     ⅓ cup chopped onion
     ⅓ cup chopped celery
     ½ cup butter or margarine
      2 cups bread cubes
     ⅔ cup walnuts, chopped
     ⅓ cup chopped parsley
      1 teaspoon salt
      1 egg
   1⅓ cups water
      2 10-ounce packages Brussels sprouts
      1 10¾-ounce can beef gravy

Cut each steak crosswise into 3 uniform pieces. Sprinkle with flour; pound each side until steaks are ¼ inch thick. Sauté onion and celery in ¼ cup of the butter until tender, 4 to 5 minutes. Add bread cubes, walnuts, parsley, and salt. Cook until bread is lightly browned. Remove from heat. Stir in egg. Spread each piece of meat with walnut mixture, leaving ½ inch around edges. Roll up and secure with toothpicks. Place remaining ¼ cup butter in a large skillet. Brown beef rolls well on all sides. Add ⅔ cup water. Reduce heat to low and simmer, covered, 30 minutes, stirring occasionally. Add Brussels sprouts, beef gravy and remaining water. Heat to boiling. Cover and cook 10 minutes.

Orange-Ginger Pork Chops

      6 lean pork chops
     ¼ cup orange juice
     ½ teaspoon salt
      1 teaspoon ground ginger
      6 orange slices (1 large orange)
     ¾ cup dairy sour cream

In a skillet brown chops over medium heat, 10 minutes per side. Add orange juice, cover, and simmer 30 minutes. Uncover; sprinkle chops with salt and ginger and top each with an orange slice. Cover and cook 10 to 15 minutes until chops are fork tender. Remove chops to an oven-proof platter and top each with sour cream. Place under broiler 1 minute. Serve immediately.

Pepper Steak

   1½ pounds boneless round steak, cut
           cross-grain into thin strips
      1 clove garlic, minced
     ¼ cup olive oil
      2 large tomatoes, skinned and chopped
      4 medium green peppers, seeded and
           cut into strips
     ¼ cup soy sauce
     ¼ teaspoon ground black pepper
     ½ teaspoon sugar
   1¼ teaspoons ground ginger
   1¼ cups beef bouillon or stock
      2 tablespoons cornstarch

Brown the meat and garlic in olive oil. Stir in tomatoes, peppers, soy sauce, pepper, sugar, ginger, and ¾ cup of stock. Cover and cook 20 minutes or until meat is tender. Blend cornstarch with remaining stock. Stir into meat mixture, bring to boil and simmer 2 minutes, stirring constantly. Serve over rice.

Beef Rib Roast

      1 3- to 4-rib beef roast

To make carving easier, have butcher loosen the backbone by sawing across ribs. Tie roast; place fat side up on a rack in an open roasting pan. Insert meat thermometer in the thickest part of roast. Do not add water. Roast, uncovered, at 325° to desired degree of doneness. The meat thermometer will register 140° for rare, 160° for medium and 170° for well done. For a 4- to 6-pound roast, allow 26 to 32 minutes per pound for rare, 34 to 38 minutes for medium and 40 to 42 minutes for well done. For a 6- to 8-pound roast, allow 23 to 25 minutes per pound for rare, 27 to 30 minutes for medium and 32 to 35 minutes for well done. For easier carving, allow roast to stand in a warm place 15 to 20 minutes after removing from the oven. Since roasts usually continue to cook after removal from the oven, it is best to remove them when the thermometer registers about 5° below the temperature of doneness desired. Before carving roast, remove strings. With a sharp knife, remove backbone and feather bones from roast.

Individual Ham Loaves

Makes 10 to 12 loaves.

    1 pound ground ham
    ½ pound ground lean pork
    ½ pound ground lean beef
    1 cup fine cracker crumbs
    2 tablespoons chopped onion
    2 tablespoons chopped celery
    2 tablespoons chopped green pepper
    ½ teaspoon salt
    ¼ teaspoon black pepper
    2 eggs, beaten
    1 cup milk

Combine ingredients in order listed; mix well. Shape into 10 or 12 loaves. Arrange in a baking dish; pour Sauce over loaves. Bake at 350° for 50 to 60 minutes. Baste frequently.

Sauce

    1 8-ounce can tomato sauce
    3 tablespoons vinegar
    1 teaspoon dry mustard
    1 cup firmly packed brown sugar

Combine all ingredients; mix well.

Sliced Beef in Onion Sauce

Makes 4 servings.

    1 pound chuck, shoulder or round roast, cut
       cross-grain in ¼-inch slices
    1½ teaspoons salt
       Dash pepper
    3 tablespoons vegetable oil
    1 cup water
    ½ pound large onions, cut into thick slices
    2 tablespoons flour
    1 teaspoon sugar

Season meat with salt and pepper. Heat oil in a skillet or Dutch oven; brown meat on both sides. Add ¼ cup of the water and cover tightly. Simmer gently 1 to 1½ hours, or until meat is tender. Add remaining water, ¼ cup at a time, to keep moist. Push meat to one side of pan and carefully place onions in the juice. Cover; simmer ½ hour, until onions are transparent and tender. Transfer meat and onions to hot platter; cover. Stir combined flour and sugar into juice, adding more water if needed. Heat to boiling. Pour over meat and onions.

Pork Steaks with Apple Stuffing

    6 pork steaks, ½-inch thick
    2 tablespoons vegetable oil
       Salt and pepper to taste
    3 tart red, unpeeled apples, cored and halved
       Sugar

Slowly brown pork steaks on both sides in hot oil. Season with salt and pepper. Place in shallow baking dish. Cover each steak with a layer of Apple Stuffing; top with an apple half. Sprinkle with sugar. Cover dish tightly with foil. Bake at 350° for 1 hour or until pork is well done.

Apple Stuffing

    3 cups toasted bread crumbs
    1½ cups chopped unpeeled apples
    ½ cup seedless raisins
    ½ cup chopped celery
    ½ cup chopped onion
    1 teaspoon salt
    1 teaspoon poultry seasoning
    ¼ teaspoon pepper
    ½ cup canned condensed beef broth

Combine all ingredients except beef broth. Add broth and toss lightly to moisten.

Beef Piquant in Rice Ring

Makes 6 servings.

    1½ pounds tenderized round steak, cut in 1-inch strips
    2 tablespoons chili powder
    2 teaspoons salt
    ½ teaspoon garlic powder
    4 cups hot cooked rice
    1 teaspoon onion powder
    1 cup cooked seasoned green peas
    2 tablespoons chopped parsley
    2 tablespoons vegetable oil
    1 8-ounce can tomato sauce

Season beef strips with chili powder, salt, and garlic powder. Let meat stand about 30 minutes to absorb the flavor of the spices. Combine rice, onion powder, green peas, and parsley. Toss gently. Pack into a 1½-quart ring mold. Cover and place mold in a pan of hot water until serving time. Sauté steak in hot oil about 10 minutes. Add tomato sauce. Cover and cook 10 minutes longer. Invert rice ring onto a heated platter. Fill ring with meat mixture.

Frosted Meat Loaf

1½ pounds ground beef
1 10¾-ounce can cream of mushroom soup
1 cup small bread cubes
¼ cup chopped onion
1 egg, beaten
½ teaspoon salt
    Dash pepper
2 cups mashed potato
¼ cup water
1 tablespoon drippings

Combine ground beef, ½ cup of the soup, bread cubes, onion, egg, and seasonings; mix thoroughly. Shape into a loaf. Place in a shallow baking pan. Bake at 350° for 1 hour. Frost loaf with potato. Bake 15 minutes. Blend remaining soup, water, and drippings; heat. Serve with meat.

Spicy Jelly-Glazed Pork Roast

Makes 6 to 8 servings.

1 4- to 5-pound pork loin roast
1 teaspoon salt
¼ teaspoon ground allspice
    Canned or fresh pineapple and orange slices
    Watercress, mint sprigs or parsley

Rub outside of roast with the salt and allspice. Place roast on a rack in a shallow, uncovered, baking pan. If meat thermometer is used, insert point in center of lean part of loin away from bone. Roast at 325° until done, 2¾ to 3 hours, or to an internal temperature of 170° if a meat thermometer is used. Prepare Glaze and brush on meat several times during last 30 minutes of roasting. Garnish with canned or fresh pineapple and orange slices, and watercress, mint sprigs or parsley, if desired.

Glaze

½ cup currant or apply jelly
¼ cup light corn syrup
3 tablespoons catsup
¼ teaspoon ground allspice

Combine jelly, syrup, catsup, and allspice in a saucepan. Simmer 2 minutes.

Baked Boneless Smoked Ham

1 5- to 7-pound smoked boneless ham

Place ham, lean side down, on a rack in an open roasting pan. Insert roast meat thermometer so that the bulb is centered in the thickest part. Do not add water. Roast, uncovered, in a 325° oven, allowing 15 to 18 minutes per pound. For a fully cooked ham weighing 6 pounds, this will take approximately 1¾ hours. Prepare the Orange-Raisin Sauce. During the last 30 minutes of cooking time, brush ham with ½ cup of the sauce. Serve remaining sauce hot with ham.

Orange-Raisin Sauce

¼ cup raisins
2 cups orange juice
2 tablespoons cornstarch
2 tablespoons water
½ teaspoon salt
1 tablespoon prepared mustard

Place raisins and orange juice in a saucepan. Bring to a simmer, cover and cook slowly 10 minutes. Combine cornstarch, water, salt, and mustard. Stir into first mixture. Cook, stirring constantly, until thickened.

Sauerbraten

Makes 6 servings.

1½ pounds 1-inch beef cubes
1 tablespoon vegetable oil
1 envelope brown gravy mix
2 cups water
1 tablespoon minced onion
2 tablespoons white wine vinegar
2 tablespoons brown sugar
½ teaspoon salt
¼ teaspoon pepper
½ teaspoon ginger
1 teaspoon Worcestershire sauce
1 bay leaf
    Hot buttered noodles

Brown meat in hot oil; remove from skillet. Add gravy and water to skillet; bring to boil, stirring constantly. Stir in remaining ingredients except noodles. Return meat to skillet; simmer 1½ hours. Stir occasionally. Remove bay leaf. Serve over noodles.

Poultry

Roast Goose with Apples

1 8-pound goose, with giblets
2 cups bread crumbs
1 chopped onion
2 tablespoons vegetable oil
¼ teaspoon sage
1 teaspoon salt
  Pinch pepper

Cook giblets until tender. Chop and add to stuffing made by mixing bread crumbs, onion, oil, sage, and seasoning. After cleaning the goose thoroughly, stuff and sew the neck and back. Roast 15 minutes at 450°; reduce heat to 350° and cook 3 hours. Serve with hot Baked Apples.

Baked Apples

6 to 8 apples, washed and cored
¼ cup brown sugar
3 sweet potatoes, cooked, mashed and seasoned

Sprinkle apples with brown sugar; stuff with sweet potatoes. Bake at 350° until tender.

Poultry Stuffing Casserole

2 cups chicken broth
1 10¾-ounce can cream of mushroom soup
½ cup milk
¼ cup butter
5 cups seasoned bread cubes
2 eggs, beaten
2½ cups cut-up chicken

Heat broth, soup, milk, and butter in a saucepan until butter melts. Pour over bread cubes. Add eggs and chicken; mix well. Pour into a casserole. Bake at 350° for 35 minutes.

Party Chicken

1 4-ounce jar dried beef
8 slices bacon
4 whole, boned chicken breasts
1 10¾-ounce can mushroom soup
1 cup sour cream

Separate beef and layer in the bottom of a greased 8-inch square pan. Wrap bacon around chicken breasts; place on beef slices. Mix soup and sour cream; pour over chicken breasts. Refrigerate overnight. Bake at 350° for 2 hours.

Spicy Chicken

1 cup plain yogurt
1½ teaspoons salt
1 small clove garlic, crushed
½ teaspoon ground cardamom
½ teaspoon chili powder
¼ teaspoon ground cinnamon
¼ teaspoon ground ginger
1 2½- to 3-pound frying chicken, quartered
2 teaspoons flour

Combine first 7 ingredients in a shallow dish. Add chicken and marinate at least 4 hours or overnight. Place chicken, skin-side up, in a baking pan. Combine flour with marinade. Spoon over chicken. Bake in a preheated 350° oven 1½ hours or until tender, basting occasionally with the marinade.

Roast Turkey

1 10- to 12-pound turkey
8 cups stuffing
1 cup butter or margarine, melted

Preheat oven to 325°. Fill dressed, cleaned bird with Wild Rice Stuffing. Skewer or sew openings. Truss and arrange on a rack in a shallow roasting pan. Roast, uncovered, until tender, 3½ to 4 hours. When turkey begins to brown, cover lightly with a tent of aluminum foil. Remove foil and baste occasionally with butter during roasting.

Wild Rice Stuffing

Makes enough for a 10-pound turkey.

1 cup raw wild rice
3 cups chicken broth or bouillon
1 cup diced celery
¼ cup minced onion
½ cup butter, melted
1 4-ounce can mushrooms
½ teaspoon salt
¼ teaspoon black pepper
¼ teaspoon sage

Add rice to boiling broth. Cover and let simmer slowly 30 to 45 minutes until broth is absorbed. Sauté celery and onion in butter 2 or 3 minutes. Combine all ingredients.

Chicken Kiev

Makes 6 chicken rolls.

- ½ cup butter or margarine
- 1 tablespoon chopped parsley
- 1 clove garlic, minced
- ¼ teaspoon crushed rosemary
  Dash pepper
- 3 chicken breasts (2½ pounds), split, skinned and boned
- 1 egg, lightly beaten
- ½ cup fine dry bread crumbs

Blend together butter, parsley, garlic, rosemary, and seasoning. Form a pattie ¾-inch thick; freeze until firm. Flatten chicken with edge of heavy saucer to ¼ inch thick. Cut butter mixture into 6 equal pieces; place 1 piece in center of each breast. Tuck in ends and roll tightly. Secure with toothpicks. Dip in egg and then in bread crumbs. Deep fry 2 chicken rolls at a time in 350° fat for 10 to 12 minutes until well browned. Drain. Serve with Sauce.

Sauce

- 2 tablespoons butter or margarine
- 2 tablespoons chopped onion
- 1 tablespoon chopped parsley
- 1 10¾-ounce can cream of chicken soup
- ⅓ cup milk
- 2 tablespoons sherry

Melt butter in a saucepan; sauté onion and parsley until tender. Blend in remaining ingredients. Heat, stirring occasionally.

Holiday Duck

- 1 4½- to 5-pound duckling
  Salt
- ⅔ cup orange marmalade
- ½ cup barbecue sauce

Clean duckling and rub with salt. Place on a rack in a shallow roasting pan, breast side up. Cover loosely with aluminum foil and bake at 425° for 45 minutes. Prick skin occasionally. Reduce heat to 325° and bake 1½ hours. Pour off drippings; remove foil. Continue roasting 45 minutes to 1 hour, or until tender. Brush often with a mixture of the orange marmalade and barbecue sauce. Serve on rice, if desired.

Chicken Newburg

- ⅓ cup butter
- ½ cup sliced fresh mushrooms
- ¼ cup flour
- 2 cups milk
- 1½ cups cooked, sliced chicken
- ¾ cup shredded Cheddar cheese
- 1 tablespoon chopped pimiento
- 1 teaspoon salt
- ¼ cup cooking sherry
- 1 teaspoon minced onion
- ¼ teaspoon black pepper
- ½ cup toasted slivered almonds

In a skillet, melt butter and sauté mushrooms for 2 minutes. Stir in flour until smooth. Add milk, stirring constantly. Add chicken and remaining ingredients, except almonds. Top with almonds just before serving. Serve with rice or in patty shells.

Duckling a l'Anglaise

- 1 4- to 5-pound duckling
  Salt and pepper to taste
- 3 cups bread crumbs
- 1 tablespoon minced onion
- ¼ cup minced celery
  Thyme to taste
  Softened butter

Clean and prepare duck for roasting. Rub with salt. Combine remaining ingredients except butter; stuff duckling. Sew securely. Rub outside with butter and place in a shallow pan. Bake at 375°. Allow 30 to 35 minutes per pound.

Glazed Chicken

- ½ cup butter
- 1 frying chicken, quartered
- 1½ teaspoons salt
- 1 cup plum jam
- 1 tablespoon catsup
- 2 teaspoons grated lemon rind
- 5 teaspoons lemon juice

Melt butter in a skillet. Add chicken; brown on both sides. Add salt. Place chicken in a shallow baking pan. Combine remaining ingredients and pour over chicken. Bake in a preheated 375° oven 30 to 40 minutes.

Butterhorns

      2 envelopes dry yeast
      1 cup warm milk
      1 cup butter, melted
    ½ cup sugar
      2 eggs, beaten
    4½ cups flour
         Melted butter
         Confectioners' Sugar Frosting (Recipe on
         this page)
         Almond or orange extract
         Finely chopped nuts

Dissolve yeast in the warm milk. Add butter, sugar, eggs, and salt. Add 2 cups of the flour. Beat with an electric mixer until well blended. Add the rest of the flour to make a stiff dough; knead 10 minutes. Place in a greased bowl and grease top of dough. Cover and let rise until double in bulk. Roll dough; brush with melted butter. Cut in pie-wedges and roll each piece, starting from the wide end. Place on a greased baking sheet, turn each to form a crescent shape, brush with melted butter, cover, and let rise until double in bulk. Bake at 375° about 20 minutes or until lightly browned. Frost while still warm with a well blended combination of Confectioners' Sugar Frosting and almond or orange extract. Top with nuts.

Sweet Fruit Loaf

      1 package dry yeast
    ½ cup lukewarm water (110 to 115°)
    ½ teaspoon salt
    ¼ cup sugar
    ½ cup lukewarm water
      1 egg, beaten
    ¼ cup shortening, melted
      2 cups plus 2 tablespoons sifted flour
    ½ teaspoon ground nutmeg
      1 cup fruit mix (chopped raisins and chopped
         candied cherries)

Soften yeast in ½ cup lukewarm water; add the next 4 ingredients and beat well. Add shortening, flour, and nutmeg; beat well. Fold in fruit mix. Let rise until double in bulk. Punch down and place in a greased loaf pan. Let rise until double in bulk. Bake at 375° for 45 minutes.

Confectioners' Sugar Frosting

      3 tablespoons margarine
      2 cups confectioners' sugar
    ⅛ teaspoon salt
      1 teaspoon vanilla extract
      3 tablespoons warm milk

Cream margarine with sugar and salt; mix thoroughly. Add vanilla and milk. Beat until fluffy.

Swiss Christmas Bread

Makes 2 loaves.

      5 cups sifted flour
      2 packages dry yeast
      1 cup milk, scalded
    ½ cup hot water
    ¼ cup sugar
      1 teaspoon salt
    ½ teaspoon ground nutmeg
    ½ teaspoon mace
    ¼ teaspoon ground cloves
      1 egg, lightly beaten
    ¼ cup butter, melted
    ½ cup raisins
    ½ cup chopped candied cherries
    ¼ cup chopped citron
    ¼ cup chopped nuts

Combine 2 cups of the flour with the yeast in a bowl. Cool milk to lukewarm. Blend yeast mixture, milk, and next 7 ingredients; beat 3 minutes. Add butter, raisins, cherries, citron, and nuts; mix. Gradually add the remaining 3 cups flour; knead until smooth. Place in a lightly greased bowl. Grease surface of dough lightly. Cover and let rise in a warm place until double in bulk, about 30 minutes. Turn out onto a lightly floured board. Punch down; divide into 2 equal parts and mold each part into a loaf. Put each loaf into a greased loaf pan. Cover and let rise in a warm place until double in bulk, about 30 minutes. Bake in a preheated 375° oven about 40 minutes.

Cranberry Casserole Bread

    2 cups flour
    ¾ cup sugar
    2 teaspoons baking powder
    ½ teaspoon baking soda
    1 teaspoon salt
    ¼ cup shortening
    ¾ cup orange juice
    1 tablespoon grated orange rind
    2 eggs, well beaten
    1 cup coarsely chopped cranberries
    ½ cup chopped candied green cherries
    1 tablespoon flour

Combine flour, sugar, baking powder, baking soda, and salt. Cut in shortening until mixture resembles coarse cornmeal. Combine orange juice, grated rind, and eggs. Pour all at once into dry ingredients, mixing just enough to dampen. Dust chopped cranberries and cherries with flour; carefully fold into batter. Spoon into a well greased 1½-quart casserole. Bake at 350° for 1 hour, or until a toothpick inserted in center comes out clean. Cool 10 minutes. Frost with Confectioners' Sugar Frosting (Recipe on page 25).

Almond Coffee Cake

Makes 2 cakes.

    1 cup milk
    ½ cup butter
    1 package dry yeast
    ½ cup sugar
    ½ teaspoon salt
    3 eggs, beaten
    4½ cups flour
    ½ cup butter, softened
    1 can almond paste filling for cakes
      Slivered almonds

Scald milk and pour over ½ cup butter in a large mixing bowl. Cool to lukewarm; add yeast and stir until dissolved. Add sugar and salt to beaten eggs; add to milk mixture. Stir in flour to make a stiff dough. Place in a greased bowl, cover and let

rise in a warm place until doubled in bulk, about 1½ hours. Divide dough in half and knead until smooth and elastic. On a lightly floured board, roll out each piece to a 12 x 8-inch rectangle. Spread each rectangle with half the softened butter and half of the almond paste. Roll up as for a jelly roll. Curve in a ring, overlapping ends to seal. Place in greased round cake pans. With scissors, make cuts at 1-inch intervals, cutting two-thirds through the ring. (Start at the outside and cut toward the center.) Turn each section on its side. Cover and let rise again until doubled in bulk, 30 to 45 minutes. Bake in a 350° oven 45 minutes. When slightly cooled, ice and sprinkle with almonds.

Icing

    1 tablespoon butter or margarine, softened
    1 cup confectioners' sugar
    1½ tablespoons milk
    ¼ teaspoon almond extract

Combine all ingredients. Beat until smooth and of spreading consistency.

Pumpkin Bread

Makes 2 loaves.

    2⅔ cups sugar
    ⅔ cup shortening
    4 eggs, beaten
    ⅔ cup water
    2 cups cooked or canned pumpkin
    3½ cups flour
    ½ teaspoon baking powder
    2 teaspoons baking soda
    1½ teaspoons salt
    1 teaspoon ground cinnamon
    ½ teaspoon ground cloves
    ⅔ cup chopped nuts
    ⅔ cup raisins
    ⅔ cup chopped dates

Combine sugar and shortening; add eggs, water, and pumpkin. Sift dry ingredients; combine with first mixture. Add nuts, raisins, and dates. Bake at 350° for 1 hour.

Cakes

Hot Milk Cake

- 1 cup milk
- 2 tablespoons butter
- 2 cups sugar
- 4 eggs
- 2 teaspoons baking powder
- 2 cups flour
- 1 teaspoon vanilla extract

Heat milk and butter in a saucepan until butter melts. Beat sugar and eggs until creamy. Add baking powder and flour to the sugar and egg mixture; add milk and butter; mix. Add vanilla. Pour into a tube pan and bake at 350° for 45 to 50 minutes. Do not open oven door during the first 30 minutes of baking. Cake is done when a toothpick inserted in center of cake comes out clean. Cool cake and frost.

Icing

- 1 8-ounce package cream cheese, softened
- ½ cup margarine, softened
- 1 pound confectioners' sugar

Blend cream cheese and margarine. Add sugar. To color add a few drops of red or green food coloring, if desired.

Cranberry Cake

- 1 package yellow cake mix
- 1 package fluffy white frosting mix

Prepare and bake cake as directed on package; cool. When cool, cut the layers in half horizontally. Spread cooled Cranberry Filling between layers. Place top layer of cake top-side down. Prepare frosting mix as directed on package; frost entire cake.

Cranberry Filling

- ⅓ cup cornstarch
- 2 16-ounce cans whole cranberry sauce
- 1 tablespoon lemon juice
- 1 cup chopped blanched almonds

Combine cornstarch and cranberry sauce in a saucepan. Cook and stir over medium heat until thickened, boiling 2 minutes. Remove from heat; add lemon juice and almonds, stirring well. Cool.

Fruit Cupcakes

Makes 3 dozen cupcakes.

- 1 14-ounce package date bar mix
- ⅓ cup sifted flour
- ¾ teaspoon baking powder
- 1 teaspoon pumpkin pie spice
- 2 eggs, beaten
- 2 tablespoons honey
- ½ cup thick applesauce
- ½ cup moist mincemeat
- ½ cup light raisins
- 1 cup chopped walnuts
- 1½ cups chopped mixed candied fruit and peels

Grease and flour cupcake pans. Combine date bar mix, flour, baking powder, and spice in a large mixing bowl; stir to blend. Add eggs, honey, applesauce, mincemeat, and raisins; beat well. Stir in walnuts and candied fruits. Spoon into prepared pans, filling about two-thirds full. Bake at 375° for 25 minutes or until toothpick inserted in center of cupcake comes out clean.

Gumdrop Cake

- 4 cups flour
- ½ teaspoon salt
- 1 teaspoon ground cinnamon
- 1 teaspoon ground nutmeg
- 1 cup shortening
- 2 cups sugar
- 2 eggs, beaten
- 1½ cups cooked applesauce
- 2 pounds colored gumdrops, chopped and floured
- 1 cup chopped nuts
- 1 pound white raisins
- 1 teaspoon vanilla extract
- 1 teaspoon orange extract
- 1 teaspoon baking soda dissolved in
  - 1 tablespoon water

Sift together flour, salt, and spices; set aside. Cream shortening. Add sugar and eggs; beat well. Add applesauce, gumdrops, nuts, raisins, flavorings, and baking soda; mix well. Gradually stir in dry ingredients. Place greased paper in bottom of pan; pour in batter. Bake at 350° for 1 hour.

Mincemeat Fruitcake

    1 18-ounce jar mincemeat, with rum and brandy
    1 cup broken pecans
    1 cup white raisins
    ½ cup margarine, melted
    1 cup sugar
    3 eggs, separated
    1 teaspoon baking soda
    1 tablespoon boiling water
    2 cups sifted flour
    1 teaspoon vanilla extract
    8 ounces candied fruit, optional

Combine first 5 ingredients in a mixing bowl. Add the egg yolks and baking soda dissolved in the boiling water. Gradually add flour. Fold in stiffly beaten egg whites and vanilla. Add candied fruit, if desired. Pour into a greased and floured bundt pan; bake at 300° for 1½ hours.

Christmas Pound Cake

    2 cups sugar
    1 cup margarine, softened
    6 eggs
    2 cups flour
    1 teaspoon vanilla extract
    4 teaspoons lemon extract
    8 ounces candied pineapple
    8 ounces candied cherries
    1 cup chopped pecans
    2 tablespoons flour

Combine sugar and margarine; cream well. Add eggs, flour, and flavorings; mix thoroughly. Add fruits and nuts that have been dredged in the 2 tablespoons flour. Pour into a lightly greased tube or bundt pan. Bake at 325° for 1 hour. Cool cake for 8 minutes. Pierce the surface of the cake with a fork; pour Glaze over cake. Cool before cutting.

Glaze

    ¼ cup margarine
    1½ cups sugar
    ½ cup lemon juice
    ½ tablespoon grated lemon rind

Combine all ingredients in a saucepan; heat until sugar dissolves.

Apple-Raisin Rum Cake

    ½ cup butter, softened
    1 cup white sugar
    ½ cup brown sugar
    2 eggs
    2 cups flour
    1½ teaspoons baking powder
    1 teaspoon salt
    ½ teaspoon baking soda
    1 teaspoon ground cinnamon
    ½ teaspoon ground nutmeg
    1 cup evaporated milk
    2 tablespoons rum
    2 cups chopped apples
    1 cup raisins
       Chopped nuts, optional

In a bowl cream butter and sugars; beat until light and fluffy. Beat in the eggs. Sift together the flour, baking powder, salt, baking soda, cinnamon, and nutmeg. Add dry ingredients alternately with the evaporated milk and rum to the creamed mixture. Mix in the chopped apples, raisins, and nuts. Pour into a greased 9 x 13-inch baking pan. Bake at 350° for 40 minutes or until cake springs back when touched.

Toffee Cake

    2 cups flour
    ½ cup butter
    1 cup brown sugar
    ½ cup white sugar
    1 cup buttermilk
    1 teaspoon baking soda
    1 egg
    1 teaspoon vanilla extract

Blend flour, butter, and sugars. Set aside ½ cup of the mixture. To remaining mixture add buttermilk, baking soda, egg, and vanilla. Blend well. Pour into a greased 10 x 14-inch pan. Prepare Topping and sprinkle over batter. Bake at 350° for 40 minutes.

Topping

    6 chocolate toffee bars
    ½ cup chopped pecans

Crush candy bars; blend with nuts. Add to the ½ cup reserved mixture.

Whipped Cream Cake

- 1 cup whipping cream, whipped
- 3 egg whites, stiffly beaten
- 2 cups flour
- 1 cup sugar
- ¼ teaspoon salt
- 2 teaspoons baking powder
- ½ cup water
- 1 teaspoon vanilla extract
- ½ cup chopped walnuts, optional

In a large mixing bowl, fold whipped cream into stiffly beaten egg whites. Sift flour, sugar, salt, and baking powder 3 times and add alternately with water and vanilla to the whipped cream mixture. Fold in walnuts. Pour into a medium-size loaf pan. Bake in a preheated 350° oven for about 30 minutes.

Holiday Date Cake

- 1 tablespoon butter, softened
- 1 cup sugar
- 1 egg
- ½ cup chopped nuts
- 1 teaspoon vanilla extract
- 1 teaspoon baking soda
- 1 cup chopped dates
- 1 cup boiling water
- 1¼ cups flour

Cream butter and sugar. Add egg, nuts, and vanilla; set aside. Sprinkle baking soda over dates; pour boiling water over dates and baking soda. Cool. Add dates to butter and sugar mixture. Gradually add flour; mix well. Pour into a large loaf pan. Bake at 350° for 40 to 50 minutes.

White Fruitcake

- 1½ cups flour
- Pinch salt
- 1 teaspoon baking powder
- 1 cup butter, softened
- 1 cup sugar
- 4 eggs
- 1 cup chopped candied fruit
- 1 tablespoon flour
- 1 lemon, juice and grated rind

Combine flour, salt, and baking powder. Blend in butter and sugar. Add 2 of the eggs, beat 10 minutes. Add remaining eggs and beat another 10 minutes. Mix in candied fruit, the 1 tablespoon flour, lemon juice and rind. Pour into a greased and floured bundt cake pan. Bake at 350° for 1 hour or until done.

Holiday Mint Angel Cake

- 8 egg whites
- ¼ teaspoon salt
- 1 teaspoon cream of tartar
- 1 teaspoon almond extract
- 1 teaspoon vanilla
- 1¼ cups sugar
- 1 cup cake flour
- 3½ cups whipped topping
- ½ cup coarsely crushed, hard mint candies

Beat egg whites in a small mixing bowl until foamy. Add salt and cream of tartar; beat until soft peaks form. Fold in almond extract and vanilla. Gradually beat in sugar; continue beating until stiff. Sift flour into egg whites and gently fold in. Bake in an ungreased 10-inch tube pan at 325° for 50 to 60 minutes. Invert pan on a rack or place center over a soft drink bottle to cool thoroughly. Remove from pan and slice horizontally into 3 layers. Place 1 layer on a cake plate. Drizzle about 2 tablespoons Mint Syrup over the bottom layer. Spread on ½ cup of the whipped topping. Sprinkle on about 1 tablespoon crushed mints. Add second layer and repeat the procedure. Invert the top layer; sprinkle with remaining Mint Syrup. Place right-side-up on second layer. Spread entire cake with remaining whipped topping and sprinkle with remaining crushed mints. If desired, place scoops of vanilla ice cream on top. Place in freezer until ready to serve.

Mint Syrup

- ¼ cup hard mint candies
- ¼ cup water

Place mints in a blender and blend at high speed until coarsely crushed. Add water and blend until thick.

Tortes

For a simple way of making thin-layered tortes, use double-thick sheets of aluminum foil to form two long pans in which the batter can be thinly spread. The cake bakes very quickly in these foil pans and is soft and tender. The same delicate sponge cake baked in a jelly roll or layer cake pan is likely to dry out and get hard around the edges.

Each long cake is cut into squares to form the 8 layers needed. The layers are assembled with a frosting between layers, on top, and sides.

Since tortes need to be refrigerated several hours before serving, a chilling and serving tray can be made by covering a piece of heavy cardboard with aluminum foil.

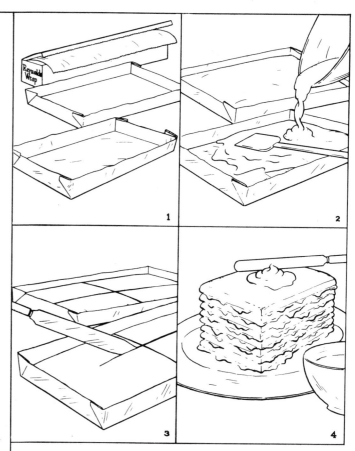

Schaum Torte

    8 egg whites
    ¼ teaspoon salt
    2 cups sugar
    1 tablespoon vinegar
    1 teaspoon vanilla extract
      Fresh or frozen berries
      Whipped cream

Beat egg whites and salt about 10 minutes until stiff but not dry. Gradually add sugar. Add vinegar and beat 10 to 15 minutes. Add vanilla. Pour into a springform pan. Preheat oven to 400°; place pan in oven and turn oven off. Leave torte in oven until oven is cool, 2 to 3 hours. Serve with berries and whipped cream.

Peppermint Candy Torte

    1 chiffon or angel food cake
    ⅓ cup confectioners' sugar
    1 cup crushed peppermint stick candy
    2 drops red food coloring
    1½ cups whipping cream, whipped
      Strawberries

Cut cake into 2 layers. Fold sugar, candy, and food coloring into the whipped cream. Spoon whipped cream mixture between layers, on top, and on sides of cake. Garnish with strawberries.

Cranberry Torte

Makes 12 servings.

    3 cups graham cracker crumbs
    ½ cup butter, softened
    2 cups sifted confectioners' sugar
    1 egg
    1 medium apple, ground
    1 cup raw cranberries, ground
    1 12-ounce can crushed pineapple, drained
    1 cup sugar
    1 teaspoon vanilla extract
    1 pint whipping cream, whipped

Pat graham cracker crumbs into a 12 x 7-inch pan. Reserve ½ cup of the crumbs for topping. Cream butter; gradually add confectioners' sugar and beat until fluffy. Add egg; mix well. Pour into crumb-lined pan. Combine apple, cranberries, pineapple, and sugar; spread over butter mixture. Add vanilla to whipped cream; spread over fruit mixture. Sprinkle reserved crumbs over top. Chill.

Cream Cheese Refrigerator Torte

Makes 12 to 14 servings.

    2 cups graham cracker crumbs
    ⅓ cup sugar
    ½ cup butter or margarine, melted
    1 teaspoon ground cinnamon

Combine ingredients. Pat into a buttered 9-inch springform pan. Bake at 425° for 5 minutes. Cool. Pour Filling into crust; refrigerate 8 hours. Top with pie filling.

Filling

    1 3-ounce package lemon-flavored gelatin
    1 cup hot water
    ¼ cup pineapple juice
    1 8-ounce package cream cheese, softened
    ½ cup sugar
    1 large can evaporated milk, chilled
    2 teaspoons vanilla extract
    1 20-ounce can crushed pineapple, drained
      Canned cherry or pineapple pie filling

Soften gelatin in hot water. Add pineapple juice; let cool until it begins to thicken. Blend cream cheese and sugar. Whip chilled milk in a large, cold bowl until stiff. Fold cheese mixture and whipped milk into gelatin. Add vanilla and pineapple.

Empire Torte

Makes 10 to 12 servings.

    1 cup sifted flour
    1 teaspoon baking powder
    ¾ cup sugar
    4 eggs, separated
    ½ teaspoon salt
    ½ teaspoon cream of tartar
    ⅓ cup sugar
    ¼ cup water
    1 teaspoon vanilla extract
    1 teaspoon orange extract
      Walnuts, chopped and whole

Following instructions on page 32, form 2 16 x 10-inch pans; set aside. Sift together flour, baking powder, and the ¾ cup sugar in a small mixing bowl. In a large mixing bowl beat egg whites, salt, and cream of tartar until soft mounds form. Gradually add the ⅓ cup sugar, beating until stiff peaks form. Do not underbeat. Combine egg yolks, water, and flavorings. Add to dry ingredients; beat 1 minute at medium speed of electric mixer. Fold batter into beaten egg whites. Pour into the two foil pans. Spread batter evenly. Bake at 375° for 10 to 12 minutes. (Cakes may be baked one at a time.) Cool 10 minutes. Cut each cake into quarters. Remove from foil pans. Cover tightly with aluminum foil until ready to frost. Stack the 8 layers, spreading 2 to 3 tablespoons Chocolate Frosting between each layer. Frost sides and top. Garnish sides with walnuts. Chill at least 2 hours.

Chocolate Frosting

    1 cup butter or margarine, softened
    2 squares (2 ounces) unsweetened chocolate,
      melted and cooled
    1 teaspoon vanilla extract
    ½ teaspoon maple flavoring
    2 cups sifted confectioners' sugar

Cream butter until fluffy. Add chocolate, flavorings, and sugar; blend. Beat at high speed of electric mixer until of spreading consistency.

Eggnog Torte

    1 envelope unflavored gelatin
    ¼ cup cold water
    ¾ cup butter, softened
    1 cup confectioners' sugar
    4 eggs, separated
    ⅓ cup dark rum or brandy
    ¾ cup chopped, toasted, salted almonds
    ¼ teaspoon salt
    1 cup whipping cream, whipped
    1 10-inch angel food cake, broken into small pieces
      Slivered almonds, optional

Soften gelatin in the cold water about 5 minutes. Dissolve over hot water. Cream butter; gradually add sugar. Add egg yolks, one at a time, beating well after each addition. Add rum and nuts; mix. Fold in slightly cooled gelatin. Add salt to egg whites and beat until stiff but not dry. Fold egg whites and whipped cream into first mixture. Pour over angel food cake pieces. Blend lightly. Pour into an ungreased 10-inch springform pan. Refrigerate 2 to 3 hours. Serve with whipped cream and sprinkle with slivered almonds.

Pies

Grasshopper Pie

Makes 1 9-inch pie.

1⅓ cups graham cracker crumbs
¼ cup sugar
¼ cup cocoa
¼ cup margarine, melted
¼ cup green creme de menthe
1 9-ounce jar marshmallow creme
2 cups whipping cream, whipped

Combine first 4 ingredients thoroughly. Press into a 9-inch pie plate; reserve 2 tablespoons of mixture for topping. Bake at 375° for 8 minutes. Gradually add creme de menthe to marshmallow creme; beat until well blended. Fold whipped cream into marshmallow mixture; pour into crust. Sprinkle reserved crumbs around the edge and center of the pie. Freeze until firm.

Eggnog Wreath Pie

Makes 1 9-inch pie.

1¼ cups graham cracker crumbs
¼ cup packed light brown sugar
⅓ cup butter or margarine, melted

Combine cracker crumbs, brown sugar, and butter. Evenly press into a 9-inch pie plate. Bake at 400° for 8 minutes. Remove to wire rack to cool. Prepare Filling and spoon into cooled crust. Refrigerate until set. Decorate by arranging the 6 apricot halves upside-down on top of the pie in a circular wreath pattern. Make leaves by slicing cherries lengthwise into quarters. Place leaves next to apricot halves. Spoon or pipe whipped cream into center of wreath. Garnish with cherry pieces.

Filling

1 30-ounce can apricot halves, drained
1½ cups eggnog
2 eggs, separated
1 envelope unflavored gelatin
  Dash salt
  Dash ground nutmeg
2 tablespoons brandy
¼ cup sugar
½ cup whipping cream, whipped
  Red and green candied cherries

Reserve 6 apricot halves for garnish. Place remaining drained apricots into a blender and puree until smooth. In top of a double boiler, combine pureed apricots, eggnog, egg yolks, gelatin, salt, and nutmeg. Cook, stirring constantly, over simmering water until gelatin dissolves and mixture coats spoon. Remove from heat; stir in brandy. Refrigerate apricot mixture in a bowl until mixture mounds when dropped from a spoon. Beat egg whites until soft peaks form. Add sugar, 1 tablespoon at a time; continue beating until stiff peaks form. Stir ¼ of this egg white mixture into apricot mixture. Gently fold in remaining egg whites.

Hot Water Whipped Piecrust

Makes 2 9-inch crusts.

¼ cup boiling water
1 tablespoon milk
¾ cup vegetable shortening
2 cups flour
1 teaspoon salt

In a mixing bowl add boiling water and milk to shortening. Beat with rapid strokes until mixture is creamy and holds soft peaks. Sift flour and salt together; add to mixture and stir until dough holds together. Roll out between waxed paper.

Fruit Turnovers

2 cups flour
1 cup margarine
1 cup small curd cottage cheese
  Fruit-flavored jam or canned fruit

Cream flour, margarine, and cottage cheese. Chill 4 hours. Drop by teaspoonfuls onto floured board and roll to 3-inch circles. Place 1 teaspoon of the fruit filling in center. Fold over sides, making a triangle. Pinch edges together at top. Bake at 425° until dough becomes "freckled" (from the cottage curds). Serve warm.

Sweet Potato Pie

Makes 1 9-inch pie.

1¼ cups cooked, mashed sweet potatoes
3 eggs, beaten
½ cup brown sugar
1 tablespoon honey
1 teaspoon mace
1 teaspoon salt
1 cup milk
1 9-inch unbaked piecrust

Combine all ingredients for filling; blend well. Pour into piecrust. Bake at 425° for 20 minutes. Reduce heat to 350° and bake 25 to 30 minutes.

Special Chocolate Pie

Makes 1 9-inch pie.

3 squares unsweetened chocolate
3½ cups milk
¾ cup sugar
⅔ cup sifted cake flour
¾ teaspoon salt
1 egg or 2 egg yolks, lightly beaten
2 tablespoons butter
1½ teaspoons vanilla extract
1 9-inch baked piecrust
½ cup whipping cream, whipped
1 cup chopped raisins or dates
¼ cup chopped nuts

Add chocolate to milk and heat in a double boiler. When chocolate is melted, beat with a rotary egg beater until blended. Combine sugar, flour, and salt. Add a small amount of chocolate mixture, stirring until smooth. Return to double boiler and cook until thick, stirring constantly. Continue cooking 10 minutes, stirring occasionally. Add a small amount of mixture to the egg, stirring vigorously. Return to double boiler and cook 2 minutes, stirring constantly. Remove from heat. Add butter and vanilla. Cool slightly and turn into piecrust; chill. Before serving, cover with whipped cream to which raisins or dates have been added. Top with nuts.

Graham Cracker Crust

Makes 1 9-inch crust.

⅓ cup butter or margarine
2 tablespoons sugar
1¼ cups graham cracker crumbs

Stir butter and sugar together in a saucepan over low heat until butter is melted. Blend in cracker crumbs. Press evenly into a 9-inch pie pan. Chill.

Christmas Pie

Makes 1 9-inch pie.

1 3-ounce package raspberry-flavored gelatin
1 cup boiling water
1 16-ounce can whole cranberry sauce
1 cup crushed pineapple, drained
1 9-inch Graham Cracker Crust, chilled (Recipe on this page)
2 cups miniature marshmallows
¼ cup milk
½ teaspoon vanilla extract
Green food coloring
1 cup whipping cream, whipped

Dissolve gelatin in boiling water; refrigerate until slightly thickened. Fold in cranberry sauce and pineapple. Pour into crust and chill until firm. In a double boiler, melt marshmallows and milk; stir until smooth. Add vanilla and a few drops of the green food coloring. Chill until thickened. Fold in whipped cream. Spread over pie filling. Chill pie until firm.

Different Pecan Pie

3 egg whites
1 cup sugar
1 teaspoon baking powder
1 cup graham cracker crumbs
1 cup chopped pecans

Beat egg whites until stiff; beat in the sugar and baking powder. Stir in cracker crumbs and nuts. Pour into a greased pan and bake at 350° for 30 minutes. Serve topped with whipped cream, if desired.

Mincemeat Pie

Makes 1 9-inch pie.

1½ cups flour
1 teaspoon salt
⅔ cup shortening
5 to 6 tablespoons ice water

Sift flour and salt into a bowl. Cut in shortening with a pastry blender until mixture resembles fine cornmeal. Add ice water, tossing lightly until dough holds together in a ball. Roll out on a floured board into a 10-inch circle. Fit into the pan; trim off excess dough. Pour in the Filling. Top with bits of butter; sprinkle with ground nutmeg. Add the top crust, making slits to let steam escape. Fold top edge under lower crust; pinch edges to seal. Sprinkle top crust with sugar and drops of milk to make a brown glaze. Bake at 425° for 35 minutes.

Filling

2 cups mincemeat
½ cup orange marmalade
2 tablespoons flour
1 tablespoon lemon juice
¼ teaspoon ground nutmeg

Combine all ingredients; mix well.

Holiday Pie

Makes 1 9-inch pie.

⅓ cup shortening
2 tablespoons cold water
¼ teaspoon salt
1 cup sifted flour

Cream shortening; add water and salt. Stir with a fork until well mixed. Add flour all at once, mixing lightly with a fork until well blended. Press into a ball and roll out to a ⅛ inch thick circle. Fit into a 9-inch pie pan; flute edge. Cut some dough into the shape of a bell. Place on baking sheet. Bake shell and cut-out bell at 450°

until golden brown. Spoon cooled Filling into baked piecrust. Top with the bell cutout.

Filling

6 apples, peeled, cored, and cut into thick slices
1 cup cranberries
½ cup raisins
½ cup chopped dates
3 tablespoons flour
1¼ cups sugar
¾ cup water
½ cup chopped nuts

Combine apple slices with cranberries, raisins, and dates. Sprinkle with flour. Bring sugar and water to boil in a saucepan. Lower heat and add fruit mixture. Simmer 10 minutes or until fruit is soft, adding more water if it becomes too dry. Cool slightly; stir in nuts.

Nesselrode Pie

Makes 1 8-inch pie.

3 eggs, separated
1 cup milk
¼ teaspoon salt
⅔ cup sugar
1 tablespoon unflavored gelatin
2 tablespoons cold water
½ cup whipping cream, whipped
¼ cup chopped maraschino cherries
2 tablespoons rum extract
1 8-inch baked piecrust
Grated chocolate

In the top of a double boiler, place the slightly beaten egg yolks, milk, salt, and ½ cup of the sugar. Set over simmering water, stirring constantly, until thick. Soak gelatin in the water; stir into the hot mixture until dissolved. Chill until syrupy. Whip egg whites until stiff peaks form. Gradually add remaining sugar. Fold whipped cream into egg whites. Stir cherries and rum extract into gelatin mixture; fold in whipped cream and egg whites. Pile into baked piecrust; garnish with grated chocolate. Chill until firm.

Puddings

Steamed Carrot Pudding

Makes 4 to 5 servings.

- ½ cup chopped suet
- 1 cup flour
- ½ cup currants or raisins
- ½ cup sugar
- 2 teaspoons salt
- 1 teaspoon ground cinnamon
- 1 cup grated raw carrots
- 1 teaspoon butter

Combine all ingredients, except butter, in a bowl; mix well. Brush a mold or double boiler with butter and spoon in carrot mixture. Boil 2 hours. Serve hot with a lemon sauce or Hard Sauce.

Hard Sauce

- ½ cup butter, softened
- 1 teaspoon flavoring
  Confectioners' sugar

Combine butter, flavoring, and as much confectioners' sugar as the butter will absorb; cream well. Cover and refrigerate. Keeps well several months.

Christmas Pudding

- ¼ pound suet, butter or margarine
- ½ cup brown sugar
- 1 large egg
- 1 cup grated raw carrots
- ½ cup seeded raisins
- ½ cup currants
- 1¼ cups flour
- 1 teaspoon baking powder
- ½ teaspoon salt
- 1 tablespoon warm water
- ½ teaspoon baking soda
- ½ teaspoon ground cinnamon
- ½ teaspoon ground nutmeg or ½ teaspoon ground allspice

Combine first 3 ingredients; mix well. Add carrots, raisins, and currants. Sift together the flour, baking powder, and salt; stir into first mixture. Combine warm water and baking soda in a small bowl; stir into the flour and carrot mixture. Add spices; stir to blend. Pour into a greased mold. Cover or tie aluminum foil over mold. Place mold on a rack in a pan with a tight-fitting cover; add enough water to the pan to reach within ¼ inch of cover of mold. Cover. Steam 1½ hours. Remove from water and cool. Bake 10 minutes at 350°. Remove from mold and place on a platter. Decorate with sprigs of holly; serve with Hard Sauce.

Hard Sauce

- ½ cup butter or margarine, softened
- 1 cup brown sugar
- ¼ cup cream
- ½ teaspoon lemon juice
  Chopped nuts, optional

Cream together butter and sugar. Add cream, lemon juice, and nuts; mix well.

Cranberry Steamed Pudding

- 1½ cups flour
- 2 teaspoons baking soda
- 2 cups fresh cranberries, halved
- ½ cup molasses
- ⅓ cup hot milk
- ½ cup chopped nuts

Sift flour with baking soda. Stir in cranberries. Combine molasses and milk; stir into cranberry mixture until well blended. Stir in nuts. Pour into a 6-cup buttered mold. If mold has a lid, butter the inside and cover mold or cover with buttered aluminum foil pressed tightly over mold and secured with a string. Place mold on a rack in a pan with a tight-fitting cover. Pour about 1 inch of water into the pan. Bring water to a boil and cover; reduce heat to simmer. Steam for 2 hours. Cool 10 minutes; unmold.

Sauce

- ½ cup butter
- 1 cup sugar
- ½ cup light cream
- 1 teaspoon vanilla extract

In a 1-quart saucepan melt butter. Stir in sugar and cream until sugar dissolves. Bring to a boil, stirring constantly. Stir in vanilla. Serve hot on pudding.

Desserts

Marble Brownies

Makes 2 dozen.

- 1 4-ounce bar sweet chocolate
- 5 tablespoons butter
- 1 3-ounce package cream cheese
- 1 cup sugar
- 3 eggs
- ½ cup plus 1 tablespoon unsifted flour
- 2 teaspoons vanilla extract
- ¼ teaspoon salt
- ½ teaspoon baking powder
- ¼ teaspoon almond extract
- ½ cup chopped nuts

Melt chocolate and 3 tablespoons of the butter over low heat; stir. Cool slightly. Combine cream cheese and remaining 2 tablespoons butter; cream until smooth. Gradually add ¼ cup sugar. Blend in 1 egg, 1 tablespoon flour, and 1 teaspoon vanilla. In a separate bowl beat 2 eggs until light in color. Add ¾ cup sugar and beat well. Add ½ cup flour, salt, and baking powder. Blend in chocolate mixture, 1 teaspoon vanilla, almond extract and nuts. Spoon half of the chocolate mixture in a greased 8-inch square pan. Spoon white batter on top. Zigzag knife through batter to give marble effect. Bake at 350° for 40 minutes or until done.

Boule de Neige

- ¼ cup rum, brandy or kirsch
- 1 cup mixed candied fruit
- 1 quart vanilla ice cream, softened
- 1 cup whipping cream, whipped
- 2 tablespoons sugar
- 1 teaspoon vanilla extract
  Toasted flaked coconut

Add liquor to the candied fruit; let stand several hours, stirring occasionally. Line a 1½-quart bowl with aluminum foil, allowing for enough foil to fold over top. Fold fruit into ice cream; quickly pack mixture into bowl. Cover with foil; freeze. To serve, loosen ice cream from bowl by pulling on foil. Unmold on cold plate; remove foil. Whip cream; add sugar and vanilla. Frost ice cream with whipped cream. Top with toasted coconut. slice in wedges.

Peppermint Ice Cream

- ½ cup crushed peppermint stick candy
- 12 large marshmallows
- ¼ teaspoon salt
- 1 cup milk, scalded
- 1 cup whipping cream, whipped

Add ¼ cup crushed candy, marshmallows, and salt to the scalded milk; stir until dissolved. Pour into a freezer tray; freeze until firm about 2 hours. Place in a chilled bowl and beat until smooth. Fold in remaining candy and whipped cream. Return to tray and freeze until firm, 3 to 4 hours.

Mincemeat Bars

- 2 cups ground rolled oatmeal
- 1¾ cups sifted flour
- 1 cup brown sugar
- 1 cup butter or margarine
- 2 cups mincemeat pie filling

Mix oatmeal, flour, and sugar in a mixing bowl. Cut in butter until mixture is crumbly. Divide into 2 parts. Pack 1 part firmly in the bottom of a greased 9 x 13-inch baking pan. Spread the mincemeat evenly over the bottom layer; add remaining mixture and pack. Bake at 350° for 40 minutes. Cool thoroughly and cut into strips or bars.

Heavenly Rice Pudding

Makes 8 servings.

- ½ cup cooked white rice, chilled
- 1 8¾-ounce can pineapple chunks, drained, reserve syrup
- 1 cup miniature marshmallows
- 10 maraschino cherries, halved (⅓ cup)
- 1 package whipped topping mix
- 2 tablespoons maraschino cherry juice

In a large bowl, combine rice, pineapple, marshmallows, and cherries; stir until well combined. Refrigerate, covered, overnight. Prepare whipped topping mix according to package directions. Stir reserved pineapple syrup and cherry juice into rice mixture. Fold in whipped topping just until combined. Refrigerate 1 hour before serving.

Cherry Bars

¾ cup butter, softened
⅓ cup brown sugar
1½ cups sifted flour
2 tablespoons unflavored gelatin
½ cup cold water
2 cups white sugar
½ cup hot water
½ cup drained, quartered maraschino cherries or candied cherries
½ teaspoon almond extract or cherry juice
2 drops red food coloring
½ cup chopped walnuts or almonds, optional

Beat butter until creamy. Gradually add brown sugar, beating after each addition. Stir in flour. Press firmly into a 9 x 13-inch pan and bake at 325° until golden brown. Cool. Sprinkle gelatin over cold water and allow to soften. Combine white sugar and hot water in a saucepan. Place over high heat, stir and bring to a boil. Boil 2 minutes. Remove from heat and add softened gelatin. Beat with an electric mixer until very stiff. Fold in cherries, almond extract, coloring, and nuts. Spoon over cooled cake layer; cool. Cut into squares.

Pumpkin Squares

Makes 18 servings.

2 cups pumpkin
1 cup sugar
1 teaspoon salt
1 teaspoon ground ginger
1 teaspoon ground cinnamon
½ teaspoon ground nutmeg
1 cup chopped, toasted pecans
½ gallon vanilla ice cream, softened
36 gingersnaps

Combine pumpkin, sugar, salt, ginger, cinnamon, nutmeg, and chopped nuts. In a chilled bowl fold pumpkin mixture into the ice cream. Line bottom of a 9 x 13-inch pan with half of the gingersnaps. Top with half of the ice cream mixture. Cover with another layer of gingersnaps; add remaining ice cream mixture. Freeze until firm, about 5 hours. Cut into squares. Garnish with whipped cream and pecan halves.

Christmas Custard

Makes 8 servings.

½ cup sugar
3 eggs, well beaten
1 quart milk, scalded
½ teaspoon vanilla extract
⅛ teaspoon salt
⅛ teaspoon ground nutmeg
1 cup crushed pineapple, drained
Whipped cream, toasted coconut or maraschino cherries

Add sugar to the beaten eggs; beat until sugar is dissolved. Slowly add milk. Cook in top of a double boiler until mixture coats a spoon. Add vanilla, salt, and nutmeg. Stir in crushed pineapple; cool. If custard separates, smooth with further beating. Garnish with whipped cream, toasted coconut, or a maraschino cherry.

Note: Custard keeps well in refrigerator several days.

Chocolate and Apricot Crepes

Makes 12 to 14 crepes.

2 eggs
¼ cup sugar
1 teaspoon salt
1 1-ounce square unsweetened chocolate, melted
¼ teaspoon ground cinnamon
1 cup water
½ cup light cream
¾ cup flour
Apricot jam
Confectioners' sugar
1 cup whipping cream, whipped

Beat eggs until thick and light. Gradually add sugar and salt, beating well. Blend in melted chocolate and cinnamon. Combine water with cream; alternately add to chocolate mixture with flour. Pour 2 tablespoons at a time into a hot, well-buttered 8-inch skillet; cook, turning once, until lightly browned. Set crepes aside. Repeat until batter is used up. Spread each warm crepe with 1 tablespoon apricot jam. Roll up and sprinkle with confectioners' sugar. Top with whipped cream.

Chestnut Soufflé

Makes 6 servings.

- ½ pound fresh chestnuts
- ¼ cup sugar
- 1 cup cream or milk
- 3 eggs, separated
- 1 teaspoon vanilla extract
  Whipped cream

Pierce shells of chestnuts; boil or steam 20 minutes. Cool. Remove skins, peel, and force through a chopper. Add sugar and stir. Heat cream and add to chestnut mixture. Beat egg yolks until creamy; stir into mixture. Whip egg whites until stiff; fold into mixture. Add vanilla. Pour into a greased baking dish. Bake at 350° for 40 minutes. Serve with whipped cream.

Flaming Peaches

Makes 8 servings.

- Brown sugar
- 8 peach halves
  Butter, softened
- 4 cubes of sugar, halved
  Lemon extract

Sprinkle brown sugar in hollows of peach halves in baking dish. Dot with butter. Broil slowly until sugar crusts. Soak sugar cubes in lemon extract for 20 minutes. Place ½ sugar cube in the center of each peach half; ignite the sugar and serve.

Cherry Cheesecake Parfait

Makes 8 servings.

- 1 3-ounce package instant vanilla pudding
- 2 cups sour cream
- 1 8-ounce package cream cheese, softened
- ¼ cup sugar
- 2 teaspoons almond flavoring
- 1 teaspoon vanilla extract
- 1 21-ounce can cherry pie filling
- 1 3½-ounce can flaked coconut

Combine pudding mix, sour cream, and cream cheese; beat until smooth. Slowly stir in sugar and flavorings. Spoon into 8 parfait glasses, filling each half full. Add 1 tablespoon pie filling to each glass. Spoon remaining pudding over and top with another spoonful of pie filling. Garnish with coconut.

Winter Snowballs

- ½ cup butter, softened
- 1 cup sugar
- 2 eggs, separated
- 1 cup crushed pineapple, well drained
- ½ cup chopped nuts
- 1 box butter cookies
- 2 envelopes whipped topping
  Coconut

Combine butter, sugar, and egg yolks; cream well. Add pineapple and nuts. Beat egg whites until stiff; fold into mixture. Spread between individual butter cookies and stack until 4 inches high. Refrigerate overnight. Before serving, cover with whipped topping, prepared according to package directions, and sprinkle with coconut. Tint coconut for added color, if desired.

Frozen Yule Log

Makes 12 to 14 servings.

- 1 20-ounce can sliced pineapple, drained, reserve ¼ cup syrup
- 1 cup quartered maraschino cherries
- ⅔ cup slivered almonds, toasted
- ¼ cup honey
- 1 cup mayonnaise
- 2 cups whipping cream, whipped
  Almonds
  Mint leaves

Combine reserved pineapple syrup with cherries, almonds, honey, and mayonnaise. Fold in whipped cream. In a 2-pound coffee can, layer pineapple and whipped cream mixture. Cover with plastic wrap and freeze. To unmold, run spatula around the inside of can, cut around bottom of can and push log out. Sprinkle with additional almonds and garnish with mint leaves.

Chocolate-Fudge Fondue

- 1 can hot fudge topping
- 1 square baking chocolate

Warm hot fudge topping. Melt chocolate and stir into hot fudge topping. Serve as dipping sauce with cubed angel food cake, well-drained pineapple chunks, banana slices, fresh whole strawberries, and marshmallows.

Date Log

    1 cup brown sugar
    ½ cup butter, melted
    1 8-ounce box dates, chopped
    2 cups crisp rice cereal
    1 cup pecans
      Confectioners' sugar

Add sugar to melted butter and stir together over medium heat. Add dates. Boil 5 minutes and stir until sugar is melted. Remove from heat. Add rice cereal and pecans; mix well. Cool slightly. Form into the shape of a log. Roll in confectioners' sugar. Place on waxed paper. Slice and serve.

Cream Puff Wreath

    1 cup water
    ½ cup butter
    1 cup sifted flour
    4 eggs

Place water and butter in a saucepan; bring to a boil. Gradually add flour to form a soft ball. Beat in eggs, one at a time; continue beating until smooth. Drop by spoonfuls onto ungreased baking sheet according to size desired. Bake in a preheated 400° oven for 45 minutes. Cool, cut off tops, and fill with whipped cream, ice cream, or a favorite filling. Arrange cream puffs around a bowl of chocolate sauce; drizzle sauce over puffs before serving.

Mincemeat Cobbler

Makes 9 servings.

    1 18-ounce jar mincemeat with rum and brandy
    1 14½-ounce package coconut-pecan snack
      cake mix
    1 egg
    2 tablespoons butter, softened
      Whipped cream

Spread mincemeat in an 8-inch square pan. Mix together dry cake mix, egg, and butter until crumbly. Sprinkle over mincemeat. Bake at 325° for 45 to 50 minutes or until light brown. Serve warm. Garnish with whipped cream.

Charlotte Russe

Makes 6 servings.

    8 ladyfingers, split
    1 envelope unflavored gelatin
    ½ cup sugar
    1 cup milk, scalded
    ½ cup water
    4 egg yolks, beaten
    1 teaspoon vanilla extract
    1 teaspoon lemon juice
    2 cups prepared whipped topping

Place ladyfingers on bottom and around sides of a 6-cup mold or bowl or a 9 x 5-inch loaf pan. Combine gelatin and sugar in a saucepan. Stir in milk and water. Cook and stir over medium heat until mixture comes to a boil. Pour a small amount of hot mixture into egg yolks, stirring quickly to blend. Return to saucepan, cook and stir 1 minute. Chill until slightly thickened. Blend in vanilla, lemon juice, and whipped topping. Pour into lined mold. Chill until firm, at least 2 hours. Invert onto serving dish. Top with sweetened fruit, if desired.

Frozen Fruit Mold

Makes 8 servings.

    1 cup sour cream
    ½ 4½-ounce container frozen whipped topping,
      thawed
    ½ cup sugar
    2 tablespoons lemon juice
    1 teaspoon vanilla extract
    1 13-ounce can crushed pineapple, drained
    2 bananas, sliced or diced
    ½ cup sliced red candied cherries
    ½ cup sliced green candied cherries
    ½ cup chopped walnuts
      Lettuce
      Candied cherries

In a mixing bowl, blend sour cream, whipped topping, sugar, lemon juice, and vanilla. Fold in fruit and nuts. Pour into a 4½-cup ring mold. Freeze overnight. Unmold onto a lettuce-lined plate. Garnish with additional candied cherries. Let stand 10 minutes before serving.

Plum Good Party Mold

2 17-ounce cans greengage plums, drained, pitted, reserve syrup
2 tablespoons cornstarch
2 tablespoons lemon juice
5 drops green food coloring
½ gallon vanilla ice cream, softened

Sieve plums into a saucepan. Blend a few tablespoons syrup into cornstarch to make a smooth paste. Stir cornstarch mixture, remaining syrup, lemon juice, and food coloring into plums. Cook, stirring constantly, until thick and clear. Chill. Set aside ¼ cup sauce for garnish. Pour ½ cup sauce into mold; freeze. Fill mold, alternating layers of ice cream and sauce. Freeze. To serve, unmold and spoon reserved sauce over mold.

Brandied Fruit

Into a 2- or 3-gallon crock or jar with a cover, pour 1 pint of brandy. For each pint of fruit, add 1 pint of sugar. Add only fresh fruit in season. Do not use plums or canned or frozen fruit. Allow at least 1 week intervals between each addition of fruit and sugar. Store container, covered, in a dark, cool, dry place. For best flavor, allow fruit to set 4 months after last addition before using.

Peach Melba

Makes 6 servings.

6 peach halves
1 quart vanilla, peach or pistachio ice cream

Place 1 peach half in each serving dish. Top with a large scoop of ice cream. Spoon Melba Sauce over ice cream.

Melba Sauce

1½ teaspoons cornstarch
1 10-ounce package frozen raspberries, thawed
½ cup currant jelly

Blend cornstarch with 1 tablespoon juice from raspberries to make a smooth paste; set aside. In a saucepan heat raspberries with jelly. Stir in cornstarch mixture. Cook, stirring constantly, until thick and clear. Cool.

Sugar Plum Ring

1 package dry yeast
¼ cup lukewarm water (110 to 115°)
½ cup milk, scalded
⅓ cup sugar
⅓ cup shortening
1 teaspoon salt
3¾ cups flour
2 beaten eggs
¼ cup butter, melted
¾ cup sugar
1 teaspoon ground cinnamon
½ cup whole blanched almonds
½ cup whole candied red cherries
⅓ cup dark corn syrup

Soften yeast in warm water. Combine scalded milk, the ⅓ cup sugar, shortening, and salt; cool to lukewarm. Stir in 1 cup flour; beat well. Add yeast and eggs. Add remaining flour or enough to make soft dough. Place in a greased bowl turning once to grease surface. Cover and let rise until double in bulk. Punch down. Let rest 10 minutes. Divide dough into 4 parts. Cut each part into 10 pieces; shape into balls. Dip balls in melted butter. Combine the ¾ cup sugar and cinnamon; sprinkle on balls to coat. Arrange ⅓ of the balls in a well-greased tube pan. Sprinkle with ⅓ of the almonds and candied cherries. Repeat 2 more layers. Mix the corn syrup and butter left from dipping balls; drizzle over top. Cover and let rise until double in bulk. Bake at 350° for 35 minutes. Cool 15 minutes.

Peppermint Fluff

2 tablespoons finely crushed peppermint candy
1 pint peppermint ice cream, softened
4 cups milk
1 cup whipping cream
Peppermint ice cream
Crushed peppermint candy

In a large mixing bowl, beat the 2 tablespoons crushed candy into the 1 pint ice cream. Gradually blend in milk and whipping cream. Beat until frothy. Pour into chilled glasses. Top each with a scoop of ice cream. Sprinkle on crushed candy for garnish.

Filled Cookies

    4 cups brown sugar
    ¾ cup butter or margarine, softened
    4 eggs
    1 teaspoon cream of tartar
    1 teaspoon baking soda
    6 cups flour
    1 teaspoon vanilla extract

Blend sugar and butter. Add eggs one at a time; mix well after each addition. Sift together cream of tartar, baking soda, and flour; add to sugar and butter. Beat well. Add vanilla. Roll out on a floured surface; cut into circles. Place about 1 tablespoon of the Filling in the center of a circle. Place a second circle on top of Filling; press dough together. Bake on a greased baking sheet at 350° for 8 to 10 minutes.

Filling

    2½ cups raisins
    2 tablespoons cornstarch
    2 tablespoons water
    1 cup sugar
    1 cup chopped nuts

Place raisins in a saucepan; add enough water to cover raisins. Simmer until tender. Combine cornstrach and water to make a paste. Add paste and sugar to raisins; mix well. Stir in nuts.

Gingerbread Cookies

    2 cups flour
    1 teaspoon baking powder
    ¼ teaspoon baking soda
    1 teaspoon ground cinnamon
    ½ teaspoon ground ginger
    ⅓ cup sugar
    ½ cup shortening
    ½ cup molasses
    3 tablespoons hot water

Combine all ingredients in a large bowl; blend well. Chill dough 1 hour. Roll out on a floured surface to ⅛-inch thickness. Use gingerbread man cookie cutter. Place on ungreased baking sheets. Bake at 400° for 8 to 10 minutes. Cool and decorate.

Almond Crescents

Makes 40 cookies.

    1 cup butter or margarine, softened
    ½ cup plus 1 tablespoon confectioners' sugar
    1 egg yolk
    1 teaspoon vanilla extract
    1 teaspoon almond extract
    2 cups sifted flour
    1 cup finely chopped nuts
      Confectioners' sugar

Cream butter and sugar; beat well. Add egg yolk and flavorings; beat to blend. Gradually add flour, mixing until moistened. Add nuts and blend. Form into crescents about 2½ inches long. Bake on ungreased baking sheets at 350° for 20 minutes or until slightly golden. Remove from oven. Sprinkle with confectioners' sugar while still warm.

Springerle

Makes 3 dozen.

    2 eggs
    1 cup sugar
    2 cups sifted flour
    ¼ teaspoon salt
    1 teaspoon baking powder
    1 teaspoon anise extract or anise seed

Beat eggs at high speed in a small bowl of an electric mixer until thick and light colored. Add sugar gradually; turn mixer to low and beat until sugar is dissolved about 10 minutes. Fold in sifted dry ingredients and anise. Place a small portion of dough at a time on a well floured board; coat dough with flour and pat with palms of hands to ⅓-inch thickness. Dust springerle rolling pin with flour; press on dough to emboss the designs and get a clear imprint. Working quickly, cut out the squares, place on greased baking sheets and allow to dry at room temperature for 4 to 6 hours. Bake at 350° for 10 to 12 minutes. Cool. Store in a covered container to mellow and soften.

Gingerbread Cookies, Springerle,
Sugar Cookies, 48, Glazed Lebkuchen, 49

Christmas Candle Cookies

2 cups sugar
1 cup margarine
2 eggs
1 cup milk
7 cups flour
2 tablespoons baking powder
1 teaspoon salt
2 teaspoons vanilla extract

Combine all ingredients; mix well. Roll to ½ inch thick; cut with a cookie cutter or make desired pattern with cardboard. Place cut cookies on lightly greased baking sheets. Bake at 375° for 7 to 10 minutes or until edges are lightly browned. Frost.

Icing

2 tablespoons shortening
2 tablespoons light corn syrup
Flavoring to taste
Milk
Confectioners' sugar

Combine shortening, syrup, and flavoring. Add enough milk and sugar for desired consistency.

Note: This recipe can also be used to make jam tarts by cutting rounds, placing a teaspoonful of jam on one round, covering with another, and sealing the edges. Increase baking time by 2 to 3 minutes.

Cathedral Window Cookies

½ cup butter or margarine
1 12-ounce package chocolate chips
2 eggs, well beaten
½ cup ground nuts, optional
1 10½-ounce package colored miniature marshmallows
Confectioners' sugar

Slowly melt the butter and chocolate chips. Remove from heat; stir in eggs and nuts. Cool. Gradually add marshmallows, mixing well after each addition. Divide mixture into 3 rolls; roll each in confectioners' sugar, wrap in waxed paper, and refrigerate. Chill 3 to 4 hours or overnight. Slice and serve.

Cinnamon Krinkles

2⅔ cups sifted flour
2 teaspoons cream of tartar
2 teaspoons baking soda
½ teaspoon salt
1 cup butter
1½ cups sugar
2 eggs
2 tablespoons ground cinnamon
3 tablespoons sugar

Sift together flour, cream of tartar, baking soda, and salt; set aside. Cream butter and sugar. Add eggs, one at a time; beat well after each addition. Add dry ingredients. Refrigerate 1 hour. Drop by teaspoonfuls onto a greased baking sheet. Combine cinnamon and sugar; sprinkle on cookies. Bake at 350° for 12 to 15 minutes.

Sugar Cookies

Makes 6 dozen.

4 cups sifted cake flour
2½ teaspoons baking powder
½ teaspoon salt
⅔ cup shortening
1½ cups sugar
2 eggs
1 teaspoon vanilla extract
4 teaspoons milk

Sift together flour, baking powder, and salt; set aside. Mix shortening, sugar, eggs, and vanilla until light and fluffy. Alternately add flour mixture and milk; blend well. Refrigerate dough until easy to handle. On a floured surface, roll ⅓ of the dough at a time, keeping the remaining dough refrigerated. For crisp cookies roll dough thin. Cut into desired shapes. Arrange ½ inch apart on a greased baking sheet. Decorate with white or colored sugar, chopped nuts, flaked coconut, cinnamon, or candied fruit. Bake at 400° for 9 minutes.

Note: Clean strings may be pressed into the cookies to form a loop so cookies can be hung on the Christmas tree.

Christmas Drop Cookies

Makes 8 dozen.

1½ cups flour
½ pound blanched almonds, chopped
½ pound walnuts, chopped
½ pound Brazil nuts, chopped
1 pound dates, chopped
3 slices candied pineapple, cut up
½ cup butter
¾ cup brown sugar
1 large egg, beaten
½ teaspoon vanilla extract
½ teaspoon baking soda
¼ teaspoon salt

Combine ½ cup of the flour, the nuts, and fruit; mix thoroughly and set aside. Cream butter and sugar; add beaten egg and vanilla. Mix in the remaining 1 cup flour, baking soda, and salt. Add floured nuts and fruit; mix well. Drop by teaspoonfuls onto a greased baking sheet. Bake at 350° for 15 minutes. Cool and store in air-tight containers 1 week before using.

Glazed Lebkuchen

Makes 2 dozen.

¾ cup honey
½ cup granulated sugar
¼ cup packed brown sugar
2 eggs, beaten
2½ cups sifted flour
1 teaspoon baking soda
¼ teaspoon ground cloves
1¼ teaspoons ground cinnamon
⅛ teaspoon ground allspice
½ cup minced citron
½ cup minced candied lemon peel
¾ cup chopped blanched almonds
1 cup confectioners' sugar
3 tablespoons hot milk
¼ teaspoon vanilla extract
   Candied cherries, citron

Bring honey to a boil in a saucepan; cool. Add sugars and eggs; beat well. Blend in sifted dry ingredients, fruit, and almonds. Spread into a greased 10 x 15 x 1-inch pan. Bake at 350° for about 25 minutes. Blend confectioners' sugar, milk, and vanilla; spread over warm cake. Decorate with fruits. Cut into bars.

Christmas Seed Cookies

Makes 8 dozen.

2½ cups sifted cake flour
½ teaspoon baking powder
⅛ teaspoon salt
1 cup sugar
1 cup butter, softened
2 egg yolks
1 teaspoon vanilla extract
   Caraway, sesame or poppy seed

Sift the first 4 ingredients; cut in butter. Add egg yolks and vanilla; blend. Chill several hours. Roll to ⅛ inch thick and cut into desired shapes. Place on baking sheets; sprinkle with seed. Bake at 400° for about 8 minutes.

Pecan Balls

Makes 4 dozen.

1 cup margarine, softened
¼ cup sugar
2 cups sifted flour
2 cups pecans, broken into small pieces
   Confectioners' sugar
   Granulated sugar

Cream margarine, sugar, and flour; add pecans and mix well. Shape 1 tablespoon per cookie into balls; place on ungreased baking sheets. Bake at 300° for 45 minutes. Combine confectioners' and granulated sugars. Roll balls in sugars while still hot.

Chocolate Nut Puffs

Makes 3 dozen puffs.

1 cup (6-ounces) semisweet chocolate chips
2 egg whites
⅛ teaspoon salt
½ cup sugar
½ teaspoon vinegar
½ teaspoon vanilla extract
¾ cup chopped nuts

Melt chocolate over warm water; set aside. Beat egg white with salt until foamy. Gradually add sugar; beat until stiff peaks form. Beat in vinegar and vanilla. Fold in melted chocolate and nuts. Drop by teaspoonfuls on a greased baking sheet. Bake at 350° for about 10 minutes.

Raisin-Currant Bars

Makes 3½ dozen bars.

1½ cups sifted flour
 1 teaspoon baking powder
 1 cup firmly packed brown sugar
1½ cups quick-cooking rolled oats
 ¾ cup butter

Combine all ingredients; mix until crumbly. Pat ⅔ of the dough in a greased 9 x 13-inch baking pan. Spread with Fruit-Spice Filling. Cover with remaining crumbs. Bake at 350° for 35 minutes. Cool and cut into bars.

Fruit-Spice Filling

 1 cup raisins
 1 cup currants
1½ cups hot water
 1 cup sugar
 2 tablespoons flour
 1 teaspoon ground cinnamon
 ½ teaspoon ground cloves
 1 teaspoon vinegar
 1 tablespoon butter

Combine all ingredients in a saucepan. Bring to a boil and cook until thick, stirring occasionally.

Snow-Covered Gingersnaps

 ¾ cup shortening, softened
 1 cup sugar
 ¼ cup molasses
 1 egg
 2 cups flour
 2 teaspoons baking soda
 1 scant teaspoon salt
 1 teaspoon ground cloves
 1 teaspoon ground cinnamon
 1 teaspoon ground ginger
 Confectioners' sugar

Cream shortening; add sugar gradually, creaming well after each addition. Add molasses; mix well. Add egg; beat. Measure flour before sifting; add soda, salt, and spices. Stir into dough. Roll into balls the size of a walnut; roll in confectioners' sugar. Place 2 inches apart on an ungreased baking sheet. Bake at 350° for 10 to 12 minutes. Sprinkle with confectioners' sugar before removing from baking sheet.

Coconut Dainties

Makes 4 dozen.

 1 cup butter or margarine, softened
 ¼ cup sifted confectioners' sugar
 2 teaspoons vanilla extract
 1 tablespoon water
 2 cups sifted flour
 1 cup chopped pecans
 Confectioners' sugar
 Finely shredded coconut

Thoroughly cream butter, sugar, and vanilla. Stir in water and flour; mix well. Stir in nuts. Shape into 1-inch balls. Place 1 inch apart on an ungreased baking sheet. Bake at 300° for 20 minutes or until firm. Dip cookies in confectioners' sugar and roll in coconut.

Cream Cheese Cookies

 1 small package cream cheese, softened
 ¼ pound margarine, softened
 1 egg yolk
2½ tablespoons sugar
 3 ounces chocolate chips
 1 cup flour

Mix ingredients together, adding flour last. Chill in refrigerator 2 hours or overnight. Use wax paper to form dough into roll. Refrigerate. Cut into ¼-inch slices to form cookies. Bake on ungreased baking sheets at 350° for 20 minutes or until light brown around edges.

Mother's Butterscotch Cookies

 ½ cup butter, softened
 2 cups brown sugar
 2 eggs
 2 teaspoons vanilla extract
 3 cups flour
 2 teaspoons baking powder
 ½ teaspoon baking soda
 ⅛ teaspoon salt
 ½ cup chopped pecans or hickory nuts

Cream butter and sugar. Stir in unbeaten eggs. Add vanilla, sifted dry ingredients, and nuts; mix well. Knead into a roll and refrigerate several hours or overnight. Cut into very thin slices. Bake at 375° for 15 minutes.

Candies

Butter Toffee

2¼ cups sugar
1 teaspoon salt
½ cup water
1¼ cups butter
1½ cups (½-pound) chopped, blanched almonds
1 cup finely chopped walnuts
¼ pound milk chocolate, melted

Bring sugar, salt, water, and butter to a boil. Add half of the almonds. Cook, stirring constantly, to the hard-crack stage (290° on a candy thermometer). Remove from heat. Add remaining almonds and half of the walnuts. Pour into a greased, shallow 9 x 13-inch pan. Cool. Brush with melted chocolate and sprinkle with remaining walnuts. Let chocolate harden; then break into pieces.

Holiday Pralines

1 cup brown sugar
1 cup white sugar
1 cup light cream
⅛ teaspoon salt
3 tablespoons butter
1 cup chopped pecans
1 tablespoon maple syrup

Bring first 3 ingredients to a full boil for 1 minute. Add remaining ingredients and cook to soft-ball stage (234° on a candy thermometer). Quickly stir and drop by teaspoonfuls onto waxed paper. Cool.

Lemon Taffy

1½ cups sugar
¾ cup water
½ teaspoon cream of tartar
⅓ teaspoon lemon extract

Boil all ingredients without stirring until brittle when dropped in cold water (300° on a candy thermometer). Cool slightly. Butter hands. Pull with tips of fingers and thumbs until taffy is light and creamy. Set aside to harden; break into chunks. Store in air-tight containers.

Fairy Food

Makes 1 pound.

1 cup sugar
1 cup light corn syrup
1 tablespoon vinegar
1½ tablespoons baking soda
1 6-ounce package semisweet chocolate chips, melted

Mix sugar, syrup, and vinegar in a 3-quart saucepan; cook to hard-crack stage (300° on a candy thermometer). Remove from heat. Add baking soda; mix quickly. Pour into a greased 11 x 7-inch pan. Cool. Invert on a tray and spread with melted chocolate. Break into chunks.

Frosties

20 large marshmallows
¼ cup evaporated milk
1½ cups shredded coconut

Cook 8 marshmallows and evaporated milk in the top of a double boiler, stirring constantly, until marshmallows dissolve. Remove from heat but leave mixture over hot water. Cut 12 marshmallows in half and dip, one at a time, into mixture. Roll in shredded coconut; place on waxed paper. The coconut may be toasted a light brown, if desired.

Hard Candy

1¾ cups sugar
½ cup light corn syrup
½ cup water
1 teaspoon flavoring
Food coloring

Combine sugar, corn syrup, and water in a saucepan. Bring to a boil over medium heat until mixture reaches 300° on a candy thermometer. Remove from heat; add flavoring and a few drops of food coloring. For variety, divide mixture in half and add ½ teaspoon each of different flavorings and colors. Pour onto a marble slab to cool. Cut with scissors or break with a knife into strips. Store in glass jars.

Tiny Tim Oranges

Makes 40 oranges.

    Peel of 4 medium oranges
2 cups sugar

Place orange peel in a saucepan; cover with cold water and simmer until tender. Drain well. Reserve 1 cup of the water in which the peel was cooked. Put orange peel through a food chopper, using coarse blades. Combine sugar and 1 cup reserved orange liquid. Stir over low heat until sugar dissolves. Cook to 238° on a candy thermometer, or until a little of the mixture forms a soft ball when dropped in cold water. Add orange peel, simmer 10 minutes or until most of the liquid has evaporated. Spread in a buttered shallow pan. When cool enough to handle, form into ¾-inch balls. Roll in granulated sugar to which orange food coloring has been added.

Maple Butternut Candy

6 cups sugar
4 cups maple syrup
¼ cup butter
2 cups chopped butternuts or pecans

Combine sugar, syrup, and butter; cook to soft-ball stage (about 236° on a candy thermometer). Remove from heat. Add nuts; stir until thick enough so that nuts do not rise to the top. Pour into 2 greased 9 x 13-inch pans.

Candy Strawberries

1 pound shredded coconut
2 6-ounce packages wild strawberry-flavored gelatin
1 can sweetened condensed milk
1 teaspoon almond extract
    Red crystal sugar
    Strawberry stems or green crystal sugar

Grind coconut in a blender. Mix all ingredients together. Shape into strawberries. Roll in red sugar. Insert strawberry stems, if available from a cake decorating shop. If stems are unavailable, dip top part of strawberry in green sugar.

Christmas Pudding Candy

3 cups sugar
1 cup light cream
1 tablespoon butter
1 teaspoon vanilla extract
1 pound dates, cut up
1 pound figs, cut up
1 pound raisins
1 pound flaked coconut
1 or 2 cups chopped nuts

Cook sugar, cream, and butter to soft-ball stage (about 236° on a candy thermometer). Add vanilla; beat until creamy. Add fruit, coconut, and nuts; mix well. Roll into a loaf. Wrap in dampened cloth, then in waxed paper; store in a cool place for 2 weeks. Slice in desired shapes when ready to use.

Marzipan

¼ cup margarine, softened
¼ cup light corn syrup
¼ teaspoon salt
½ teaspoon lemon or vanilla extract
1 pound confectioners' sugar
1 cup almond paste
    Food coloring

Cream margarine, syrup, salt, and flavoring. Add sugar, ⅓ at a time, and mix well after each addition. Knead in almond paste. Color with a few drops of food coloring. Mold into small shapes of fruits and vegetables or use as the center of candied cherries, dates, and prunes.

Caramel Turtles

1 cup pecan halves
36 light caramels
½ cup sweet chocolate, melted

Arrange pecans, flat-side-down, in clusters of 4 on a greased baking sheet. Place 1 caramel on each cluster of pecans. Heat at 325° until caramels soften, 4 to 8 minutes. Remove from the oven; flatten caramel with buttered spatula. Cool slightly and remove from pan to waxed paper. Swirl melted chocolate on top.

Maple Seafoam

      3 cups firmly packed light brown sugar
    ¾ cup water
      1 tablespoon maple syrup
      2 egg whites
    ⅛ teaspoon salt
      1 teaspoon vanilla extract
      1 teaspoon maple flavoring
    1½ cups broken walnuts, optional

Mix sugar, water, and maple syrup in a sauce-pan; bring to a boil. Cook to soft-ball stage (about 236° on a candy thermometer). Beat egg whites with the salt until stiff. Pour sugar syrup over egg whites in a thin stream, beating constantly. Continue beating until thick and creamy. Add flavorings and nuts. Drop from teaspoon onto a well-greased pan.

Peanut Brittle

      2 cups sugar
      1 cup light corn syrup
    ½ cup water
    ¼ teaspoon salt
      1 teaspoon butter
      2 cups raw Spanish peanuts
      2 teaspoons baking soda

Using a large saucepan, boil first 4 ingredients together until mixture reaches thread stage (238° on a candy thermometer). Add butter and pea-nuts. Cook, stirring constantly until golden brown. Remove from heat; add baking soda. (Mixture will bubble up.) Mix well. Pour onto a well-greased baking sheet. As it cools, pull as thin as possible. When cool, break into pieces. Store in an airtight container.

Tan Fudge

      2 cups sugar
      1 cup milk
      1 7-ounce jar marshmallow creme
      1 12-ounce jar crunchy peanut butter
      1 teaspoon vanilla extract

Combine sugar and milk in a large, heavy sauce-pan. Slowly bring to a boil. Cook, stirring, to soft ball stage (238° on a candy thermometer). Re-move from heat; add remaining ingredients. Beat until blended. Pour into a buttered 9-inch pan; cool. Cut into squares.

Rainbow Popcorn Balls

    ½ cup unpopped corn
    ¼ cup plus 2 tablespoons salad oil
    1½ cups salted peanuts, coarsely chopped
      1 cup light corn syrup
    ½ cup sugar
      1 3-ounce package strawberry- or lime-flavored gelatin
        Red or green food coloring

To pop corn, heat oil over medium heat. Add popcorn in a single layer. Heat until all corn is popped. Turn into a bowl; add peanuts to popcorn and toss to mix. Set aside. In a 1-quart saucepan combine corn syrup and sugar. Cook, stirring with a wooden spoon, until sugar dissolves. Without stirring, bring mixture to a full rolling boil. Remove from heat and add gelatin. Stir until dissolved and add food coloring. Pour over pop-corn and mix. Butter hands and form into balls.

No-Cook Chocolate Fudge
Makes about 2 pounds.

      1 pound confectioners' sugar
      2 eggs, well beaten
      1 cup broken nuts
      1 teaspoon vanilla extract
      6 squares unsweetened chocolate
      2 tablespoons butter

Sift sugar; add to the eggs. Mix until smooth. Add nuts and vanilla. Melt chocolate slowly in the top of a double boiler, stirring constantly. Add butter to melted chocolate and blend. Add chocolate mixture to nut mixture; mix well. Quickly pour into a 10 x 6-inch well-greased pan. Let harden. When firm, cut into pieces.

Maple Seafoam, Tan Fudge,
No-Cook Chocolate Fudge,
Rainbow Popcorn Balls,
Peanut Brittle

New Year's Eve Buffet

Lemon Champagne Sparkler

- 2 12-ounce cans frozen lemonade concentrate
- 2 12-ounce cans frozen pineapple juice
- 1½ quarts water
- 2 quarts ginger ale, chilled
- 1 quart sparkling water, chilled
- 1 bottle (⅘-quart) dry champagne, chilled

Mix concentrated lemonade, pineapple juice, and water. Chill, covered. Before serving add ginger ale and sparkling water; pour into a large punch bowl. Add ice cubes. Pour champagne over punch and stir.

New Year's Herring Dip

- 1 8-ounce package cream cheese, softened
- 2 tablespoons chopped pimiento
- 1 8-ounce jar herring fillets in wine sauce, drained
- 1 cup cottage cheese

Combine cream cheese and pimiento. Cut herring into small pieces. Fold herring and cottage cheese into cream cheese. Heat mixture over low heat until hot and bubbly. Transfer to a chafing dish; keep warm. Add herring liquid as needed for dipping consistency. Serve with assorted crackers.

Pickled Shrimp

Makes 12 servings.

- ½ clove garlic
- 1 teaspoon salt
- ½ cup cider vinegar
- ¼ cup salad oil
- 4 drops Tabasco sauce
- 2 tablespoons chopped stuffed olives
- 3 tablespoons minced parsley
- 2 tablespoons chopped dill pickle
- 2 pounds jumbo shrimp, cooked and cleaned

Mash garlic and salt together. Add all ingredients and place in a quart jar; shake well. Place in refrigerator at least 24 hours before serving. Serve with slices of pumpernickel bread.

Ham and Cheese Specials

Makes 8 open-face sandwiches.

- 2 3-ounce packages cream cheese, softened
- 2 teaspoons ground cinnamon
- 1 16-ounce can brown bread, cut into 8 slices
- 8 slices boiled ham
- 2 8-ounce cans sliced pineapple in unsweetened juice, drained, reserve 5 tablespoons juice
- 1 10½-ounce can chicken gravy

Combine cream cheese and cinnamon. Spread about 1 tablespoon on each slice of bread. Top with ham and pineapple. Broil 4 inches from heat for 5 minutes or until hot. In a saucepan blend gravy and reserved pineapple juice into the remaining cream cheese mixture. Heat, stirring occasionally. Spoon over sandwiches.

Gourmet Meat Roll

Makes 8 servings.

- 2 eggs, beaten
- ¾ cup soft bread crumbs
- ½ cup tomato juice
- ¼ cup sherry
- 2 tablespoons chopped parsley
- 1 small clove garlic, chopped
- ½ teaspoon salt
- ¼ teaspoon black pepper
- 2 pounds ground beef
- 8 thin slices boiled ham
- 1½ cups shredded mozzarella cheese
- 3 slices mozzarella cheese, halved diagonally

Combine eggs, bread crumbs, tomato juice, sherry, parsley, garlic, salt, and pepper. Stir in ground beef, mixing well. On foil or waxed paper, pat meat to a 12 x 10-inch rectangle. Arrange ham slices on top of meat, leaving a small margin around edges. Sprinkle shredded cheese over ham. Starting from short end, roll up meat, using foil to lift. Seal edges and ends. Place roll seam-side-down in a 13 x 9-inch pan. Bake at 350° for 1 hour and 15 minutes. Place cheese wedges over top of roll, return to oven for 5 minutes until cheese melts.

Orange Eggnog Punch

2 pints raspberry, orange or lime sherbet
2 cups pineapple juice
2 cups orange juice
1 quart dairy eggnog

In a mixing bowl, place all but 1 cup of the sherbet; beat until smooth. Add juices and blend thoroughly. Gradually add eggnog. Pour into a punch bowl. Float small scoops of sherbet on top.

Fruit Salad

1 can mandarin oranges, drained, reserve juice
1 can pineapple chunks, drained, reserve juice
1 package vanilla pudding
1 package vanilla tapioca pudding
1 tablespoon (heaping) frozen orange juice concentrate, thawed
1 banana, sliced

Add enough water to reserved fruit juices to measure 3 cups. Cook puddings with the 3 cups liquid and orange juice concentrate. Cool slightly; add fruits and gently toss. Refrigerate.

Stuffed Mushrooms

1 pound mushrooms
1 tablespoon chopped onion
½ cup butter
1 10-ounce package frozen spinach, cooked and drained
Ground nutmeg
Salt and pepper
⅓ cup grated Cheddar cheese

Twist out mushroom stems and chop. Sauté chopped stems and onion in half of the butter. Remove from skillet and set aside. Add remaining butter to skillet; gently sauté mushroom caps. Remove and set aside on absorbent paper. Put spinach, sautéed onion, and mushroom stems in blender. Add seasonings. Puree. Fill mushroom caps with teaspoonfuls of mixture. Sprinkle each with grated cheese. Bake on a cookie sheet at 375° for 15 minutes.

Note: These may be made ahead and refrigerated to bake just before serving.

Sausage and Oyster Casserole

1 pound pork sausage, cut into 1-inch pieces
1 small can button mushrooms
½ cup chopped onion
2 10¾-ounce cans cream of celery soup
1 cup milk
1½ teaspoons salt
¼ teaspoon black pepper
½ cup chopped parsley
1 pint oysters
3 cups cooked elbow macaroni

Fry sausage in a skillet until lightly browned. Remove sausage to paper towels using a slotted spoon. Pour off half of the fat. Add mushrooms and onion to remaining fat; sauté until onion is transparent. Stir in soup, milk, seasoning, and parsley. Cook until thoroughly heated. Add oysters and half of the browned sausage; mix. Heat thoroughly. In a greased 3-quart casserole, alternately layer macaroni and sausage-oyster mixture. Top with remaining sausage. Bake at 350° for 30 minutes.

Snowball Cake

2½ packages unflavored gelatin
5 tablespoons water
1 cup boiling water
2½ cups sliced pineapple, drained
1 cup sugar
1 tablespoon lemon juice
5 packages whipped topping
1 angel food cake
1 cup chopped pecans
½ teaspoon vanilla extract
1 can flaked coconut

Dissolve gelatin in the 5 tablespoons water. Add the 1 cup boiling water, pineapple, sugar, and lemon juice to gelatin and mix. Refrigerate until thick. Prepare 4 packages of the whipped topping. Break cake into bite-size pieces; add to the whipped topping. Add nuts and vanilla. Combine cake mixture and gelatin mixture. Spoon into a buttered tube pan. Refrigerate overnight to set. Prepare remaining 1 package of whipped topping and frost cake. Sprinkle with flaked coconut.

Gifts from the Kitchen

Coconut Christmas Cookie Tree

Makes 1 cookie tree.

1½ cups butter or margarine
  1 cup sugar
  2 eggs
4½ cups sifted flour
  1 teaspoon vanilla extract
  1 teaspoon almond extract
  2 cups flaked coconut
  ¼ cup hot milk
  1 pound unsifted confectioners' sugar
    Green food coloring, optional
    Flaked coconut

Cut star-shaped patterns from heavy paper 9, 8, 7¼, 6½, 5½, 4¾, 4, and 3 inches in diameter, measuring from point to point. Cut two round patterns, 2½ and 1½ inches in diameter.

Cream butter until soft; gradually add sugar, beating until light and fluffy. Add eggs and beat well. Add flour, a small amount at a time, mixing well after each addition. Blend in vanilla, almond extract, and the 2 cups flaked coconut. Divide dough into 2 equal portions, wrap in waxed paper and chill 30 minutes or until firm enough to roll. Roll dough ⅛ inch thick on a lightly floured board. Cut 2 cookies from each star pattern, making a total of 16 cookies. Cut 12 cookies from the 1½-inch round pattern and 20 cookies from the 2½-inch round pattern. With a large drinking straw, cut a hole in the center of each cookie. Place on ungreased baking sheets. Bake at 350° for 8 minutes, or until edges are lightly browned. Cool. Gradually add hot milk to the confectioners' sugar, using just enough milk for a spreading consistency. Tint green with food coloring, if desired. Spread on each star-shaped cookie. Sprinkle flaked coconut on edges.

To Assemble Tree

Place a 12- to 15-inch stick or thin candle in a candle holder; secure with paper. Slip 2 of the larger round cookies over the stick. Slip on largest star cookie and continue to stack cookies in decreasing size, placing 2 round cookies between star-shaped cookies. Top with a rosette of frosting or a small candle. Decorate with silver dragées or small candles, if desired.

Nut Roll

Makes about 5 pounds.

  1 7½-ounce jar marshmallow creme
  1 teaspoon vanilla extract
3½ cups confectioners' sugar
  1 pound caramels
9½ cups chopped nuts

Combine marshmallow creme and vanilla; add sugar gradually. Shape into rolls about 1 inch in diameter. Wrap in plastic wrap and freeze for at least 6 hours. Melt caramels over hot water; keep warm. Dip candy rolls in caramels and roll in nuts until well coated. Cool and store in an airtight container.

Striped Cookies

Makes about 5½ dozen.

2½ cups sifted cake flour
  1 teaspoon baking powder
  ½ teaspoon salt
  ½ cup butter or margarine, softened
  ⅔ cup sugar
  1 egg
  1 tablespoon milk
  1 square unsweetened chocolate, melted
    Milk

Sift together flour, baking powder, and salt; set aside. Cream butter and sugar; beat until light and fluffy. Add egg and milk, blend well. Add flour mixture, a small amount at a time, beating well after each addition. Divide dough in half. Blend chocolate into one half. If necessary chill or freeze both parts of dough until firm enough to roll. Roll each portion of dough on a lightly floured board into a 9 x 4½-inch rectangle. Brush chocolate dough lightly with milk; place plain dough on top. Using a long, sharp knife, cut rectangle lengthwise into 3 equal strips 1½ inches wide. Brush each layer with milk. Stack strips, alternating colors, and press together lightly. Carefully wrap in waxed paper. Freeze until firm enough to slice, or refrigerate overnight. Cut into ⅛-inch slices, using a very sharp knife. Place on greased baking sheets. Bake at 400° for 6 to 8 minutes or just until white portions begin to brown.

Coconut Christmas Cookie Tree
Striped Cookies

59

Cranberry Claret Jelly

Makes 4 cups.

3½ cups sugar
1 cup cranberry juice cocktail
1 cup claret wine
3 ounces liquid fruit pectin

Combine sugar, cranberry juice cocktail, and wine in a large saucepan. Stir over medium heat, bringing mixture to just below the boiling point. Continue stirring until the sugar is dissolved, about 5 minutes. Remove from heat. Stir in fruit pectin; mix well. Skim off foam and pour quickly into glasses. Seal with paraffin.

Holiday Conserve

Makes 6 cups.

2 30-ounce cans apricot halves, drained, reserve 1½ cups syrup
1 cup candied mixed fruits
½ cup quartered red candied cherries
1½ cups sugar
¼ teaspoon salt
¼ teaspoon ground nutmeg
1 tablespoon grated lemon peel
1 tablespoon grated orange peel
1½ cups finely chopped pecans

Coarsely chop the apricots. Place all ingredients except pecans in a Dutch oven. Bring to a boil, stirring occasionally. Reduce heat; simmer, uncovered, 25 minutes or until thickened. Stir in pecans. Ladle into hot sterilized jars; seal with lid or cover with paraffin.

Stuffed Dates

Fill centers of pitted dates with 1 or more of the following: walnuts, pecans, peanut butter mixed with chopped peanuts, plain fondant or fondant mixed with chopped candied fruits. Roll in confectioners' sugar or finely grated coconut. Store in an air-tight container in the refrigerator.

Mini-Fruitcakes

Makes 3 dozen.

3 cups unsifted flour
1⅓ cups sugar
1 teaspoon salt
1 teaspoon baking powder
2 teaspoons ground cinnamon
1 teaspoon ground nutmeg
½ cup orange juice
½ cup brandy or water
1 cup vegetable oil
4 eggs
¼ cup light corn syrup
1 cup dark seedless raisins
2 cups diced, dried California apricots
2 cups mixed candied fruits
2 cups pecan halves
⅓ cup light corn syrup

In a large mixing bowl, combine all ingredients except fruits, nuts, and ⅓ cup corn syrup. Blend for ½ minute on low speed, scraping bowl constantly. Beat 3 minutes on high speed, scraping bowl occasionally. Stir in fruits and nuts. Spoon batter into 3 dozen 2½-inch muffin pans lined with paper baking cups. Bake at 275° for 65 to 70 minutes or until toothpick comes out clean when inserted in center of fruitcake. Cool fruitcakes in pans for 5 minutes; remove to cooling rack. Cool thoroughly. Heat corn syrup in a small pan; brush over tops of cakes. Place cupcakes in container; cover with cheesecloth soaked in brandy. Cover tightly; store in a cool place for up to 2 weeks. For longer storage, freeze in tightly covered containers.

Meltaway Maple Crisps

½ cup butter, softened
¼ cup sugar
1 teaspoon maple flavoring
2 cups sifted cake flour
¾ cup chopped pecans

Cream butter; add sugar gradually. Add flavoring and beat until fluffy. Stir in flour; mix well. Fold in pecans; press into a ball. Pinch off small pieces of dough and place on an ungreased baking sheet. Flatten cookies with a glass dipped in sugar. Bake at 350° for 7 minutes.

Candied Orange Coffee Cake

    ¾ cup sugar
    ¼ cup butter or margarine, softened
    1 egg
    ½ cup milk
    1½ cups sifted flour
    2 teaspoons baking powder
    ½ teaspoon salt
    4 teaspoons minced candied orange peel
    1 tablespoon grated orange rind

Blend sugar, butter, and egg until light and fluffy. Alternately add milk and dry ingredients. Add orange peel and rind, stirring until just combined. Pour into a greased mold. Sprinkle with the Topping. Bake at 375° for 25 to 30 minutes.

Topping

    ½ cup sugar
    ⅓ cup flour
    1 tablespoon grated orange rind
    ¼ cup chopped candied orange peel
    ¼ cup butter or margarine

Combine all ingredients; mix until crumbly.

Note: To freeze, cool, and tightly cover. To serve, heat at 350° for 20 minutes if frozen; 10 minutes if thawed.

Nut Stollen

Makes 2 stollens.

    1 package dry yeast
    ¼ cup lukewarm water (110 to 115°)
    1 teaspoon sugar
    ¾ cup shortening or margarine
    2 cups flour
    2 eggs, beaten
      Poppy or prune cake filling

Dissolve yeast in water; add the sugar. Cut shortening into flour until crumbly; add eggs and the yeast mixture. Divide dough into 2 parts. Roll out each part into a rectangle. Spread with poppy or prune filling or use your own favorite filling. Roll up jelly-roll style from long side; seal edges. Place on a greased baking sheet. Make 3 slashes crosswise or 1 long cut through center. Bake at 350° for 30 minutes.

Marmalade Nut Bread

    2½ cups unsifted flour
    ⅓ cup sugar
    3½ teaspoons baking powder
    1 teaspoon salt
    1 cup coarsely chopped walnuts
    1 egg
    1 cup orange marmalade
    1 cup orange juice
    3 tablespoons vegetable oil

In a large mixing bowl, thoroughly stir together flour, sugar, baking powder, and salt. Add walnuts; toss to coat evenly. In a medium bowl, beat egg slightly; stir in marmalade, orange juice, and vegetable oil. Add to flour mixture; stir only until dry ingredients are moistened. Divide batter evenly between 2 well-greased 9 x 5-inch loaf pans. Bake at 350° for 1 hour or until toothpick inserted in center comes out clean. Cool in pans on rack 10 minutes; remove from pans; cool thoroughly on rack. Wrap tightly and let stand several hours before serving.

Spicy Applesauce Cake

    2 cups sifted flour
    1½ teaspoons baking soda
    ½ teaspoon salt
    ½ teaspoon each: ground cinnamon, cloves, nutmeg and allspice
    ½ cup butter or margarine, softened
    1 teaspoon vanilla extract
    1 cup firmly packed light brown sugar
    ½ cup white sugar
    2 eggs, lightly beaten
    1½ cups sweetened applesauce
    ¾ cup each: chopped dates, raisins, broken walnuts
      Confectioners' sugar

Line an ungreased 9 x 5-inch loaf pan with aluminum foil. Sift flour with soda, salt, and spices. Cream butter, vanilla, and sugars until light and fluffy. Add eggs; continue beating until very light. Add flour mixture alternately with the applesauce, stirring until just blended. Combine dates, raisins, and nuts; fold in lightly. Spoon into loaf pan. Bake at 325° for 1 hour or until cake is firm and springy when touched. Cool and sprinkle with confectioners' sugar.

Cranberry-Orange Relish

Makes 2 pints.

- 4 cups (1-pound) cranberries
- 2 oranges, seeds removed
- 2 cups sugar

Put cranberries and oranges, including rind, through a food chopper. Add sugar; mix well. Chill.

Maple Squash

Makes 8 servings.

- 1 3-pound butternut squash, cut into eighths, seeds and pulp removed
- ¼ cup butter or margarine
- ¼ cup maple syrup
- ½ teaspoon salt
  Ground nutmeg to taste
  Black pepper to taste

Place squash in boiling salted water; cover. Heat to boiling and cook 15 minutes or until tender. Drain, pare, and mash. Combine remaining ingredients with squash and heat thoroughly.

Cornish Game Hens with Wild Rice

- 4 ounces fresh mushrooms
- ½ cup butter or margarine
- ½ cup walnut halves
- 4 1- to 1¼-pound Cornish game hens
- ¾ cup wild rice
- 1 teaspoon instant minced onion
- 2 cups water
- 4 chicken bouillon cubes
  Garlic salt and black pepper to taste

Clean mushrooms; remove and slice stems. Melt 2 tablespoons butter in an electric skillet. Add mushrooms and walnuts; sauté lightly. Remove from skillet and set aside. Clean birds inside and out; dry with absorbent paper. Truss legs to body of bird. Add remaining butter to skillet; brown birds on all sides at 300°. Wash rice and place in a bowl with the onion, water, and bouillon cubes.

Reduce skillet temperature to 200°. Add rice mixture; spread evenly under and around birds. Cover and cook for 45 minutes or until birds are tender. Remove birds. Crisp birds, breast-side-up, 4 to 5 inches from broiler, if desired. Add mushrooms and walnuts to rice.

Upside-Down Pear Gingerbread Cake

- ¼ cup butter
- ½ cup firmly packed light brown sugar
- 2 tablespoons finely chopped maraschino cherries
- 2 cups thinly sliced fresh pears
  Orange or lemon juice
- 1 package gingerbread mix
  Vanilla ice cream

Melt butter in an 8-inch square baking pan; stir in sugar. Sprinkle cherries over butter and sugar. Dip pear slices in juice to prevent darkening. Arrange pear slices in rows over cherries; set aside. Prepare gingerbread according to package directions. Pour over pears and bake according to package directions. Cool in pan on wire rack 5 minutes. Invert onto serving plate. Serve warm topped with vanilla ice cream.

Prune Pudding

- 1 pound cooked prunes, reserve ½ cup prune juice
- ⅔ cup cornstarch
- 2 cups sugar
  Juice of 1 lemon
- 1 cup chopped nuts
- 1 teaspoon ground cinnamon
  Whipped cream

Pit and chop the prunes. Blend the reserved ½ cup prune juice with the cornstarch until smooth. Combine prunes, sugar, lemon juice, and cornstarch mixture in a saucepan; simmer until thick and clear. Cool slightly; add nuts and cinnamon. Chill. Serve with whipped cream.

Index

Book II

Gourmet Christmas
COOKBOOK

by Naomi Arbit and June Turner

CONTENTS

Book I Christmas Cookbook

Book II Gourmet Christmas Cookbook

Book III Christmas Kitchen Cookbook

HOLIDAY WASSAIL

Fill the bowl and lift the cup to toast the holiday season with steaming hot wassail.

- 1 gal. apple cider
- 1 c. light brown sugar
- 1 6-oz. can frozen lemonade
- 1 6-oz. can frozen orange juice
- 12 whole cloves
- 6 whole allspice
- 1 t. ground nutmeg
- 1 4-inch cinnamon stick
- 2 bottles of port (optional)

In a large kettle, combine cider, sugar, lemonade and orange juice. Tie cloves and allspice into a small piece of cloth and add to cider. Add nutmeg and cinnamon stick; simmer gently for 20 minutes. Add wine; heat to steaming. *Do not boil.* Remove spice bag, discard and serve hot. Makes 30 to 35 servings.

'"'Tis the season to be jolly . . . " and here's a jolly good collection of holiday drinks—both hot and cold.*

Beverages

CRANBERRY PUNCH

2 qts. cranberry juice cocktail
2 small cans frozen lemonade, thawed
2 qts. ginger ale

Pour juices and ginger ale over ice in punch bowl and serve. Makes 25 to 30 servings.

MILKSHAKE PUNCH

Punch for the peanut butter set. Candy canes make colorful stirrers.

1 qt. milk
1 pt. vanilla ice cream, softened
1 pt. chocolate ice cream, softened
½ t. vanilla
2 T. sugar
¼ t. cinnamon

Beat together all ingredients until frothy. Makes 8 to 10 servings.

EGGNOG

Eggnog, festive and wickedly rich, is a Christmas tradition for many families. Recipe may be doubled.

10 eggs, separated
¾ c. sugar
Dash salt
2 to 4 c. rum, brandy, bourbon, or rye (a combination of two is best)
1 qt. heavy cream, whipped
Nutmeg

Beat egg yolks until lemon-colored and thick. Beat in sugar and salt. Slowly add liquor, constantly beating with a wire whisk. When all liquor is whisked in, stir in cream. Beat egg whites until stiff and fold into eggnog. Chill for several hours before serving. Dust each serving with nutmeg. Makes 25 to 30 servings.

SERVE COFFEE WITH A FLAIR OR A FLOURISH

A wonderful way to start an afternoon or end an evening.
Before dinner offer a selection of spices and garnishes such as:
cinnamon sticks
nutmeg
orange or lemon peel
brown or white sugar
grated chocolate
stiffly whipped cream

After dinner, to accompany coffee, serve:
Curacao
creme de cacao
creme de menthe
anise flavored liqueur

Anytime additions from almost everywhere:
As in the West Indies, use rum, brown sugar and whipped cream.
When in Vienna, use a dash of brandy.
Go Hungarian with cinnamon stick, grated chocolate and whipped cream.
Think Persian with cardamom seeds.
Be Irish: whipped cream, sugar and dash of Irish whisky.

MULLED CIDER

Rendezvous around the bowl of hot spicy cider.

1 qt. apple cider
¼ c. firmly packed brown sugar
6 whole cloves
2 2-inch cinnamon sticks

Combine all ingredients in a saucepan. Bring to a boil and simmer 5 minutes. Serve in mugs or in cups. Makes 6 servings.

ARTILLERY PUNCH

This punch is aptly named.

1 c. sugar
Juice of 6 lemons
1 T. Angostura bitters
1 qt. sherry
1 qt. Burgundy
1 qt. Scotch
1 qt. brandy
1 qt. sparkling water

Combine sugar, lemon juice, bitters and liquors. Chill to blend flavors. Pour punch over ice, then add sparkling water. Makes 50 servings.

CAFE BRULOT

1 c. brandy
Peel of 1 orange
6 whole cloves
4 whole allspice
4 cinnamon sticks
3 T. sugar
3 c. hot double-strength coffee

In chafing dish, over direct heat, combine all ingredients except coffee. Heat until hot. Carefully ignite brandy with a long match. Let it flame for 1 to 2 minutes. Slowly pour coffee into flaming brandy. Ladle into cafe brulot cups or demitasse cups. Makes 8 servings.

COCOA

¼ c. cocoa
4 T. sugar
Pinch salt
Pinch cinnamon
1 c. water
3 c. milk
Marshmallow
Whipped cream

Combine dry ingredients in a small saucepan and add water gradually, stirring well. Cook over low heat for 3 to 4 minutes. Slowly add milk and heat until steaming hot. Serve with marshmallow or a dollop of whipped cream. Serves 4.

FRENCH CHOCOLATE

A warm way to toast the season.

2½ 1-oz. squares unsweetened chocolate
½ c. water
⅔ c. sugar
1 t. vanilla
¼ t. salt
½ c. heavy cream, whipped
4 c. hot milk

Heat chocolate and water over low heat, stirring until chocolate is melted. Add sugar and salt and bring to a boil. Add vanilla. Cool to room temperature. Fold in whipped cream. To serve, place 1 generous tablespoon in each cup and fill with hot milk. Makes 8 to 10 cups.

COFFEE LIQUEUR

2 oz. instant coffee crystals
2 c. boiling water
4 c. sugar
1 vanilla bean, diced
2 c. brandy

Stir instant coffee into boiling water. Add sugar, stirring until dissolved. Cool. Place half of diced vanilla bean in each of two 4/5-quart bottles. Pour 1 cup brandy into each bottle. Pour in cooled coffee mixture. Add more brandy if necessary to fill bottles to top. Cap and store at least 30 days.

COFFEE ALEXANDER

2 c. strong hot coffee
⅓ c. brandy
¼ c. heavy cream
2 T. creme de cacao
Whipped cream
Chocolate curls

In a heat-proof pitcher, combine strong coffee, brandy, heavy cream and creme de cacao. Pour into 4 or 5 heat-proof cups or mugs. Garnish with a dollop of whipped cream and a chocolate curl. Makes 4 servings.

Appetizers

"Deck the halls with boughs of holly . . ." sprays of evergreen and candles, candles, candles; and what is a more glowingly beautiful decoration than a buffet table laden with delicious appetizers and hors d'oeuvres?

CHEESY SHRIMP

A delicious beginning.

  1 c. cooked shrimp, chopped
  ½ c. grated Cheddar cheese
  1 T. minced celery
  1 T. minced onion
  3 T. mayonnaise
  ¼ t. dry mustard
  ½ t. lemon juice
  ¼ t. Worcestershire sauce
  2½ dozen bread rounds, toasted on 1 side

Combine all ingredients and spread on bread rounds. Broil 3 to 5 minutes until bubbly. Serve immediately. Makes 30 rounds.

QUICK PARMESAN PUFFS

A simple snack.

  1 c. mayonnaise
  ½ c. grated Parmesan cheese
    Dash cayenne or Tabasco sauce
  2 t. instant minced onion
    Party rye rounds

Combine all ingredients and mound generously on rye. Broil about 4 inches from heat 3 to 4 minutes until puffed. Makes about 32 puffs.

CAVIAR STAR

This will be the star of your show.

  2 8-oz. pkgs. cream cheese, softened
  ¼ t. beef bouillon crystals
  ½ c. sour cream
  ¼ c. mayonnaise
  1 to 2 green onions, minced
  2 small jars red caviar

Combine cream cheese, bouillon crystals, sour cream, mayonnaise and green onions; mix until well blended. Form into a square on a serving plate. Place caviar on top, forming into the shape of a star. Garnish platter with parsley, lemon slices, deviled eggs, black olives or any combination. Serve with melba toast or party pumpernickel.

MUSHROOM TARTS FOR A CROWD

Make the shells at your leisure and freeze. Let thaw at room temperature, bake and fill.

PASTRY

  2 c. flour
  ½ lb. butter or margarine, softened
  1 8-oz. pkg. cream cheese, softened

Blend together all ingredients to form a dough. Chill about 1 hour. Shape into 4 dozen 1-inch balls. Place each ball in an ungreased 1¾-inch muffin cup. Press dough against the bottom and sides of the cup. Bake in a preheated 400° oven 12 to 15 minutes or until golden brown.

FILLING

  ¾ lb. finely chopped mushrooms
  2 T. minced green onion
  2 to 3 T. butter
  ¼ c. flour
  ½ t. salt
  1 c. sour cream
  1 T. mayonnaise

Sauté mushrooms and green onion in butter. Blend in flour and salt. Cook, stirring constantly, until thickened and smooth. Add sour cream and mayonnaise; heat through. Spoon mixture into baked shells. Makes 48 Tarts.

GREAT LAKES DIP

For a tasteful gathering.

  ½ lb. smoked fish, skin and bones removed
  1 c. sour cream
  2 T. lemon juice
  2 T. snipped green onion
    Freshly ground pepper to taste
  ½ t. salt
    Parsley to garnish

Flake the fish. Combine all ingredients and chill for at least 60 minutes. Garnish with parsley and serve with crackers or an assortment of raw vegetables. Makes 1¾ cups.

Pictured opposite: Caviar Star

FOR THE HORS D'OEUVRES TABLE

Beautiful, bright cherry tomatoes make colorful containers for endless fillings. Scoop inside out with a grapefruit knife or spoon. Invert and drain on paper towels while you make the fillings. Fills about 2 to 3 dozen.

HAM SALAD

1 c. ground or minced ham
1 T. prepared mustard
1 t. horseradish
1 t. minced onion
3 T. mayonnaise

Combine all ingredients and mix well.

DEVILED EGGS

4 hard-boiled eggs, minced
1 t. vinegar
1 t. mustard
1 t. Worcestershire sauce
2 T. mayonnaise

Combine all ingredients and mix well.

CHEESE

1 c. cottage cheese
2 T. chopped chives
2 T. mayonnaise
1 t. dried dill weed

Combine all ingredients and mix well.

CREAM CHEESE AND ANCHOVIES

1 8-oz. pkg. cream cheese, softened
1 can anchovies with capers, chopped
1 T. mayonnaise

Combine all ingredients and mix well.

CHEESE AND BACON

1 c. grated Cheddar cheese
4 slices bacon, cooked and crumbled
3 T. mayonnaise
1 t. mustard

Combine all ingredients and mix well.

CHICKEN SALAD

1 c. cooked chicken, minced
2 T. celery, minced
2 T. mayonnaise
1 T. sour cream
½ t. sherry

Combine all ingredients and mix well.

MINI CLAM BAKE

Ready in a minute!

1 8-oz. pkg. cream cheese, softened
1 8-oz. can minced clams, drained
2 t. instant minced onion
½ t. Tabasco sauce
48 round crackers
   Paprika
   Sliced black olives for garnish

Combine first 4 ingredients and mix well to blend. May be stored in refrigerator. Just before serving, spread 1 teaspoonful on each cracker. Place on a cookie sheet and bake in a preheated 400° oven 5 minutes. Sprinkle with paprika or garnish each with a sliver of black olive. Makes 4 dozen.

SMOKY PUFF

3½ oz. dried smoked beef, chopped
4 oz. grated Cheddar cheese
1 t. instant minced onion
5 T. mayonnaise
32 melba toast rounds

Combine first 4 ingredients and spread on melba toast rounds. Broil until cheese melts. Serve piping hot. Makes 32 Puffs.

FROSTED PATÉ

2 T. butter
¼ lb. mushrooms, chopped
1 medium onion, minced
3 T. butter
1 lb. liverwurst
½ c. ripe olives, sliced
1 8-oz. pkg. cream cheese, softened
½ c. sour cream
1 t. chicken bouillon crystals

Sauté mushrooms and onion in 2 tablespoons butter. Blend remaining 3 tablespoons butter with liverwurst; stir in mushrooms and onion. Using half of the mixture, form bottom half of loaf and stud with olive slices. Form top half of loaf from remaining mixture. Combine cream cheese, sour cream and bouillon crystals, mixing well. Frost loaf with cheese mixture. May be garnished with parsley, green or black olives, and pimiento slices. Serve with melba toast, party rye or pumpernickel.

SHRIMP SPREAD

For easy hostessing!

- 1 8-oz. pkg. cream cheese, softened
- 2 T. mayonnaise
- 1 T. lemon juice
- 1 t. chopped chives
- 1 garlic clove, crushed
- ½ lb. tiny, cooked shrimp

Blend all ingredients except shrimp. Stir in shrimp and serve with crackers and celery chunks. Makes 1½ cups.

PARTY IDEAS
CHRISTMAS OPEN HOUSE
Stop in and see the tree—open house from 5 to 8! This kind of party can be for all ages and very informal; it can be just for children or just for adults. The theme also can be more formal. All these parties are fun to have and fun to attend.
ALL AGES
Cranberry Punch, p. 4
Eggnog, p. 4
Coffee, p. 5
With these hours, some people may be coming before dinner, and some after, so you can have a wide assortment of things to nibble: trays of cheese and crackers, raw vegetables and dips, nuts, a turkey with assorted breads, and . . .
Fruitcake, p. 55
Cookies, p. 56
Candies, p. 63

COCKTAIL NUTS

Spicy nibbles!

- 2 T. butter
- 2 T. Worcestershire sauce
- ½ t. hot pepper sauce
- ¼ t. garlic powder
- 2 c. walnut or pecan halves
  Salt

Melt butter in a 13 x 9 x 2-inch baking pan. Stir in Worcestershire sauce, pepper sauce and garlic. Add nuts, stirring to coat each nut. Spread nuts in a single layer in pan. Bake in a preheated 250° oven 45 to 60 minutes, stirring occasionally, until nuts are lightly browned. Cool completely on paper toweling. Sprinkle with salt to taste. Store in a tightly covered container. Makes 2 cups.

ORIENTAL BEEF CUBES

A delicious blend of East and West

- ½ c. soy sauce
- ¼ c. sesame oil
- ¼ c. dry sherry
- 1 T. finely chopped ginger
- 1 T. sugar
- 2 large cloves garlic, minced
- 1½ to 2 lbs. boneless sirloin or top round, cut into ½-inch cubes

Combine first 6 ingredients in a glass bowl; stir to blend. Add meat cubes and refrigerate for at least 4 hours or overnight. Turn meat several times. Remove meat from marinade, reserving liquid. Broil meat 3 to 4 inches from heat for about 10 minutes; place in a chafing dish. Heat marinade just to boiling and pour over meat. Serve with wooden picks. Makes about 40 "bites."

SALMON MOUSSE

Beautiful addition to a cocktail buffet. Serve with rye crackers.

- 1 envelope unflavored gelatin
- ½ c. water
- 1 lb. red salmon, skin and bones removed, drained and flaked
- 1 c. grated cucumber
- ¼ c. lemon juice
- ½ c. mayonnaise
  Dash Tabasco sauce
- ½ c. heavy cream, whipped
  Lemon slices
  Minced parsley
- 1 t. dill weed

Dissolve gelatin in water. Combine with salmon, cucumber, lemon juice, mayonnaise, Tabasco sauce and whipped cream. Mix well. Pour into a greased 5-cup fish or ring mold. Chill until firm. Turn out on a platter, garnish with lemon slices, parsley and dill weed. Serve with crackers or party rye bread.

BROIL UNTIL BUBBLY

Slices of party rye, melba toast or crackers, when topped with one of the following and broiled are nice to pass as a hot appetizer.

MUSHROOM

1 8-oz. pkg. cream cheese, softened
2 T. butter, softened
1 clove garlic, minced
1 small can mushrooms, drained and chopped

Mix together all ingredients. Heap on party bread slices and broil. Makes about 48.

CHEESE

2 c. grated Cheddar cheese
¼ c. mayonnaise
2 T. chili sauce
1 t. Worcestershire sauce

Mix together all ingredients. Heap on party bread or crackers. Broil. Makes about 48.

TURKEY

1 4-oz. pkg. Roquefort or blue cheese
¼ c. mayonnaise
Slices of turkey, small and thin

Combine cheese and mayonnaise, mixing well. Place turkey on bread; top with cheese mixture. Broil. Makes about 24.

CORNED BEEF

Tomato paste
Corned beef slices
Swiss cheese slices

Spread rye or pumpernickel with 1 teaspoon tomato paste. Top with corned beef and then cheese. Broil until cheese melts.

CURRIED CHICKEN

2 c. minced chicken
½ c. mayonnaise
1 t. curry powder (or to taste)

Mix together all ingredients. Heap on melba toast and broil. Makes about 48.

CHEESE BALL

Surround with crackers or sliced party bread.

1 8-oz. pkg. cream cheese
1 4-oz. pkg. blue cheese
⅛ t. Tabasco sauce
¼ t. Worcestershire sauce
¾ c. chopped nuts

Cream together softened cheeses. Blend in seasonings and ¼ cup of the nuts. Shape into a ball and roll in the remaining nuts. Wrap in clear plastic and chill.

MOCK LIVER PATÉ

½ lb. fresh liver sausage
1 3-oz. pkg. cream cheese
2 to 4 T. mayonnaise
2 hard-boiled eggs, finely chopped
1 t. instant minced onion
Sieved egg yolk or minced parsley for garnish

Combine first 5 ingredients and shape into a ball. Garnish with additional sieved hard-boiled egg yolk or minced parsley. Serve with crackers.

CHICKEN WINGS

"finger-lickin' good"

32 chicken wings
6 to 8 T. melted butter
1½ c. bread crumbs
½ c. grated Parmesan cheese
1 t. salt or lemon-pepper
1 t. garlic powder

Discard tip of wing; cut remaining wing in 2 pieces. Dip chicken in melted butter. Combine bread crumbs, cheese, salt and garlic powder in a plastic bag. Shake wings in crumb mixture. Place chicken on greased 15 x 10-inch baking sheet and bake in a pre-heated 400° oven for 30 minutes. Serve hot.

Soups

"Strike the harp and join the chorus..." you'll sing the praises of soups which are easy to cook in the oven or from quick combinations on the pantry shelf.

SHRIMP BISQUE

1 10-oz. can tomato soup
1 10-oz. can green pea soup
1 10-oz. can beef consommé
1 soup can light cream
½ lb. cooked shrimp
¼ c. sherry
1 hard-boiled egg, chopped

Combine all soups in a saucepan; bring to a boil. Add cream, shrimp and sherry. Heat to steaming and serve garnished with egg. Serves 4 to 6.

SHERRIED PEA SOUP

1 10-oz. can split pea soup
1 soup can milk
1 10-oz. can chicken broth
½ c. dry sherry
    Sour cream (optional)
    Garlic croutons (optional)

Combine soups and milk. Heat gently until steaming. Add sherry. Garnish with sour cream or croutons or both if desired. Makes 4 to 6 servings.

MINESTRONE SOUP

1 lb. beef chuck, cut in 1-inch cubes
1 T. vegetable oil
1 28-oz. can tomatoes
3 c. water
1 t. salt
1 t. Italian seasoning
1 10-oz. pkg. frozen mixed vegetables
1 onion, chopped
1 6-oz. pkg. spiral noodles, cooked and drained
    Grated Romano cheese

Brown meat in 1 tablespoon oil. Add tomatoes, water and seasonings. Cover and simmer 1 hour. Add vegetables, onion and cooked noodles; continue cooking until vegetables are tender. Sprinkle with grated Romano cheese before serving. Makes about 6 servings.

MULLIGATAWNY SOUP

Spicy chicken soup with vegetables; you may also use turkey if you like. Serve over a small mound of cooked rice, if desired.

1 cut-up fryer
¼ c. flour
1 t. salt
1 T. curry powder
¼ t. nutmeg
¼ t. pepper
¼ c. butter or margarine
3 carrots, sliced
2 tart apples, cut in eighths
1 medium onion, chopped
½ green pepper, chopped
¼ c. chopped parsley
2 stalks celery, chopped
1 28-oz. can tomatoes
4 c. water

Dredge chicken in mixture of flour, salt, curry powder, nutmeg and pepper. Melt butter in heavy kettle or Dutch oven and brown chicken. Add remaining ingredients; bring to a boil and simmer, covered, for 45 minutes to 1 hour. Remove chicken, discard skin and bones, cut into chunks and return to soup. Makes 4 to 6 servings.

RED BEAN SOUP

A quick and hearty soup made from in-the-house ingredients.

2 1-lb. cans kidney beans, drained
3 10-oz. cans beef consommé
1 c. water
1 medium onion, finely chopped
1 carrot, finely chopped
¼ t. basil
1 T. tomato paste
¼ c. sherry (optional)
2 slices bacon, fried and crumbled

Combine all ingredients except sherry and bacon; simmer for 60 minutes. Blend in blender or strain, if you like. Just before serving, add sherry and garnish with bacon. Serves 4 to 6.

MUSHROOM SOUP

2 10-oz. cans cream of mushroom soup
2 soup cans milk
¼ lb. mushrooms
2 T. butter
¼ c. sherry

Combine soup and milk; heat. Sauté mushrooms in butter and add to steaming soup. Stir in sherry and serve. Serves 2 to 4.

BEAN SOUP

This soup cooks in the oven while you go about your holiday business.

3 qts. water
1 lb. dried navy beans
1 ham bone
1 lb. ham or ham steak, cubed
2 stalks celery, diced
2 carrots, diced
1 onion, diced
1 8-oz. can tomato sauce
Salt and pepper to taste

Combine all ingredients in a large pot or roaster. Cover and bake in a preheated 325° oven 3 to 4 hours.

OYSTER STEW

Traditional Christmas Eve supper in many families. Delicious any time you can get fresh oysters.

1 pt. oysters with liquor
4 c. milk
¼ c. butter
Salt and pepper to taste
Sprinkle celery salt

Place oysters and liquor in a saucepan and cover. Simmer until the edges curl slightly. Add remaining ingredients; heat to steaming and serve. Makes 4 to 6 servings.

ONION SUPPER SOUP

A tureen of soup is a welcome gift. Take along a loaf of French bread.

1 lb. ground chuck
2 1¼-oz. pkg. onion soup mix
5 c. water
1 c. Burgundy wine
1 c. grated Parmesan cheese

Brown meat in soup pot; drain fat. Sprinkle with soup mix and stir in water. Bring to a boil and simmer slowly for 12 to 15 minutes. Add wine and heat through. When ready to serve, ladle into soup bowls and sprinkle with Parmesan cheese. Makes 4 to 6 servings.

NEW YEAR'S EVE GALA
A midnight supper is a festive way with
which to start the new year. Serve a steaming
tureen or two of soup, such as,
Oyster Stew, p. 13
Shrimp Bisque, p. 12
sliced ham, turkey or beef with cheeses
and assorted breads.
If you prefer a little more formality, serve
Mushroom Tarts, p. 6
Turkey Tetrazzini, p. 24
Beef en Croute, p. 16
Lamb Navarin, p. 17
Tomatoes Florentine, p. 30
Cranberry Sour Cream Mold, p. 35
Fruitcake, p. 55
Spumoni Parfait, p. 47
Any combination of these will make a
beautiful supper table.

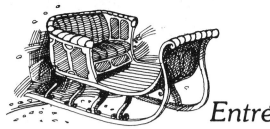

"See the blazing Yule before us..." you probably won't roast your dinner on an open spit, but here are some how-to tips which will make you a blazing success.

Entrées

STANDING BEEF RIB ROAST

1 8-lb. standing rib roast
Salt
Pepper
Garlic powder

Place roast, fat side up, on rack in an open, shallow roasting pan. Insert meat thermometer into the thickest part of meat, not touching bone or fat. Do not add water. Sprinkle with salt, pepper and garlic powder. Place in a preheated 325° oven 3 to 3¼ hours or until thermometer registers 140° for rare or 160° for medium. Allow roast to stand 15 to 20 minutes before carving. May be served with Horseradish Sauce (p. 16). Makes 8 servings.

CARBONNADES FLAMANDES

Cook once—eat twice.

4 lbs. lean beef, cut in large cubes
Flour
2 t. salt
½ t. pepper
Oil to brown meat
4 medium onions, thinly sliced
2 cloves garlic
¼ c. butter
2 12-oz. cans beer
½ c. bouillon
2 T. brown sugar
2 T. catsup
1 t. marjoram
1 t. thyme
¼ c. minced parsley
¼ c. vinegar (optional)

Dredge meat in flour mixed with salt and pepper and brown in oil. In another skillet, sauté onions and garlic in butter. Add to meat along with beer, bouillon, sugar, catsup, marjoram, thyme and parsley. Cover and cook over low heat until meat is tender, 1 to 1½ hours. Just before serving, stir in vinegar. Serves 6 to 8.

PEPPER STEAK

3 to 4 green peppers, seeded and cut in chunks
½ to 1 lb. fresh mushrooms
3 T. butter
2 to 3 T. oil
1 2½ to 3-lb. beef tenderloin, thinly sliced
2 t. salt
½ to 1 t. pepper
1 t. oregano
2 cloves garlic, minced
2 T. tomato paste
¼ c. dry sherry
2 tomatoes, cut in eighths

Sauté green peppers and mushrooms in 1 tablespoon butter and 2 tablespoons oil until tender crisp. Set aside. Brown meat quickly (a few slices at a time) in 2 tablespoons butter and 1 tablespoon oil. Remove meat slices from pan as soon as they are seared. Combine all ingredients except tomatoes and place in large pan. Cook, covered, 5 minutes. Uncover; stir in tomatoes and heat thoroughly. Serve immediately. Serves 8.

RUSSIAN STEW

2 lbs. stewing beef, cut into chunks
2 c. chicken broth
1 8-oz. can tomato sauce
4 carrots, cut into chunks
2 onions, quartered
2 stalks celery, cut into chunks
1 t. dill
1 t. thyme
1 t. salt
1 cabbage, cut into eighths
Sour cream

Set aside cabbage and sour cream. Combine remaining ingredients in a covered casserole. Bake in a preheated 325° oven for 2 hours. Add cabbage and bake an additional 30 minutes. Serve with sour cream. Serves 4 to 6.

Pictured opposite:
Pepper Steak

BEEF EN CROUTE

1 2½ to 3-lb. fillet of beef tenderloin, trimmed
　Salt and pepper to taste
2 t. garlic powder
2 7-oz. pkgs. onion crescent rolls
1 egg white

Turn thin tail of beef under and tie securely with string. The fillet should be about 9 or 10 inches long after securing. Sprinkle salt, pepper and garlic powder on top and place on a rack in a shallow pan. Roast in a preheated 425° oven 40 minutes. Remove from oven and cool. Cover and chill in refrigerator 4 hours or overnight. Remove string. Open rolls and carefully unroll dough. Do not separate rolls. Arrange dough pieces to form a rectangle on a lightly floured board. Pinch perforations together to make 1 piece of dough. With lightly floured rolling pin, roll dough to a 13 x 10-inch rectangle. Place the chilled fillet on dough, top side down. Bring edges of dough together down the center of the fillet. Brush with lightly beaten egg white and pinch to close. Turn ends of dough under meat to form a smooth seam. Place fillet, seam side down, in a shallow baking pan. Lightly roll out any leftover pieces of dough and use to cut flowers or leaves. Moisten with egg white and arrange over top of dough. Brush entire surface with egg white. Bake in a preheated 400° oven about 25 minutes, or until crust is browned. With 2 broad spatulas, lift fillet to serving platter. To serve, cut into thin slices. Serve with Madiera Sauce. Serves 6 to 8.

MADIERA SAUCE

1 c. sliced mushrooms
4 T. butter
2 T. flour
1 10-oz. can consommé
2 T. tomato paste
1 envelope beef concentrate
½ c. Madiera wine (or dry sherry)

Brown mushrooms in 2 tablespoons of the butter. Set aside. Slightly brown remaining 2 tablespoons butter; add flour and stir to a paste. Gradually add consommé, stirring constantly. Add tomato paste and beef concentrate; simmer, uncovered, about 10 minutes or until mixture is reduced by one-quarter. Add mushrooms and wine. Check for saltiness and add water, if necessary.

POT ROAST

½ 6-oz. can tomato paste
1 T. sugar
½ pkg. onion soup mix
½ c. Burgundy
½ c. water
1½ lbs. chuck roast

Mix together the first 5 ingredients. Pour over meat in a casserole. Cover and bake in a preheated 325° oven for 3 hours. Serves 2 to 4.

HORSERADISH SAUCE

3 T. prepared horseradish
1 T. prepared mustard
3 T. lemon juice
½ t. salt
1 c. sour cream

Combine all ingredients and mix well. Refrigerate, covered, until serving time. Makes about 1½ cups.

MERRIE ROAST PORK LOIN

1 3-lb. rolled pork loin roast
1 10-oz. jar apple jelly
¼ c. soy sauce
2 T. salad oil
2 T. lemon juice
2 cloves garlic, minced
½ t. ginger

Place roast in a glass baking dish. Combine remaining ingredients in a saucepan and cook over low heat until the jelly is melted. Remove from heat. Pour sauce over and refrigerate 3 hours, turning meat several times. Remove from sauce and roast in a preheated 350° oven about 2 hours, or until meat thermometer inserted in the center of roast registers 170°. During roasting, brush meat a few times with sauce. Let stand 10 minutes before serving. Serves 6.

CROWN ROAST OF PORK

The prince of roasts for your royal occasion.

Crown Roast, 2 ribs per serving
12 to 15 c. stuffing

Place roast in shallow roasting pan, rib side up. Heap stuffing in center. Cover stuffing and rib ends with foil. Roast in a 325° oven for about 3 hours until internal temperature registers 180° on a meat thermometer. Remove foil and roast an additional 60 minutes until well done (185°). Let stand 10 to 20 minutes before carving. Rib ends may be garnished with cherry tomatoes or small crab apples.

Note: Optional additions to stuffing may include cooked sausage, walnuts, chopped apples or green grapes.

MAPLE GLAZED HAM

A tempting entrée.

1 7 to 8-lb. fully cooked smoked ham shank
1 c. maple syrup
2 T. cider vinegar
1 T. prepared mustard
Whole cloves

Combine syrup, vinegar and mustard. Place ham, fat side up, on rack in shallow roasting pan. Pour about ½ cup mixture over ham and bake, uncovered, in a preheated 325° oven for 1½ hours. Baste every 30 minutes with additional sauce. Remove ham from oven and score fat into diamond shapes. Insert a clove into each diamond. Bake ham an additional 30 minutes or until a meat thermometer inserted into the thickest part of meat registers 140°. Let ham rest 15 minutes before carving. Makes 10 to 12 servings.

CURRIED HAM STEAK

Economical ham steak with a tasty topping of curried fruit.

2 ham steaks, ¼ to ½ inch thick
¼ c. butter
¼ c. brown sugar
1 T. curry powder
¼ c. raisins
1 1-lb. can pineapple slices, drained
1 1-lb. can apricot halves, drained
1 1-lb. can pear halves, drained

Melt together butter and brown sugar. Stir in curry powder. Place ham steaks in a large shallow baking dish. Top with fruit. Pour brown sugar sauce over all and bake for 30 to 45 minutes in a 350° oven until it bubbles and sizzles. Serves 4 to 6.

CURRY SAUCE

Try a curried sauce to make holiday ham or turkey leftovers take on a new air.

1 10-oz. can cream of celery or chicken soup
½ c. milk
1 T. curry (more or less to taste)
½ c. raisins
Snipped green onions

Heat soup, milk and curry powder, stirring until smooth. Add onion and raisins; serve over meat with rice.

LAMB NAVARIN

A combination of lamb and vegetables simmered with wine and herbs in the oven.

3 lbs. lamb, cut into 1-inch cubes
1 large onion, chopped
1 clove garlic, minced
2 c. chicken broth
¼ c. tomato paste
1 c. dry white wine
1 bay leaf
1 t. thyme
1 t. salt
1 10-oz. pkg. frozen peas
1 20-oz. pkg. frozen onions
3 carrots, cut into chunks

Combine first 9 ingredients in a covered casserole. Bake in a preheated 350° oven 2 hours. Add peas, onions and carrots. Bake an additional 45 minutes. Serves 6.

ROAST GOOSE

For a festive entrée.

1 goose, thawed, cleaned and dried

Choose the largest available goose. Remove all loose fat from the body cavity. Prepare Stuffing. Lightly fill wishbone area and body cavity with stuffing. Fasten neck skin to the back with a skewer. Fold wing tips onto back. Tuck drumsticks under band of skin at tail or tie together with string. Place goose, breast side up, on a rack in a shallow pan. Prick skin (not meat) all over with a fork. Insert meat thermometer deep into thigh muscle away from bone. Roast goose at 400° for 60 minutes. Reduce heat to 325° and roast an additional 2 to 2½ hours until meat thermometer registers 185°. Check stuffing temperature also for 165°. During entire roasting period, spoon off accumulated fat. Do not baste. When cooked, allow goose to rest 10 minutes before carving.

STUFFING

1 11-oz. can mandarin oranges
1 c. white raisins
2 c. chopped, unpeeled apple
4 to 6 c. seasoned stuffing mix
1 c. water
½ c. apple juice
Sautéed onion and celery (optional)

Combine all ingredients and toss lightly. May be served with Plum Sauce.

PLUM SAUCE FOR PORK OR GOOSE

¾ c. port wine
⅓ c. goose or pork drippings
1 1 lb. 14-oz. can purple plums, pitted and drained
Few grains cayenne pepper
1 T. cornstarch
2 T. cold water
2 T. lemon juice

Simmer port wine over moderate heat until just ¼ cup remains. Add drippings and simmer 5 minutes. Crush plums with fork and add to pan with cayenne. Mix cornstarch with cold water and stir into plum mixture. Stir until boiling, then simmer over low heat 15 minutes. Add lemon juice. Makes 2 cups sauce.

HOLIDAY ROAST DUCKLINGS

1 to 2 ducklings, thawed cleaned and dried
Salt
Garlic powder
1 can whole cranberry sauce
½ c. orange marmalade
1 t. prepared mustard
2 T. brandy

Cut ducklings lengthwise in half. Slash skin around bottom of duck to keep from curling while roasting. Remove all loose pieces of fat. Sprinkle inside with salt and garlic powder. Place cut side down on rack in shallow pan and roast at 350° for about 2 to 2½ hours. During baking time, pierce skin and spoon out all fat. Duck is done when skin is brown and meat is no longer pink when pierced between leg and body. Combine remaining ingredients in a saucepan and heat, stirring to blend. Pass at table. Allow ½ duck per person.

ROCK CORNISH HENS

6 to 8 Rock Cornish hens, thawed and cleaned
Salt and pepper to taste
Butter or margarine
Paprika
Garlic, minced
1 10-oz. jar currant jelly

Sprinkle insides of hens with salt and pepper. Tie legs together with string. Rub hens with softened butter mixed with garlic and paprika to taste. Refrigerate or cook immediately. Arrange hens in a shallow pan and place in a preheated 425° oven for 60 minutes or until tender and well browned. Baste occasionally with melted butter. Heat currant jelly in a saucepan. Remove hens to a platter, cut strings and spoon melted warm currant jelly over each hen. Pass remaining jelly at the table. Serves 6 to 8.

Pictured opposite:
Chicken Della Robbia, p. 20

CHICKEN DELLA ROBBIA

Golden chicken with a wreath of beautiful fruit.

       2 to 3 fryers, cut up
       4 T. butter
       2 T. salad oil
       2 onions, sliced
    1¼ c. water
       ½ t. instant chicken bouillon
       ½ lb. mushrooms, sliced
       1 c. white raisins
       2 t. salt
       ¼ c. lemon juice
       1 clove garlic, minced
       ½ t. ground cloves
       ½ t. allspice
       ½ t. ginger
       ¼ c. brown sugar
       1 c. walnut halves
       ½ c. water
       1 T. cornstarch
       2 c. green seedless grapes
       2 c. orange sections
    12 cherries

In a large Dutch oven or fryer, sauté chicken pieces in butter and oil until golden brown. Add onions and sauté. Combine 1¼ cup water with ½ teaspoon instant chicken bouillon. Add with mushrooms, raisins, salt, lemon juice, garlic, spices and brown sugar. Simmer, covered, turning 1 or 2 times, for 35 minutes or until tender. Add walnut halves. Push chicken to side of pan. Blend cornstarch with ½ cup water and stir into pan liquid. Heat until smooth and thickened. Add grapes, oranges and cherries and heat through for 2 to 3 minutes. Serve at once on heated platter or in a chafing dish. Serves 8 to 12.

CHICKEN COGNAC

Tempt your family with the unexpected.

       4 chicken breasts
       ½ c. milk
       ½ c. biscuit mix
       ½ t. salt
       ½ t. minced garlic
       ½ t. paprika
       ½ c. sliced green onion
       2 T. butter or margarine
       1 egg yolk
       ½ c. light cream or milk
       ½ c. cognac

Dip chicken breasts in milk and drain. Combine biscuit mix, salt, garlic and paprika. Coat chicken with mixture and place, skin side down, in a greased baking dish. Bake in a preheated 425° oven for 30 minutes or until tender. Keep warm. Sauté onion in butter or margarine until tender. Beat egg yolk with cream and stir into onion. Cook over low heat, stirring constantly, until thickened. Heat cognac in a small saucepan until just hot (do not boil). Pour over chicken and ignite. When flame dies, pour hot sauce over chicken and serve immediately. Serves 2 to 4.

CHICKEN TARRAGON

       2 fryers, cut up
       2 T. salad oil
       2 T. butter or margarine
       6 shallots, chopped
       2 carrots, sliced in rounds
       ¼ c. cognac
       1 c. dry white wine
       ¼ c. water
       1 T. dried tarragon
       1 t. dried chervil
       1 t. salt
       1 t. pepper
       1 c. light cream (optional)
       1 egg yolk (optional)
       1 T. flour (optional)

Wash chicken; dry well. In a 6-quart Dutch oven, heat oil and butter. Sauté a few pieces of chicken at a time until golden brown. Remove the chicken as it browns. Add shallots and carrots, stirring about 5 minutes. Return chicken to pan; sprinkle with warmed cognac and ignite. Add wine, water, crushed tarragon, chervil, salt and pepper. Bring to boil; reduce heat and let simmer gently 30 minutes. Remove chicken to a heated platter; keep warm. Optional: Strain drippings in pot. In a small bowl combine cream, egg yolk and flour; mix well. Stir into drippings; bring to a boil, reduce sauce by half. Pour over chicken. Makes 8 servings.

CHICKEN WITH POLYNESIAN VEGETABLES

2 frying chickens, cut up
2 T. butter or salad oil
Flour, seasoned with salt and pepper

Coat chicken lightly with seasoned flour. Melt butter or oil in a shallow baking dish. Arrange chicken pieces in pan. Bake, uncovered, in a 400° oven 20 minutes. Turn chicken, reduce heat to 350° and bake for 30 to 35 additional minutes, or until chicken is tender. Serves 6.

POLYNESIAN VEGETABLES

1 c. water
1 t. instant beef bouillon
1 T. soy sauce
½ t. ginger
2 c. diagonally sliced celery
2 c. diagonally sliced carrot
2 c. green pepper, cut into 1-inch pieces
1 c. sliced green onion
1 5-oz. can water chestnuts, thinly sliced
½ c. unsweetened pineapple juice
2 to 3 t. cornstarch

Combine first 4 ingredients in a saucepan. Bring to a boil; add celery, carrot and green pepper. Return to boiling; cover and simmer 5 minutes. Add green onion and water chestnuts. Cook 2 additional minutes. With slotted spoon, remove vegetables to heated dish and keep warm. Combine cornstarch and pineapple juice. Stir into broth and cook, stirring, until thickened. Pour over vegetables. Toss and serve. Serves 6.

SCALLOPED OYSTERS

A simple and delicious way to treat the delicate oyster.

1 qt. oysters with liquor
3 c. cracker crumbs
½ c. butter
1 to 2 c. milk
Dash pepper

In a greased casserole, make layers of oysters and crackers, ending with crackers. Dot each layer with butter. Pour enough milk over to bring liquid to the top layer of oysters. Sprinkle with pepper and dot with remaining butter. Bake in a preheated 350° oven for 50 to 60 minutes. Makes 6 to 8 servings.

BAKED FISH WITH OYSTER STUFFING

Whole baked fish with succulent oyster stuffing. This stuffing is also delicious with turkey.

1 4 to 5-lb. fish, dressed
Salt and pepper
1 T. lemon juice
¼ c. unsalted butter, melted

Wash and dry fish. Sprinkle cavity with salt, pepper and lemon juice. Place in a shallow, foil-lined baking dish. Stuff fish; secure opening and baste with butter. Bake in a preheated 350° oven for 45 to 60 minutes. Baste frequently. Allow ½ pound fish per person.

OYSTER STUFFING

2 stalks celery, diced
1 medium onion, chopped
½ c. butter
1 t. salt
1 t. poultry seasoning
½ t. sage
1 pt. oysters with liquor
4 slices bread, cubed and toasted

Sauté celery and onion in butter until golden. Add seasonings and oysters with liquor; simmer until edges of oysters curl. Remove from heat. Stir in bread cubes.

CLAMS AND SHELLS

Hear the good tidings!

1 large clove garlic, halved
⅛ c. salad oil
2 T. lemon juice
2 T. butter or margarine
2 cans clams (crushed or whole) and juice
½ t. salt
½ t. basil, crushed
¼ t. pepper
2 t. minced parsley, fresh or dried
1 7-oz. pkg. seashell pasta, cooked
¼ c. melted unsalted butter
1 c. grated Parmesan cheese

Brown garlic in oil; discard garlic. Stir in next 7 ingredients. Simmer 10 minutes, stirring occasionally. Cook and drain pasta; toss with butter. Mix with sauce and garnish with Parmesan cheese. Serves 2 to 4.

SOLE AND SHRIMP AU GRATIN

Pastel elegance.

2 lbs. fillet of sole
½ t. salt
¼ c. dry sherry
2 T. lemon juice
2 T. butter or margarine
2 T. flour
Dash Tabasco sauce
1 t. instant chicken bouillon
½ c. light cream
½ c. grated Parmesan cheese
12 to 16-oz. shrimp, cooked and cleaned
Snipped parsley

Arrange fillets in baking dish and sprinkle with salt. Combine sherry and lemon juice and pour over fish. Bake in a preheated 350⁰ oven for 15 minutes. Drain juices and reserve. Return fish to oven and bake for another 10 minutes or until it flakes easily with fork. While it bakes, add enough water to the reserved broth to make 1 cup. Melt butter in saucepan over low heat. Stir in flour, Tabasco, broth and bouillon. Cook over low heat, stirring, until sauce is smooth and bubbly. Remove from heat; stir in cream. Heat just to boiling, stirring constantly. Add cheese and shrimp and stir until cheese is melted. Alternate layers of fish and sauce in a chafing dish, ending with sauce. Garnish with parsley. Serves 6.

STUFFED FLOUNDER

An elegant entrée with the Florentine touch.

2 whole dressed flounder (1½ lbs. each)
1 pkg. frozen spinach soufflé, thawed
1 T. lemon juice
¼ c. melted butter

Have fish cut along the backbone and split from center to the outside edges, forming pockets. Spoon spinach soufflé into fish. Fasten opening with poultry skewers. Place flounder in a 9 x 13 x 2-inch buttered baking dish. Bake in a preheated 375° oven for 45 minutes, basting fish with butter and lemon juice every 15 minutes. Serves 2 to 4.

NEW YEAR'S DAY
All over America, New Year's Day is devoted to football. Since the games last from sunup to past sunset, why don't you have a football party? Serve lots of crunchy things to munch, hot and cold drinks and, as the main event, serve a casserole, such as:
Jambalaya, p. 22 or Russian Stew, p. 14
Crusty French Bread
Fruit and cheese for dessert

JAMBALAYA

2 to 3 strips bacon
1 onion, chopped
1 clove garlic, minced
1 stalk celery, chopped
1 green pepper, chopped
1 28-oz. can tomatoes
½ 6-oz. can tomato paste
1 c. water
½ t. thyme
1 bay leaf
1 t. sugar
1 t. salt
Dash red pepper
2 to 3 cooked pork sausages, diced
1 c. cooked chicken, diced
½ lb. cooked ham, cut in strips
1 lb. cooked shrimp
3 c. cooked rice
¼ c. minced parsley

Fry bacon; drain and set aside. Sauté onion, garlic, celery and pepper in bacon fat for a few minutes. Add tomatoes, tomato paste, water, thyme, bay leaf, sugar, salt and red pepper. Simmer for 25 to 30 minutes. Add meats, shrimp and rice and simmer for 10 to 15 minutes until piping hot. Add a little water if necessary. Sprinkle with parsley and serve. Serves 6 to 8.

Pictured Opposite
Curried Ham Steak, p. 17

Yuletide treasures are recipes which cook themselves and leave time to enjoy family and friends.

Eggs, Pasta, Casseroles

TURKEY TETRAZZINI

A rest-of-the-bird casserole.

- ¾ c. butter or margarine
- ¾ c. flour
- 3 t. salt
- ⅛ t. nutmeg
- 4 c. milk
- 2 c. turkey or chicken stock
- 4 egg yolks
- 1 c. milk
- ½ c. dry sherry
- 1 lb. thin spaghetti
- 6 c. leftover turkey or chicken (cut in 1½-inch pieces)
- ½ lb. mushrooms, sliced
- 1 T. butter
- 2 c. grated Swiss cheese
- ¼ c. grated Parmesan cheese

Melt ¾ cup butter in a large saucepan. Remove from heat and stir in flour, salt and nutmeg. Gradually add 4 cups milk and stock and bring to a boil, stirring constantly. Boil 2 minutes or until slightly thickened. In a small bowl, beat egg yolks with remaining milk. Pour 2 tablespoons hot mixture into yolks and then pour yolk mixture into saucepan, beating constantly until sauce is hot. Do not boil. Remove from heat and stir in sherry. Cook spaghetti as directed on package and drain. Return spaghetti to kettle and toss lightly with 2 cups sauce. Divide spaghetti in half and place in two 12 x 8 x 2-inch baking dishes. Sauté mushrooms in remaining butter. Add mushrooms and turkey to 2 cups of the sauce. Reserve remaining sauce. Spoon half of turkey mixture to center of each dish; sprinkle with Swiss cheese. Cover with foil and refrigerate 1 hour or overnight. One hour before serving, place in a preheated 350° oven for 45 minutes. Uncover and sprinkle with Parmesan cheese, broil 2 minutes. Heat reserved sauce and serve with casserole.
Note: Casserole can be frozen. Let thaw 1 hour and bake, covered, in a preheated 350° oven 60 minutes until bubbly. Serves 12.

TURKEY CASSEROLE

Can't be dismissed as casual leftovers.

- 6 eggs, beaten
- 2 c. milk *or* 1 c. milk and 1 c. cream of celery soup
- ½ t. salt
- 1 t. dry mustard
- 1 t. Worcestershire sauce
- 10 slices slightly stale bread, crusts trimmed
- 2 c. grated sharp Cheddar cheese
- 1 lb. cooked turkey slices or cubes

Combine eggs, milk, salt, mustard and Worcestershire sauce. Grease a 13 x 9 x 11-inch casserole. Alternate layers of bread, turkey and cheese, ending with bread. Cover with the liquid mixture and refrigerate for 4 hours or overnight. Bring to room temperature and bake in a preheated 350° oven for 45 to 60 minutes. Let stand 15 minutes before serving. Makes 8 servings.

SKILLET STEAK 'N' EGGS

One skillet makes a dinner. Also a great breakfast or lunch. Serve it directly from the skillet with buttered toast and catsup, if desired. For more helpings, increase beef and eggs.

- ½ lb. ground beef
- 1 small onion, chopped
- 2 eggs
  Salt and pepper to taste
- 1 pkg. frozen chopped spinach, thawed and drained (optional)

In frying pan, stir beef over medium heat until just browned. Add onion and cook until tender. Add spinach, if desired. Beat eggs with a fork or wire whisk; stir into meat and scramble. Season with salt and pepper. Serves 2.

EGG CASSEROLE

Have a brunch during the holidays. This casserole can be put together the day before needed. Served with sausage, sweet rolls, nut bread and fruit, it is an elegant and easy party.

- ¼ c. butter
- ¼ c. flour
- 2½ c. milk
- ¼ t. thyme
- ¼ t. marjoram
- 1 lb. grated Cheddar cheese
- 2 dozen hard-boiled eggs, sliced
- 1 lb. bacon, fried and crumbled
- ½ c. snipped parsley

Melt butter; stir in flour. Gradually stir in milk, stirring constantly. Add thyme, marjoram and cheese, stirring constantly, until cheese melts. In a large greased casserole, make layers of boiled egg, bacon, cheese sauce and parsley. Bake in a preheated 350° oven 30 minutes. Serves 8 to 10.

SCRAMBLED EGGS AU GRATIN

Assemble this casserole the day before needed and enjoy Christmas morning while breakfast cooks itself.

- 6 T. butter or margarine
- 6 T. flour
- 3 c. milk
- ½ t. salt
- ½ t. pepper
- ½ lb. mushrooms
- ¼ c. vermouth or lemon juice
- 12 eggs
- ½ c. milk
- 2 T. butter
- ½ lb. bacon, cooked and crumbled
- ½ lb. Cheddar cheese, grated

Melt 6 tablespoons butter; blend in flour until smooth. Slowly add 3 cups milk. Simmer and stir constantly until thickened and smooth. Season with salt and pepper. Sauté mushrooms in vermouth or lemon juice. Beat eggs with milk. Melt remaining butter and pour in eggs, stirring over medium heat until tender. In a greased, large and shallow casserole, combine cheese, mushrooms, bacon, eggs and sauce, stirring to blend. Refrigerate. Bring to room temperature and bake in a preheated 325° oven 30 minutes. Serves 10 to 12.

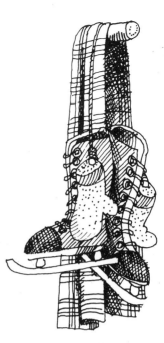

SPEEDY SPINACH LASAGNE

Great 1-dish meal.

- 1 pkg. spaghetti sauce mix
- 1 6-oz. can tomato paste
- 1 8-oz. can tomato sauce
- 1¾ c. cold water
- 2 eggs
- 1 15-oz. container Ricotta *or*
  1 lb. creamed cottage cheese
- ½ t. salt
- 1 10-oz. pkg. frozen chopped spinach, thawed and drained
- ½ c. grated Parmesan cheese
- ½ lb. sliced mozzarella cheese
- ½ lb. uncooked lasagne noodles, broken in half

Empty spaghetti sauce mix into saucepan; add tomato paste, tomato sauce and water. Heat, stirring, until well blended. Remove from heat. Beat eggs in a large bowl and add Ricotta or cottage cheese, spinach, salt and ¼ cup Parmesan cheese. Lightly grease bottom of a 13 x 9 x 2-inch baking dish; cover with a little sauce. Layer noodles, half of the cheese-spinach mixture, half the mozzarella cheese and half the tomato sauce. Repeat layers, ending with tomato sauce. Sprinkle with ¼ cup Parmesan cheese. Cover dish with a lightly greased sheet of aluminum foil and bake in a preheated 350° oven for 60 minutes or until noodles are tender. Let stand 10 minutes before cutting in squares and serving. Serves 8.

BARLEY CASSEROLE

¾ c. barley
1 onion, thinly sliced
3 t. instant beef bouillon
2 c. boiling water
½ c. sliced canned mushrooms

Mix all ingredients together in a 1½-quart casserole. Cover and bake in a 400° oven for 60 minutes, or until liquid is absorbed and barley is tender. Makes 4 to 6 servings.

BAKED RICE

¼ c. chopped onion
¼ c. butter or margarine
1 c. rice
2 c. chicken broth
¼ c. chopped parsley
    Salt to taste

Sauté onion in butter until translucent. Add rice and stir until coated. Bring chicken broth to a boil; add with parsley and salt. Pour into a 1-quart casserole; cover and bake in a 375° oven for about 20 minutes or until liquid is absorbed. Serves 6.

BROWN RICE PILAF

4 slices bacon
¼ lb. mushrooms, sliced
½ c. chopped onion
1 c. brown rice
3 c. beef broth
½ c. dry white wine
¼ c. slivered toasted almonds

Sauté bacon until crisp. Drain and save 2 tablespoons drippings. Crumble bacon. Cook mushrooms and onion in drippings until tender. Add rice; stir and sauté 1 minute. Stir in broth, wine, almonds and bacon; bring to a boil. Pour into a 1½-quart casserole and bake, covered, in a 325° oven 60 minutes. Serves 6 to 8.

Pictured opposite:
Speedy Spinach Lasagne, p. 25

NOODLES ALFREDO

A delicious difference if your entrée is roast beef or pork.

1 lb. broad noodles, cooked and drained
½ c. butter
¾ c. light cream, warmed
1½ c. grated Parmesan cheese
    Chopped parsley
    Chives

Place cooked noodles in a large serving dish. Melt butter. Pour butter, cream and grated cheese over noodles; mix well. Toss to coat and sprinkle with parsley and chives. Serves 6 to 8.

TREE PARTY
Some trees are so beautiful, they deserve to have a party just to admire them. With that in mind, we offer the following serving suggestions:
bowl of cold shrimp with Curry Sauce, p. 17
thinly sliced ham, turkey or beef with assorted breads
Caviar Star, p. 6
Cheese Ball, p. 10
nuts
mixed drinks
soft drinks
wine or eggnog

TOMATO PILAU

This festive rice dish is traditional in many Southern homes.

2 slices bacon, fried and crumbled
1 medium onion, diced
1 green pepper, diced
1 6-oz. can tomato paste
1 can water
1 t. sugar
1 t. salt
½ t. pepper
2½ to 3 c. rice
6 c. boiling water

Drain bacon and set aside. Sauté onion and pepper in bacon fat for 2 to 3 minutes. Add tomato paste, water, seasonings and rice. Sauté for about 5 minutes. Pour into boiling water and cook according to time on rice box. Serve garnished with bacon. Serves 8 to 10.

"Don we now our gay apparel . . ." vegetables are the gay apparel of the dinner table and a glorious decoration for the sturdy, everyday roast or chop.

Vegetables

GREEN BEANS AND BACON

The meaty flavor makes this a hearty vegetable.

- ¼ to ½ c. diced salt pork or bacon
- 1½ lbs. green beans *or* 2 9-oz. pkgs. frozen whole green beans
- 1 c. water
- ½ t. salt
- 1 t. instant minced onion
- 1 T. sugar

Sauté salt pork until crisp and brown; save pork and fat. Cook beans in water to which salt has been added. Heat to boiling and simmer, uncovered, 5 minutes. Cover and cook until tender, about 10 minutes. Drain. (If using frozen beans, cook as directed on package.) Toss beans with pork fat, minced onion and sugar. Makes 6 to 8 servings.

TURKISH GREEN BEANS

For a flavorful surprise.

- 2 T. olive oil
- 1 T. tomato paste
- 1 t. instant minced onion
- ¼ c. chopped green pepper
- ½ t. salt
- 1 9-oz. pkg. frozen whole green beans

Combine oil, tomato paste, onion, green pepper and salt. Pour over beans in a saucepan. Cook 10 minutes or until tender. Makes 4 servings.

CAULIFLOWER MOIRÉ

A new topping with tang.

- 1 head cauliflower
- ½ c. sour cream
- 1 T. prepared mustard
- ¼ t. salt
- ¼ t. pepper
- 2 to 3 green onions, snipped

Steam or cook cauliflower for about 20 minutes until just tender. Combine remaining ingredients. Heat but do not boil. Pour over hot cauliflower and sprinkle with paprika. Serves 6 to 8.

GREEN PEPPERS WITH STUFFING

Green pepper shells can be stuffed and frozen days ahead; then thawed and baked with the turkey.

- 6 to 8 green peppers, halved and seeded
- 2 medium onions, chopped
- 3 stalks celery, chopped
- ½ c. butter or margarine
- 2 8-oz. pkgs. herbed bread stuffing
- 1 to 1½ c. chicken broth

Sauté onions and celery in butter until tender crisp. Add stuffing. Moisten with broth and spoon lightly, but firmly, into peppers. Freeze at this point or place on a cookie sheet. Bake in a preheated 325° oven 20 to 30 minutes.

FRENCH PEAS

- 1 10-oz. pkg. peas
- ¼ c. chicken bouillon
- ¼ head lettuce, shredded
- ½ c. light cream
  Pepper

Cook peas in chicken bouillon. When tender, place lettuce on top, stir with a fork until lettuce wilts. Add cream and sprinkle with pepper. Serves 4.

GREEN PEAS AND ONIONS

Instant glamour.

- 1 10-oz. pkg. green peas
- ½ 20-oz. pkg. small pearl onions
- 1 pkg. sherry wine sauce mix *or* 1 pkg. white sauce mix
- 2 T. butter
- ½ c. bread crumbs
- ¼ c. grated Romano cheese

Place peas and onions in a casserole. Stir in sauce. Sprinkle crumbs and cheese on top and dot with butter. Bake in a 350° oven for 20 to 30 minutes. Serves 4 to 6.

WHIPPED RUTABAGAS AU GRATIN

Not to be neglected for the holidays.

3 lbs. rutabagas, cooked and mashed
¼ c. butter
1 T. sugar
3 eggs
1 c. bread crumbs
2 T. melted butter

Beat rutabagas, butter, sugar and eggs together. Turn into greased casserole. Top with crumbs and melted butter. Bake in a 350° oven 50 to 60 minutes until lightly browned. Serves 8 to 10.

STUFFED YAMS

To complement a roast.

6 medium yams, washed and dried
4 T. butter or margarine, softened
2 T. brown sugar
1 t. salt
Orange juice
Walnut or pecan halves

Bake yams in a 425° oven 40 minutes or until done. Remove from oven. Cut slice from top of each yam and scoop out inside, taking care not to break the shell. Add butter, brown sugar, salt and enough orange juice to moisten; beat until fluffy. Spoon mixture into shells. Return to oven and bake 15 to 20 minutes until heated through. Garnish each with a nut half. Makes 6 servings.

SPINACH, ARTICHOKE AND MUSHROOM CASSEROLE

½ lb. mushrooms, sliced
2 onions, chopped
2 jars artichoke hearts (drain and save marinade)
1 pkg. frozen chopped spinach, thawed and drained
5 eggs, lightly beaten
1½ c. grated Cheddar cheese
Salt and pepper to taste

Sauté mushrooms and onion in 2 to 3 tablespoons of the marinade. Combine with remaining ingredients in a lightly greased shallow casserole and bake in a 350° oven 30 to 45 minutes. Serves 4.

SPINACH RICE CHEESE BAKE

A combination of simple leaf and grain.

2 pkgs. frozen spinach, cooked and drained
1 c. cooked rice
1 c. cream of mushroom soup
1 t. instant minced onion
¼ lb. Cheddar cheese, shredded

Combine all ingredients and place in a greased casserole. Bake in a 350° oven for 30 minutes. Serves 6.

DILLED BRUSSELS SPROUTS

This is a dilly!

2 pkgs. Brussels sprouts, cooked and drained
¼ c. salad oil
2 T. lemon juice
½ small onion, minced
1 t. dill weed
Salt and pepper to taste

Combine oil, lemon juice, onion, dill and salt and pepper. Pour over Brussels sprouts. Cover and chill overnight. Serve cold. Serves 4 to 6.

PILAF AND BRUSSELS SPROUTS

A bowl of rice pilaf ringed with Brussels sprouts rounds out a feast.

2½ c. chicken or turkey broth or instant bouillon
1 T. lemon juice
1 T. butter
½ t. salt
½ t. cinnamon
½ c. raisins
1 c. uncooked, long grain rice
1 can mushrooms, drained
1 or 2 pkgs. frozen Brussels sprouts, cooked according to package directions
Pimiento strips

Heat broth, lemon juice, butter, salt, cinnamon and raisins to a boil in a large saucepan. Stir in rice. Cover and simmer over low heat until all liquid is absorbed. Stir in mushrooms; place on serving platter. Garnish with pimiento strips and Brussels sprouts. Makes 4 to 6 servings.

TOMATOES FLORENTINE

This beautiful vegetable casserole can be put together in the morning for easy baking at dinner time.

    2 pkgs. frozen chopped spinach
    ½ t. garlic salt
    ¼ c. mayonnaise
    4 to 6 tomatoes, sliced ½ inch thick
       Cheddar cheese slices
       Butter

In a shallow baking dish, combine spinach, garlic salt and mayonnaise. Arrange tomato slices over spinach and top with cheese. Dot with butter and bake in a 325° oven 20 to 30 minutes. Serves 4 to 6.

TOMATOES A LA PROVENCALE

A handsome garnish for a roast or fowl. Prepare in the morning and refrigerate until you are ready to bake it.

    12 tomatoes
    ½ c. butter or margarine
    1 c. chopped onion
    1 clove garlic, minced
    1½ c. fine dry bread crumbs
    ½ c. snipped fresh parsley
    2 t. basil
    1 t. thyme
    ½ t. salt
    ¼ t. freshly ground pepper

Cut a thin slice off the stem end of the tomatoes and cut out a wedge-shaped piece halfway down. Gently squeeze out the juice and remove seeds, not breaking skin. Melt butter in a skillet; sauté onion and garlic until soft. Remove pan from heat and stir in crumbs, parsley, basil, thyme, salt and pepper. Spoon this mixture into the tomatoes, then place tomatoes in a shallow baking dish. Bake in a preheated 350° oven about 20 minutes until the filling is lightly browned and the tomatoes are tender. Makes 12 servings.

Pictured opposite:
Savory Vegetable Platter

BAKED TOMATOES

A colorful brunch or breakfast dish when served with grilled bacon and toasted English muffins.

    8 tomatoes, sliced ½ inch thick
    ½ c. flour
    ½ t. salt
    ½ t. pepper
    1 T. sugar
    2 to 3 T. butter
    1 c. light cream
    1 T. sugar
    ⅛ t. baking soda

Dust tomato slices with flour seasoned with salt, pepper, and sugar. Brown lightly in butter and transfer to a baking dish. Stir cream, sugar and soda into pan drippings, blending well. Pour over tomatoes and bake at 325° for 15 to 20 minutes. Serves 4 to 6.

CHEESY ONIONS

Easy does it.

    2 1-lb. cans onions, drained
    1 10-oz. can condensed cream of celery
       soup
    ½ c. shredded Cheddar cheese
    ¼ c. slivered almonds

Place onions in a 1-quart casserole. Pour soup over. Sprinkle with cheese and nuts. Bake in a preheated 375° oven 20 to 25 minutes until heated thoroughly. Serves 6.

SAVORY VEGETABLE PLATTER

    3 c. beef bouillon
    ½ t. savory
    ½ t. tarragon
    1 head cauliflower, trimmed
    ½ lb. fresh green beans, trimmed
    10 carrots, peeled and cut into large pieces
    4 to 5 stalks celery, cut into
       2-inch chunks
    2 T. butter
    2 T. sesame seeds
    2 T. lemon juice

Heat bouillon, savory and tarragon to a boil. Add cauliflower; cover and simmer 10 minutes. Add remaining vegetables. Cover and simmer for 20 minutes. Make sauce of butter, seeds and juice. Serve vegetables in clusters on a large platter. Drizzle sauce over all. Serves 8 to 10.

JULIENNED CARROTS

10 to 12 carrots, cut into julienne strips
2 green onions, sliced
½ c. butter
½ c. chopped walnuts
  Sprinkle of nutmeg

Steam carrots until tender crisp. Melt butter. Add carrots, onions and nuts and sizzle for a few minutes. Dust with a sprinkle of nutmeg. Serves 6 to 8.

SESAME CARROTS

4 c. thinly sliced carrots
2 T. butter
1 T. salad oil
1 T. orange juice
½ t. ground ginger
½ t. salt
  Dash pepper
2 T. sesame seeds

Stir fry carrots in butter and oil over moderate heat until tender crisp, about 5 minutes. Stir in orange juice, ginger, salt, pepper and sesame seeds. Toss, heat well and serve. Serves 8 to 10.

BAKED-AHEAD POTATOES

Bake, stuff and refrigerate or freeze potatoes. Double or triple recipe as needed.

6 large baking potatoes
¼ c. butter
1 t. salt
½ t. pepper
½ c. sour cream
  Grated Swiss or Parmesan cheese

Scrub, pierce and bake potatoes in a 425° oven for 1 hour or until tender. Cool slightly. Break in half lengthwise and scoop potato into a large bowl. Beat in butter, salt, pepper and sour cream; refill shells. Sprinkle Parmesan or grated Swiss cheese on top. Bake in a 350° oven for 30 to 40 minutes. Freeze or refrigerate as desired.

POTATOES ANNA

6 large potatoes, pared and thinly sliced
½ c. melted butter
  Salt, pepper, paprika

Dip each potato into melted butter and layer in circles in a greased 9-inch iron skillet. Season each layer with salt, pepper and paprika. Cover and bake in a 450° oven 15 to 20 minutes. Loosen and invert onto a platter. Makes 6 servings.

JUST FOR CHILDREN
Present each child with two ornaments made of decorated cookies or popcorn balls. They can hang one on your tree and take one home. After the tree has been trimmed, serve:
  Cranberry Punch, p. 4
  Milkshake Punch, p. 4
Plates of cookies, nuts and candies
If you have a good storyteller, a Christmas story near the tree or in front of the fireplace is a nice finale. Also, singing carols is fun for all ages.

BROCCOLI OR ASPARAGUS

1 lb. fresh broccoli or asparagus *or*
1 10-oz. pkg. frozen broccoli or
  asparagus
1 t. chicken boullion crystals
  Water

Place broccoli or asparagus in a steamer with a small amount of water (about ¼ cup). Sprinkle with chicken boullion crystals. Steam until tender-crisp, 10 to 15 minutes. (Time will vary according to the density of vegetables.) Serve with Hollandaise Sauce. Serves 2.

INSTANT HOLLANDAISE SAUCE

1 c. sour cream
1 c. mayonnaise
¼ c. lemon juice

Combine all ingredients and blend together. Heat slowly and serve hot over asparagus or broccoli.

"Sing we joyous all together . . ." we've composed this medley of salads and dressings to echo the zestiness of the season.

Salads and Dressings

GALA FRUIT MOLD

An all-American combination.

2¼ c. boiling water
1 3-oz. pkg. lemon gelatin
¾ c. blueberry juice
1 3-oz. pkg. lime gelatin
¾ c. pineapple juice
1 3-oz. pkg. strawberry gelatin
¾ c. strawberry juice and water
1 pt. heavy cream
1 can blueberries
1½ c. crushed pineapple
1 10-oz. pkg. frozen strawberries, thawed

In 3 separate bowls, dissolve lemon gelatin in ¾ cup boiling water and blueberry juice. Dissolve lime gelatin in ¾ cup boiling water and pineapple juice. Dissolve strawberry gelatin in ¾ cup boiling water and strawberry juice and water. Refrigerate until slightly thickened. Whip cream and divide in thirds. Fold whipped cream into each bowl of partially set gelatin. Fold in corresponding fruits. Refrigerate each 10 minutes. Grease a very large mold or bowl. Spoon in gelatin, making 3 layers. Chill until completely set. Serves 8 to 10.

CARAWAY COLESLAW

Caraway studded cabbage slaw.

3 to 4 c. shredded cabbage
½ c. chopped green pepper
½ small onion, minced
½ carrot, grated
⅓ c. mayonnaise
2 T. lemon juice
½ t. sugar
½ t. caraway seed
¼ t. celery salt

Prepare cabbage, green pepper, onion and carrot. Combine remaining ingredients, mixing well. Pour over vegetables and toss well.

SEAFOAM MOLD

1½ c. boiling water
2 3-oz. pkgs. lime gelatin
1½ c. cold water
1 8-oz. can crushed pineapple with juice
1 c. sour cream
1 16-oz. can sliced pears, drained

Dissolve gelatin in boiling water. Add cold water, pineapple with juice and sour cream. Mix gently. Line a lightly oiled 5-cup mold with pear slices and pour gelatin fruit mixture in. Chill until set. Makes 6 to 8 servings.

CRANBERRY SALAD MOLD

1 3-oz. pkg. lemon gelatin
1 c. boiling water
1 c. cranberry juice
1 10½-oz. pkg. cranberry orange relish, partially thawed
½ c. chopped celery
½ c. chopped walnuts

Dissolve gelatin in boiling water. Stir in juice and relish. Chill until partially thickened; stir in celery and nuts. Pour into small mold. Chill until firm.

CHERRY JUBILEE MOLD

1 16-oz. can pitted dark sweet cherries
2 3-oz. pkgs. cherry gelatin
½ c. cream sherry
1 can pear halves
1 3-oz. pkg. cream cheese
Chopped nuts

Drain cherries and reserve syrup. Add enough water to make 3 cups liquid. In a saucepan, combine gelatin and liquid. Heat and stir until gelatin dissolves. Remove from heat and stir in sherry. Chill until partially set. Fold in cherries and pour into a lightly oiled mold. Chill until firm. Drain pears. Form cream cheese into small balls and roll in nuts. Place on pear halves. Turn out mold on lettuce leaves and surround with pear halves. Serves 8 to 10.

CRANBERRY SOUR CREAM MOLD

    2 3-oz. pkg. red gelatin
 1¾ c. boiling water
    1 can jellied cranberry sauce
    1 c. sour cream

Dissolve gelatin in boiling water. Chill until slightly thickened. Beat cranberry sauce and sour cream until smooth. Fold into gelatin; pour into mold and chill until firm. Serves 4 to 6.

PINEAPPLE CRANBERRY MOLD

Ring in the season.

    2 6-oz. pkgs. raspberry gelatin
    3 c. boiling water
    2 c. cold water
   ½ c. pineapple juice
    1 T. lemon juice
   ¼ t. salt
  18 pecan halves (optional)
    1 20-oz. can crushed pineapple, drained
    1 16-oz. can whole cranberry sauce

Dissolve gelatin in boiling water. Stir in 2 cups cold water, pineapple juice, lemon juice and salt. Pour ½ cup gelatin into an 8-cup ring mold. Arrange pecan halves in mold and refrigerate until set. Refrigerate remaining gelatin until slightly thickened, about 1½ hours. Spoon 1¾ cups gelatin into mold. Stir pineapple and cranberry sauce into remaining gelatin and spoon over gelatin in mold. Refrigerate until set. Makes 16 servings.

FRESH VEGETABLES VINAIGRETTE

Crudities are very stylish.

 6 to 8 c. assorted fresh vegetables
      1 c. olive or safflower oil
     ¼ c. white wine vinegar
      2 T. lemon juice
      1 t. dry mustard
     ½ t. salt
         Freshly ground pepper
      2 T. snipped parsley
      1 T. snipped green onion

Wash and prepare vegetables such as carrots, red and green pepper slices, cauliflowerets, cucumber slices, celery, cherry tomatoes, kohlrabi slices, zucchini slices, mushrooms and any other vegetable you like. Combine remaining ingredients, mixing thoroughly. Pour over vegetables and chill for 6 hours. Drain vegetables and arrange on a platter.

SPINACH SALAD DELUXE

    1 lb. fresh spinach, washed, dried and shredded
 4 to 6 green onions, chopped
    4 slices bacon, fried and crumbled
   ½ c. mayonnaise
   ½ c. sour cream
    3 T. grated Parmesan cheese
       Bacon to garnish

Toss spinach, onions and bacon. Mix mayonnaise, sour cream and cheese together. Toss with salad. Garnish with bacon and serve. Serves 2 to 4.

WALDORF SALAD AU VIN

An apple a day in this special way.

    4 Winesap or Jonathan apples
    1 rib celery, diced
    1 c. seedless green grapes
   ½ c. walnut pieces
   ½ c. mayonnaise
   ¼ c. dry white wine

Core apples but do not peel; chop into cubes. In a salad bowl, combine apples, celery, grapes and walnuts. Mix mayonnaise with wine and pour over fruit. Toss lightly. Makes 8 servings.

Pictured opposite:
Gala Fruit Mold, p. 33

MIMOSA SALAD

Add a spring-like touch of color to any season!

- 1 head romaine lettuce
- 2 heads of bibb lettuce
- 1 bunch of watercress
- 1 T. prepared mustard
- 6 T. salad oil
- 1 clove garlic, minced
- 2 T. wine vinegar
  Juice of 1 lemon
  Salt and pepper
- 1 can sliced beets, drained
- 2 hard-boiled eggs, sieved

Wash and dry greens; toss lightly. Combine mustard, oil, garlic, vinegar, juice of lemon, salt and freshly ground pepper. Toss with greens. Add sliced beets and sieved whites and yolks as garnish to justify its name. Serves 6 to 8.

SPRING SALAD

A touch of spring all year long.

- 1 1-lb. can whole tomatoes, chopped and drained (save juice for soup or sauces)
- 3 to 4 green onions, chopped
- ½ green pepper, chopped
- 1 stalk celery, chopped
- 1 cucumber, thinly sliced
- 1 carrot, thinly sliced
- 2 to 3 T. olive or salad oil
- 2 to 3 T. wine vinegar
- ½ t. salt
- ¼ t. pepper
- ½ t. sugar
  Mixed greens

Combine first 6 ingredients. Add oil, vinegar, salt, pepper and sugar. Stir gently to blend. Chill for 1 hour or more and serve over mixed greens. Serves 4 to 6.

GARDEN MOLD
For the beauty of a molded salad.

- 1 16-oz. can diced beets
- 1 3-oz. pkg. lemon gelatin
- 1 c. Burgundy wine
- 1 t. horseradish
- ¼ t. salt
- 1 c. boiling water
- 1 3-oz. pkg. lemon gelatin
- 1 c. cold water
- 1 c. sour cream
- 1 pkg. frozen tiny peas
- 3 hard-boiled eggs, chopped
- 2 T. snipped green onion
- ½ t. Worcestershire sauce
- 2 drops Tabasco sauce
- 1 t. salt
  Salad greens
  Hard-boiled egg wedges

Drain beets, saving liquid. Add enough water to beet liquid to make 1 cup; bring to a boil. Add 1 package gelatin, stirring to dissolve. Stir in wine, horseradish and salt. Chill until slightly thickened. Dissolve remaining package gelatin in 1 cup boiling water. Stir in cold water and chill until slightly thickened. Fold beets into thickened beet gelatin. Pour into an 8-cup mold and chill until just set. Mix sour cream with next 6 ingredients and fold into lemon gelatin. Spoon mixture over beet layer. Chill at least 4 hours. Unmold onto salad greens. Garnish with hard-boiled egg slices, if desired. Serves 8 to 12.

RASPBERRY MOLD

A colorful complement.

    2 10-oz. pkgs. frozen raspberries, thaw
      and reserve juice
    ½ pt. sour cream
    2 c. boiling water
    2 3-oz. pkgs. raspberry gelatin

Dissolve gelatin in boiling water. Add enough water to raspberry juice to make 1¾ cups liquid. Add to gelatin and chill until partially thickened. Fold in sour cream and berries. Chill until firm. Serves 8.

GRAPEFRUIT RING

For winter sunshine.

    2 3-oz. pkgs. lemon gelatin
    1½ c. boiling water
    1¾ c. cold water
    ½ c. frozen lemonade concentrate
    2 grapefruits, pared and sectioned (2 c.
      segments)
    1 c. red grapes, halved and seeded
    ½ c. slivered almonds (optional)

Dissolve gelatin in boiling water. Stir in cold water and lemonade. Chill until mixture is partially set. Fold in grapefruit segments, grapes and almonds. Spoon into a 6-cup mold. Chill until firm. Serves 8.

THOUSAND ISLAND SALAD

A toss for winners!

    ½ large head lettuce, shredded
      Handful spinach, washed and torn up
    1 sweet red onion, cut in rings
    3 hard-boiled eggs, sliced
    4 to 6 water chestnuts, sliced
    1 c. mayonnaise
    ¼ c. chili sauce
    1 T. Worcestershire sauce

Toss first 5 ingredients together. Combine remaining ingredients and add, tossing to blend. Serves 4.

SALAD DRESSING

    ½ c. olive oil
    ¼ c. tarragon vinegar
    1 clove garlic
    1 t. brown sugar
    ¼ t. dry mustard
    ½ t. salt

Combine all ingredients and blend. Makes about ¾ cup.

CHEF'S SALAD DRESSING

Serve with greens topped with julienne strips of turkey, ham and cheese. Garnish with hard-boiled egg and tomato.

    ½ pt. sour cream
    1 c. mayonnaise
    1½ T. vinegar
    1 t. salt
      Dash pepper
    1 t. sugar
    ¼ t. dry mustard
    1 T. minced onion
    1 clove garlic, minced

Combine all ingredients and chill overnight. Makes about 2 cups.

HONEY-CELERY SEED DRESSING

May be used over a grapefruit ring.

    ⅓ c. sugar
    3 T. honey
    1 t. salt
    1 t. dry mustard
    1 t. celery seed
    1 t. paprika
    1 c. safflower oil
    ¼ c. vinegar

Combine all ingredients in a blender until well mixed. Makes 1⅔ cups.

"Hail the new, ye lads and lasses . . ." here's a delightful assortment of condiments and relishes to accompany the most discriminating palate into the new year.

Condiments

END-OF-SUMMER RELISH

Vary this vegetable combination to suit your taste and the contents of your vegetable crisper.

- 2 c. sliced cauliflower flowerets (about ½ small head)
- 2 carrots, julienne strips
- 1 green pepper, cut in strips
- 10 to 12 green beans
- 1 zucchini, cut in disks
- 1 small jar stuffed olives
- ¾ c. wine vinegar
- ¼ c. olive oil
- 1 T. sugar
- 1 t. salt
- ½ t. oregano
- ¼ t. pepper
- ¼ c. water
- Cherry tomatoes (optional)

Combine all ingredients in a large pan. Bring to a boil and simmer, covered, 5 minutes. Cool and let marinate at least 24 hours. Cherry tomatoes may be added just before serving. Makes 2½ quarts.

APPLE CHUTNEY

To accompany a curry or just to sweeten up a meal.

- 3 lbs. green apples, cubed
- 1 lime, cut up
- 1 orange, cut up
- 2 c. packed light brown sugar
- 1½ c. golden raisins
- ¼ c. cider vinegar
- ½ t. salt
- 1 t. cinnamon
- ½ t. ground cloves
- ¼ t. ground ginger
- ¼ t. nutmeg

Combine all ingredients in a heavy saucepan. Bring to a boil over medium heat. Lower heat to a simmer and cook for about 30 minutes, or until tender. Makes about 4 cups.

BRANDY BERRIES

Cranberries with new sophistication and flavor.

- 1 lb. fresh cranberries, washed and dried
- 2 c. sugar
- 1 T. grated orange rind
- ½ c. Triple Sec, Cointreau or Grand Marnier

Combine all ingredients in a large flat oven-proof dish. Set aside for 20 to 30 minutes. Cover dish with foil and bake in a preheated 325° oven for 40 minutes. Cool slightly and pour into glass containers. Refrigerate.

NUTS AND FRUITS

A delicious snack, full of vitamins and proteins.

- ½ lb. raw cashews
- ½ lb. pecans
- ½ lb. almonds
- 1 c. sunflower seeds
- 1 c. pepitas
- 1 c. raisins
- 1 c. dried apricots, chopped

Mix together all ingredients. Store covered. Makes about 5½ cups.

CANDIED ORANGE PEEL

- 2 large navel oranges, sliced crosswise
- ½ c. sugar
- ¼ c. hot water
- ¼ c. sugar (for coating)

Remove peel from orange slices and cut circles in half. Place peel in saucepan, cover with cold water and bring to boil; drain. Repeat this 4 or 5 times. Drain and put on plate. In same saucepan, heat ½ cup sugar and water, stirring constantly until sugar is dissolved. Add orange peel and cook slowly until syrup is reduced to half. Remove peel, and roll in ¼ cup sugar on a sheet of waxed paper. Cool.

*Pictured opposite:
End-of-Summer Relish
Nuts and Fruits*

CURRIED PEARS

A winter fruit with flavor.

4 firm, fresh pears
¼ c. butter
¾ c. packed brown sugar
2 t. curry powder

Peel and core pears and cut in half. Arrange in shallow baking dish. Melt butter and stir in brown sugar and curry powder. Pour over pears. Cover and bake in a preheated 350° oven about 20 minutes. Serve slightly warm or cool with turkey, chicken or ham. Makes 8 servings.

MUSTARD BEANS

A "snappy" relish.

2 lbs. green beans
½ red pepper, sliced
1 onion, sliced into thin rings
½ c. cider vinegar
½ c. water
½ c. sugar
1 T. flour
2 T. prepared mustard

Cook beans until tender crisp and drain. Combine with pepper and onion slices. In a saucepan, heat vinegar, water, sugar, flour and mustard to boiling. Pour hot mixture over vegetables. Refrigerate at least 24 hours in a glass container.

DRIED FRUIT AND NUT CHUTNEY

A "perker-upper" for any meal.

½ lb. dried apples
½ lb. dried peaches
½ lb. dried apricots
½ lb. pitted dates
½ lb. golden raisins
1¼ c. sugar
1 c. brown sugar
3 cloves garlic, minced
1 t. salt
1 t. dry mustard
½ t. ground ginger
½ t. pepper
½ t. ground allspice
¼ t. cinnamon
1 c. chopped nuts
3 c. cider vinegar

Cut fruits in ½-inch pieces; cover with water and set aside for 4 to 6 hours. Drain fruit, reserving 1½ cups liquid. Bring liquid to a boil; add fruit and remaining ingredients. Bring again to a boil, simmer, stirring often, until tender and thick, about 30 minutes. Cool and store in glass containers in the refrigerator. May be processed in a hot water bath, if desired. Makes 6 pints.

FROSTED CRANBERRIES

For a holiday touch around a mold or an entrée.

1 lb. washed and dried cranberries
1 egg white
Sugar

Beat egg white until frothy. Dip cranberries into egg white and then roll in sugar. Place on waxed paper to dry.

ORANGE SLICES, GLACÉS

Delicious with chicken, beef or lamb.

2 large navel oranges
2 T. butter or margarine
⅓ c. light brown sugar, firmly packed
¼ t. ground allspice
1 T. light corn syrup

Cut ends off oranges and cut crosswise into ½-inch slices. In large skillet, heat butter, brown sugar, allspice and corn syrup, stirring constantly until mixture is smooth. Add orange slices. Cook 10 minutes on each side or until oranges are shiny and glazed.

DILLYS

Keep on hand for munching. Also makes a pretty gift. Alternate bunches of beans or carrots in a tall jar.

Green beans (about ½ lb.)
Carrots (about 4 to 6 medium)
2 c. water
2 c. vinegar
¼ c. salt
½ t. red pepper
2 cloves garlic
2 T. dried dill weed
1 to 2 small dried red peppers (seeds removed)

Wash and trim beans. Scrape carrots and cut into sticks. Place beans and carrots in jars. Combine remaining ingredients in a saucepan and bring to a boil. Pour over vegetables. Chill for 8 to 10 days for maximum flavor.

"Heedless of the wind and weather..."the aroma of these quick breads and coffee cakes would warm Jack Frost himself!

Breads

CRANBERRY MUFFINS

1 c. coarsely chopped cranberries
2 T. sugar
2 c. flour
½ c. sugar
3 t. baking powder
¼ t. salt
1 c. milk
1 t. vanilla
¼ c. butter, melted
2 eggs

Add 2 tablespoons sugar to cranberries; set aside. Mix flour, remaining sugar, baking powder and salt in a large bowl. Set aside. Beat together eggs, milk, vanilla and butter. Make a well in the center of the flour. Pour in liquid all at once, stirring quickly with a fork just until mixed. Do not beat; batter will be lumpy. Fold in cranberries. Fill greased 2½-inch muffin tins two-thirds full and bake in a 400° oven 25 to 30 minutes. Makes 12 muffins.

FRUIT AND CHEESE BREAD

1 c. butter or margarine
1 8-oz. pkg. cream cheese
1½ c. sugar
4 eggs
1 t. vanilla
2¼ c. flour
2 t. baking powder
¼ t. salt
1 c. candied cut up cherries
1 c. candied cut up pineapple
1 c. chopped nuts
¼ c. flour for dredging fruit and nuts

Cream butter and cream cheese together. Beat in sugar until light and fluffy. Add eggs, one at a time, beating well. Add vanilla. Combine 2¼ cups flour, baking powder and salt and add to mixture. Dredge fruit in remaining flour. Stir floured fruits and nuts into batter. Bake in 2 small greased loaf pans in a 325° oven 60 to 70 minutes. Cool on rack for 10 minutes. Remove from pans and cool thoroughly. Makes 2 loaves.

COFFEE DATE LOAF

Good for all seasons.

2 c. flour
3 t. baking powder
1 t. baking soda
1 t. salt
1 t. instant coffee
⅔ c. sugar
¼ c. chopped nuts
1 c. snipped dates
1 egg
1 c. buttermilk
4 T. vegetable oil

Combine flour, baking powder, baking soda, salt, instant coffee and sugar. Add nuts and dates. In a separate bowl, beat egg, buttermilk and oil. Pour into dry ingredients and blend lightly. Pour into a greased 10½ x 3⅝ x 2⅝-inch pan and allow to rest 20 minutes. Bake in a preheated 375° oven about 45 minutes. Makes 1 loaf.

DATE AND NUT BREAD

Some breads take their place with the dinner—others entertain with coffee.

1¾ c. packed brown sugar
3 T. butter or margarine, softened
2 eggs
3 c. flour
1½ t. baking soda
¼ t. salt
1 c. sour milk *or* 1 T. vinegar plus milk to equal 1 c.
½ c. chopped nuts, lightly floured
1½ c. dates, cut in small pieces

Cream butter and brown sugar; add eggs, beating well. Combine flour, soda, salt and add alternately with milk. Stir in nuts and dates, mixing thoroughly. Spoon into 2 well-greased 9 x 5 x 3-inch loaf pans or five 16-ounce cans. Bake loaves in a preheated 350° oven for 60 minutes and cans in a 325° oven for 60 to 70 minutes, or until toothpick inserted in center comes out clean. Cool on rack for 10 minutes. Turn out of pans and continue cooling on rack. Makes 2 loaves.

APPLESAUCE BREAD

Spicy, moist and delicious. Keeps for weeks in refrigerator and months in the freezer.

- **4 eggs**
- **1½ c. sugar**
- **1 c. salad oil**
- **2 c. applesauce**
- **⅔ c. milk**
- **3½ c. flour**
- **2 t. baking soda**
- **1 t. cinnamon**
- **1 t. nutmeg**
- **1 c. chopped nuts**

Beat eggs. Add sugar, oil, applesauce and milk. Combine remaining ingredients, stirring well. Add to applesauce mixture, mixing well. Pour into three 8 x 4-inch loaf pans. Bake in a 350° oven for 1 hour or until done. Makes 3 loaves.

HONEY WHOLE WHEAT BREAD

The aroma from the oven is a joy.

- **2 c. flour**
- **1¼ c. whole wheat flour**
- **1 pkg. dry yeast**
- **1 t. salt**
- **½ c. milk**
- **½ c. water**
- **¼ c. honey**
- **1 T. butter or margarine**
- **1 small egg**

In a large mixing bowl, combine ½ cup of the flour, whole wheat flour, yeast and salt, mixing well. In a saucepan, combine milk, water, honey and butter; heat until warm. Add to flour mixture. Add egg. Blend at low speed until moistened; beat 3 minutes at medium speed. By hand, stir in remaining flour to make a firm dough. Knead on floured surface until smooth and elastic, about 5 minutes. Place in a greased bowl, turning to grease top. Cover and let rise in a warm place until light and doubled in bulk, about 1 hour. Punch dough down. On a lightly floured surface, roll or pat dough to a 14 x 7-inch rectangle. Starting with the shorter side, roll up tightly, pressing dough into the roll with each turn. Pinch edges and ends to seal. Place in a greased 9 x 5-inch loaf pan. Cover and let rise in a warm place until doubled in bulk, about 30 minutes. Bake in a 375° oven 35 to 40 minutes until golden brown. Remove from pan and cool. Makes 1 loaf.

Pictured opposite:
Almond Coffee Cake

ALMOND COFFEE CAKE

For breakfast, brunch or for gifts.

- **1 c. milk**
- **½ c. butter**
- **1 pkg. dry yeast**
- **½ c. sugar**
- **½ t. salt**
- **3 eggs, beaten**
- **4½ c. flour**
- **½ c. butter, softened**
- **1 can almond paste filling for cakes**
  Slivered almonds

Scald milk and pour over ½ cup butter in a large mixing bowl. Cool to lukewarm; add yeast and stir until dissolved. Add sugar and salt to beaten eggs; add to milk mixture. Stir in flour to make a stiff dough. Place in a greased bowl, cover and let rise in a warm place until doubled in bulk, about 1½ hours. Divide dough in half and knead until smooth and elastic. On a lightly floured board, roll out each piece to a 12 x 8-inch rectangle. Spread with half the remaining butter and half a can of almond paste. Roll up as for a jelly roll. Curve in a ring, overlapping ends to seal. Place in greased round cake pans. With scissors, make cuts at 1-inch intervals, cutting two-thirds through the ring. (Start at the outside and cut toward the center.) Turn each section on its side. Cover and let rise again until doubled in bulk, 30 to 45 minutes. Bake in a 350° oven 45 minutes. When slightly cooled, ice and sprinkle with almonds. Makes 2 cakes.

ICING

- **1 T. butter or margarine, softened**
- **1 c. confectioners' sugar**
- **1½ T. milk**
- **¼ t. almond extract**

Combine all ingredients. Beat until smooth and of spreading consistency.

MINIATURE COFFEE CAKES

Easier than you think.

- 1 c. flour
- ¾ t. baking powder
- ½ t. baking soda
- ¼ t. salt
- ¼ c. butter
- ½ c. sugar
- 1 egg
- ½ t. vanilla
- ½ c. sour cream
- ½ c. golden raisins

Mix together dry ingredients. Cream butter and add sugar gradually. Beat until fluffy. Add egg and vanilla and beat well. Add sour cream and flour mixture alternately. Stir in raisins. Grease bottom only of 1½-inch muffin tins and fill two-thirds full. Sprinkle with Topping and bake at 425° for 12 minutes. Makes 24 miniature cakes.

TOPPING

- 3 T. brown sugar
- 2 T. granulated sugar
- ½ c. chopped nuts

Combine all ingredients.

CHOCOLATE NUT APPLESAUCE LOAF

A loaf with "pizzazz!"

- ½ c. butter or margarine
- 1 c. sugar
- 2 eggs
- 2 t. vanilla
- 2 1-oz. squares unsweetened chocolate, melted and cooled
- 1¾ c. flour
- 1½ t. baking powder
- ½ t. baking soda
- ½ t. salt
- ½ c. chopped nuts
- 1 c. canned applesauce

Cream butter and sugar until very light and fluffy. Add eggs, one at a time, beating well. Beat in chocolate and vanilla. Combine dry ingredients, mixing well. Add dry ingredients alternately with applesauce. Stir in nuts. Spoon into a greased and floured 9 x 5-inch loaf pan and bake in a preheated 325° oven for 75 minutes or until done. Cool on rack for 10 minutes. Remove from pan and cool thoroughly. May be frosted or sprinkled with confectioners' sugar. Makes 1 loaf.

OLIVE-NUT BREAD

Olives make a nice difference. Slice bread thin and serve with scrambled eggs or spread with cream cheese for party sandwiches.

- 2½ c. flour
- ¼ c. sugar
- 4 t. baking powder
- 1 egg, beaten
- 1 c. milk
- ½ c. salad oil
- 1 c. chopped olives
- 1 c. chopped walnuts

In a large bowl, combine flour, sugar, and baking powder. Stir in egg, milk and oil, mix until blended. Add olives and nuts. Turn into a 9 x 5-inch loaf pan. Bake in a 350° oven for 45 minutes or until done. Cool on rack. Makes 1 loaf.

CARAWAY RYE BREAD

- 2½ to 3 c. flour
- 1½ c. rye flour
- 2 pkgs. dry yeast
- 2 T. sugar
- 2 t. salt
- 1 T. caraway seed
- 1 c. milk
- ¾ c. water
- 2 T. butter or margarine

In a large mixing bowl, combine 1 cup of the flour, rye flour, yeast, sugar, salt and caraway seed, mixing well. In a saucepan, heat milk, water and butter until warm. Add to flour mixture. Blend at low speed until moistened; beat 3 minutes at medium speed. By hand, gradually stir in remaining flour to make a firm dough. Knead on floured surface until smooth and elastic, about 5 minutes. Place in a greased bowl, turning to grease top. Cover and let rise in a warm place until light and doubled, about 1 hour. Punch dough down and divide into 2 parts. On a lightly floured surface, roll or pat each half to a 7 x 14-inch rectangle. Starting with the shorter side, roll up tightly, pressing dough into the roll with each turn. Pinch edges and ends to seal. Place in 2 greased 9 x 5-inch or 8 x 4-inch loaf pans. Cover and let rise in a warm place until doubled in bulk, about 30 minutes. Bake in a 375° oven 35 to 40 minutes or until golden brown. Remove from pans to cool. Makes 2 loaves.

COFFEE RING
For late evening coffee and cake.

1 pkg. dry yeast
¼ c. warm water
¼ c. lukewarm milk
¼ c. sugar
½ t. salt
1 egg
¼ c. butter or margarine
2¼ to 2½ c. flour
2 T. butter or margarine, softened
½ c. packed brown sugar
1 t. cinnamon
½ c. raisins
½ c. nuts

Dissolve yeast in warm water in a large bowl. Stir in milk, sugar, salt, egg, butter and half of the flour. Beat until smooth. Mix in enough remaining flour to make dough easy to handle. Turn dough onto a lightly floured board and knead until smooth and elastic, about 5 minutes. Place in a greased bowl; turn greased side up and cover. Let rise in a warm place until doubled in bulk, about 1½ hours. Punch dough down; roll into a 15 x 9-inch rectangle. Spread with butter; sprinkle with brown sugar, cinnamon, raisins and nuts. Roll up tightly, beginning at the wide side. Pinch edges to seal. Place sealed side down in ring on lightly greased baking sheet. Join ends of ring and seal. Make cuts two-thirds through the ring at 1-inch intervals. Turn each section on its side. Let rise until doubled in bulk, about 45 minutes. Bake in a 375° oven about 25 to 30 minutes until golden. While warm, frost with confectioners' sugar icing. Decorate with almonds and cherries if desired.

CONFECTIONERS' ICING

½ c. confectioners' sugar
1 T. milk

Beat sugar and milk until smooth and of spreading consistency.

"Follow me in merry measure . . ." to ensure that you will turn out beautiful cakes, pies, cookies and candies.

Desserts

STRAWBERRY BAKED ALASKA

For a jolly holiday!

- 2 egg whites
- ¼ t. cream of tartar
- ⅓ c. sugar
- 1 pkg. frozen sliced strawberries, thawed and drained
- 6 individual sponge cake shells
  Ice cream (butter pecan, strawberry, vanilla)

Beat egg whites with cream of tartar until foamy. Gradually beat in sugar until egg whites hold a stiff peak. Place 1 spoonful berries in shell and an ice cream ball on top; freeze. Cover ice cream and shell with meringue, sealing edges. Bake on a cookie sheet in a preheated 450° oven 3 minutes until golden brown. Garnish with a whole strawberry, if desired. Makes 6 servings.

VANILLA CREAM TRIFLE

For a yummy Yuletide.

- ½ c. sherry or rum
- 1 angel food or sponge cake
- 1 3-oz. pkg. French vanilla instant pudding mix
- 2 c. milk
- ½ pt. heavy cream, whipped
- ½ c. slivered almonds
- ½ c. golden raisins

Cut cake into cubes and sprinkle with ¼ cup sherry or rum. Prepare pudding mix as directed on the package, using 2 cups milk and folding in remaining ¼ cup sherry and half of the whipped cream. Fold in raisins and nuts. In a glass serving bowl or 8 parfait glasses, make 3 layers of cake and pudding mixture, beginning with cake cubes and ending with pudding. Top with whipped cream. Chill at least 3 hours, but no longer than 24 hours. Makes 8 servings.

Pictured opposite:
Peaches Flambées

PEACHES FLAMBÉES

- 1 2½-lb. can cling peach halves
- ⅔ c. brandy
- ½ c. syrup from peaches
- 1 orange rind, coarsely shredded
- ⅓ c. currant jelly
- 1 qt. vanilla ice cream

Drain peaches; pour one-third cup brandy over and set aside for about 1 hour. Heat syrup from peaches with orange rind in chafing dish (or saucepan on stove) and boil until volume is reduced by about half. Add currant jelly and stir until melted. Add peaches and heat thoroughly. Heat remaining one-third cup brandy and pour over hot peaches; carefully ignite with a match. Do not stir or it will not flame. When flames die, spoon over ice cream. Serves 4 to 6.

SPUMONI PARFAIT

Elegant dessert for the busy hostess. Can be made one or two days ahead. For the grand occasion, fix it in your crystal ice-tea or parfait glasses or in a mold.

- 3 pts. chocolate ice cream, softened
- 1 pt. pistachio ice cream, softened
- 2 pts. strawberry ice cream, softened
- 1½ c. heavy cream, whipped
- 1 t. rum flavoring
  Almond slices, maraschino cherries or other garnish (optional)

Layer ice creams (chocolate, strawberry, pistachio, strawberry, chocolate) in glasses. Stir rum flavoring into whipped cream and top parfait with a dollop of cream.

For mold: Line mold or bowl with a 1-inch layer of chocolate; freeze. Next, line chocolate with a layer of pistachio and freeze. Fill with strawberry ice cream; freeze. To serve, unmold and frost with whipped cream to which flavoring has been added. Garnish with cherries and almond slices. Serves 14.

CRANBERRY MOUSSE

Pale pink and picture pretty.

1 can whole-berry cranberry sauce
½ pt. heavy cream
1 T. orange-flavored liqueur

Chill cranberry sauce for an hour or so. Place in blender with liqueur and whirl until smooth. Whip cream until stiff. Fold cranberry mixture into cream until well blended. Chill and serve. Makes 4 to 6 servings.

SHERRIED APPLE CRISP

5 tart apples, cored and thinly sliced
½ t. cinnamon
¼ c. sweet sherry
1 c. flour
½ c. sugar
½ c. butter
1 egg

Arrange apple slices in a shallow baking dish. Sprinkle with cinnamon and sherry. Mix flour, sugar, butter and egg until crumbly. Sprinkle over apples. Bake in a 350° oven for 45 minutes. Serve warm with cream or ice cream. Serves 6 to 8.

GRAHAM CRACKER TORTE

Not lavish—just good.

3 T. butter or margarine
1¾ c. sugar
2 eggs
1½ t. baking soda
2 c. buttermilk
1 1-lb. box graham crackers, crushed
1 c. chopped nuts
Confectioners' sugar

Cream butter with sugar until light. Add eggs and beat well. Stir baking soda into buttermilk and stir until it bubbles. Alternately add graham cracker crumbs and buttermilk to creamed mixture. Mix well. Stir in nuts. Pour into a greased springform pan and bake in a preheated 350° oven for 1 hour or until toothpick inserted in center comes out clean. Cool on rack. Top with confectioners' sugar. Serves 10 to 12.

STRAWBERRY CREAM TORTE

For a final holiday party effect.

4 egg whites, room temperature
½ c. sugar
4 egg yolks
½ c. sugar
1¼ c. flour
¼ t. salt
2 T. lemon juice
2 t. grated lemon peel
2 T. water
¼ c. confectioners' sugar
2 c. heavy cream, whipped
1 12-oz. jar strawberry preserves
6 fresh whole strawberries

In a large bowl, beat egg whites at high speed until frothy. Gradually beat in ½ cup sugar. Continue beating until soft peaks appear when beater is slowly raised. In small bowl at high speed with the same beater, beat egg yolks until thick and lemon colored. Gradually beat in ½ cup sugar and continue beating until mixture is well blended. At low speed, add flour and salt. Blend well and add lemon juice, lemon peel and water, beating about 1 minute. Gently fold yolk mixture into egg white mixture just until blended. Pour the batter into 2 round ungreased 8 x 1½-inch layer cake pans. Bake in a preheated 350° oven for 25 minutes or until surface springs back when gently touched. Invert cake pans by hanging pans between 2 other pans. Cool completely about 1 hour. Carefully loosen cake from pans and remove. Beat cream with confectioners' sugar until stiff. Refrigerate. Slice cake to make 4 layers. Place a layer, cut-side up on a plate. Spread with one-third cup preserves and ½ cup whipped cream. Repeat with remaining layers, ending with top layer down. Frost top and side of torte with whipped cream. Refrigerate 1 hour before cutting. Top with whole strawberries before serving. Makes 8 to 10 servings.

HEAVENLY TORTE

Forget about calories and enjoy!

½ c. margarine
½ c. butter
½ c. sugar
3 egg yolks
1 t. lemon juice
½ t. grated lemon peel
2 c. flour
1 t. baking powder
¼ t. salt
4 egg whites
¾ c. sugar
1 t. cinnamon
1 c. finely ground almonds
1 12-oz. jar raspberry jelly
1 12-oz. jar currant jelly

Cream butter, margarine, and sugar until fluffy. Add egg yolks, lemon juice and peel, flour, baking powder and salt. Pat into 3 springform pans, using thumbs to make dough into ridges around the edges of the pans. Beat 4 egg whites until frothy; gradually add ¾ cup sugar and cinnamon and beat until thick and glossy. Add almonds. Spread over 3 dough layers to the edge and bake in a preheated 400° oven until meringue is caramel color, about 25 minutes. Let cool. Mix jellies together; set aside 1 tablespoon. Spread jelly on 2 layers and stack. Place on top layer and put reserved jelly in the middle. Do not wrap cake—it will keep nicely uncovered for 1 week. Serves 12 to 14.

CAROB CARROT CAKE

Kids will never know they're eating carrots.

½ lb. butter or margarine, softened
2 c. sugar
3 eggs
2 t. vanilla
2½ c. flour
2 T. carob powder
1 t. baking powder
1 t. cinnamon
¼ t. salt
3 c. shredded carrot (about 1 lb.)
1 c. chopped nuts
½ c. semisweet chocolate chips

Cream butter and sugar; add eggs, one at a time. Add vanilla. Combine flour, carob, baking powder, salt, cinnamon and add to mixture. Remove beaters rand, stirring by hand, add carrot, nuts and chocolate chips.

Pour into a greased and floured 9 x 13 x 2-inch pan and bake in a preheated 350° oven for 40 to 45 minutes or until toothpick inserted in center comes out clean. May be frosted or sprinkled with confectioners' sugar. Serves 12 to 16.

CHOCOLATE GLAZE

1 1-oz. square unsweetened chocolate
2 T. butter or margarine
½ c. confectioners' sugar
½ t. vanilla
1 T. hot water

Melt chocolate and butter over low heat. Remove from heat and stir in sugar and vanilla. Stir in water, 1 teaspoon at a time, until glaze is of proper spreading consistency.

BUTTERCREAM FROSTING

½ c. butter or margarine
⅛ t. salt
1 t. vanilla or almond flavoring
1 lb. confectioners' sugar
5 to 6 T. evaporated milk or cream

Cream butter until light and fluffy. Add salt, flavoring and half of the sugar. Beat until smooth. Add a few tablespoons milk. Beat in remaining sugar, beating until smooth. Slowly add remaining milk, adding just enough to make frosting of spreading consistency.

VARIATIONS

Orange Buttercream: Add 2 teaspoons grated orange rind and ½ cup orange juice instead of the milk.

Mocha Buttercream: Add ½ teaspoon vanilla and ¼ cup strong coffee instead of milk.

Chocolate Buttercream: Add ¼ teaspoon vanilla and 2 1-oz. squares unsweetened chocolate, melted.

CHEESE-MINCE PIE

A taste surprise.

    1 9 or 10-inch baked pie shell
    1½ 8-oz. pkgs. cream cheese, softened
    2 eggs
    ½ c. sugar
    1 T. orange liqueur
    2 c. mincemeat
    ½ c. chopped nuts
    1 c. sour cream
    ½ t. vanilla
    2 T. sugar
    1 can mandarin oranges (optional)

Beat cream cheese, eggs, ½ cup sugar and liqueur until smooth. Combine mincemeat and nuts and spread on bottom of pie shell. Pour cheese mixture over mincemeat. Bake in a preheated 375° oven 20 minutes. While pie is baking, combine sour cream, vanilla and sugar. Spread evenly on hot pie and return to oven for another 10 minutes. Chill at least 6 hours. May be decorated with drained mandarin orange segments. Serves 8 to 10.

RUM CREAM PIE

A dream of a dessert!

    1 9-inch baked pie shell or graham
       cracker crust
    6 egg yolks
    ¾ c. sugar
    1 envelope unflavored gelatin
    ½ c. cold water
    ½ c. dark rum
    1 c. heavy cream, whipped
       Whipped cream (optional)
       Chocolate curls or chopped
       nuts (optional)

In a large mixing bowl, beat egg yolks until light. Add sugar gradually, beating until thick and lemon colored (about 5 minutes). In a small saucepan, soak gelatin in cold water and then stir over low heat until gelatin is dissolved and just comes to a boil. Remove from heat. Add hot mixture in a slow stream to egg yolks, beating constantly. Beat in rum. Chill until mixture mounds when dropped from a spoon. Fold whipped cream into mixture and pile into pie shell. Chill until firm. Garnish with additional whipped cream and shaved semisweet chocolate or chopped nuts. Serves 8 to 10.

50

CREME CARAMEL PIE

This delicious pie has a surprise of crunchy caramel down under the smooth custard.

    1 9-inch pie shell
    ¼ c. brown sugar
    ¼ c. butter

Heat brown sugar and butter in a saucepan until bubbly. Pour into pie shell, smoothing to cover bottom. Bake in a 425° oven for 10 minutes. Remove and pour on Custard. Reduce heat to 325° and bake an additional 30 minutes until a knife inserted in the middle comes out clean. Serves 8 to 10.

CUSTARD

    6 eggs, slightly beaten
    ½ c. sugar
    ¼ t. salt
    2 c. light cream
    1 t. vanilla

Combine all ingredients and blend well.

PUMPKIN CHEESE PIE

    1 8-oz. pkg. cream cheese, softened
    ¾ c. sugar
    1 t. cinnamon
    ½ t. cloves
    ½ t. ginger
    ½ t. nutmeg
    ½ t. salt
    3 eggs
    1 16-oz. can pumpkin
    1 t. vanilla
       Pecan halves (optional)
    1 9-inch pie crust, unbaked

Beat cream cheese until fluffy, gradually adding sugar combined with spices. Add eggs one at a time, beating well after each. Beat in pumpkin and vanilla. Pour into prepared shell. Bake in a preheated 350° oven for 40 minutes or until knife inserted in center comes out clean. During last 15 minutes of baking, pecan halves may be placed on top as decoration. Chill before serving. Serves 8 to 10.

Pictured opposite:
Pumpkin Cheese Pie

COFFEE-CLOUD PIE

Beautiful, rich and different.

- ½ lb. marshmallows
- 1 c. strong coffee
- 1 T. butter
- 1 T. brandy
- 1 c. heavy cream, whipped
- 1 9-inch baked pie shell

In top of double boiler, combine marshmallows, coffee and butter; heat until marshmallows dissolve. Add brandy. Remove from heat and cool until stiff. Fold in whipped cream and heap into pie shell. Refrigerate. Serves 8 to 10.

CHOCOLATE PECAN PIE

Chocolate lovers, rejoice!

- 1 9-inch unbaked pastry shell
- ½ c. sugar
- 1 c. dark corn syrup
- 3 eggs
- ¼ t. salt
- 1 T. flour
- 2 T. butter
- 2 1-oz. squares bitter chocolate
- 1 t. vanilla
- 1½ c. pecan halves
- ½ c. heavy cream, whipped (optional)

Beat together sugar, syrup, eggs, salt and flour. Melt butter and chocolate. Beat into egg mixture with vanilla. Put pecans into a pastry shell, pour egg mixture over. Bake in a 300° oven 50 to 60 minutes, until custard is set. Garnish with unsweetened whipped cream. Serves 8 to 10.

LEMON CHESS PIE

A dessert with a "twist."

- ¼ c. butter or margarine, softened
- 2 c. sugar
- 4 eggs
- ¼ c. lemon juice
- 1 T. grated lemon peel
- ¼ c. milk
- 1½ T. flour
- 1 9-inch unbaked pie shell
- 1 t. cornmeal
  Whipped cream (optional)

Beat together butter, sugar, eggs, lemon juice and peel, milk and flour. Pour into pie shell. Sprinkle with cornmeal. Bake in a preheated 375° oven 45 minutes or until set. Serve with whipped cream. Serves 8 to 10.

EGGNOG BAVARIAN

Shimmering, ivory elegance.

- 3 T. unflavored gelatin
- ½ c. cold water
- ¼ c. sugar
- ½ t. nutmeg
- ½ c. boiling water
- 1 c. warmed eggnog
- 1½ c. cold eggnog
- ½ c. rum
  Yellow food coloring
- 2 egg whites
- ⅛ t. cream of tartar
- 2 T. sugar
- ¾ c. chopped walnuts
- ¾ c. heavy cream, whipped
  Walnut halves

In a large bowl, soften gelatin in cold water. Let set for 5 minutes. Add ¼ cup sugar, nutmeg and boiling water. Stir until gelatin is dissolved. Add warmed eggnog, stirring well. Chill until slightly thickened and then beat until fluffy. Add cold eggnog, rum and a couple of drops of yellow food coloring, if desired. Continue beating until mixture mounds and is smooth. Beat egg whites with cream of tartar until foamy; add 2 tablespoons sugar and beat until stiff. Fold into eggnog mixture. Fold in nuts and whipped cream. Pour into a lightly oiled 2-quart mold and chill until set (4 to 6 hours). Unmold and garnish with walnut halves. Serves 8.

CRANBERRY BREAD PUDDING

Delightful for the cook!

- 1¾ c. milk
- ½ t. salt
- ½ t. vanilla
- 2 c. soft, stale bread cubes
- ¼ c. honey
- 2 eggs, beaten
- 1 c. cranberries
  Whipped cream or light cream

Combine all ingredients except whipped cream. Pour into a shallow greased 1½-quart baking dish. Bake in a preheated 350° oven 25 minutes, or until firm. Serve warm with cream or a dollop of whipped cream. Makes 6 servings.

STEAMED CARROT PUDDING

This delicious pudding is a nice change from the traditional plum pudding. Serve with a choice of sauces.

2 eggs
1 c. molasses
2 T. butter or margarine, softened
2 c. carrots, cooked and mashed
1 c. flour
1 t. baking soda
1 t. cloves
1 t. cinnamon
½ t. allspice
1 t. nutmeg
1 c. raisins
1 c. chopped walnuts

Beat eggs slightly. Add molasses, butter and carrots, mixing well. Stir in flour, soda and spices; then stir in raisins and nuts. Turn into a heavily greased 1½-quart mold. Place a rack in any deep container which can be covered. (To make a rack, pierce an aluminum pie plate with a fork.) Cover container with foil and steam for 1½ to 2 hours, until done. Pudding will have a firm, solid feeling. Serves 8.

SAUCES FOR CARROT PUDDING

HARD SAUCE

1 c. confectioners' sugar
¼ c. butter
1 T. rum, brandy, sherry *or* 1 t. vanilla
1 to 3 T. cream

Cream butter and sugar. Add rum or vanilla and cream. Blend until smooth. Serve cold.

HOT WINE SAUCE

¼ c. butter
1 c. sugar
2 eggs
¾ c. dry sherry

Cream butter and sugar. Beat in eggs; stir in the sherry. Just before serving, heat in double boiler, beating or whisking constantly until steaming hot.

LEMON SAUCE

½ c. sugar
1 T. cornstarch
1 c. water
3 T. butter
Grated rind of one lemon
2 T. lemon juice

Combine sugar, cornstarch and water. Cook over low heat until clear and thickened. Remove from heat and add butter, rind and juice.

WHITE FRUITCAKE, NOEL

Chill fruitcake before slicing. Makes thinner and prettier slices.

1 lb. butter
2 c. sugar
6 eggs
1 T. lemon flavoring
4 c. flour
½ t. salt
2 t. baking powder
1 lb. shelled pecans
1 lb. golden raisins
4 slices candied pineapple, cut up
1 lb. cut-up red and green candied cherries
Cover raisins with hot water; set aside.

Cream butter and sugar. Add eggs, one at a time, and lemon flavoring; beat well. Drain raisins. Flour nuts and fruits with ½ cup of the flour and stir into batter. Combine flour, baking powder and salt and add to egg mixture. Mix well. Line five 7½ x 3½-inch loaf pans with waxed paper; grease paper. Pour batter into pans and bake in a preheated 350° oven 1½ hours or until done. Place a pan of water in bottom of the oven to keep cakes from drying out. Wrap cakes in foil or plastic wrapping and store in a cool place.

MINIATURE FRUITCAKES
(LITTLE JEWELS)

3 c. flour
1⅓ c. sugar
1 t. salt
1 t. baking powder
2 t. cinnamon
1 t. nutmeg
½ c. orange juice
½ c. brandy
1 c. salad oil
4 eggs
¼ c. light corn syrup
1 c. golden raisins
2 c. dried apricots, cut into small pieces
1 c. dried dates, cut up
2 c. blanched almonds
⅓ c. light corn syrup for glaze
  Brandy

In a large mixing bowl, combine all ingredients except fruits, nuts, syrup and brandy. Blend with electric mixer 30 seconds at low speed, scraping bowl constantly, and 3 minutes at high speed, scraping bowl occasionally. Stir in fruit and nuts. Spoon batter into 36 paper-lined 2½-inch muffin cups. Bake in a preheated 275° oven 65 to 70 minutes. Remove to rack and cool thoroughly. Heat corn syrup in a small pan and brush over tops of cakes. Place cakes in a container and cover with a cheesecloth soaked in brandy. Cover tightly and store up to 2 weeks. May also be frozen. Makes 36 cakes.

Note: Two cups (1 lb.) mixed candied fruit may be substituted for apricots and dates.

PENUCHE GLAZE

Good on fruitcakes or coffee bread.

¼ c. butter or margarine
½ c. brown sugar, packed
2 T. milk
1 c. confectioners' sugar
¼ t. ground mace (optional)
1 to 2 T. milk

Melt butter in pan. Stir in brown sugar. Heat to boiling, stirring constantly. Boil and stir over medium heat for 2 minutes. Remove from heat. Stir in 2 tablespoons milk, sugar and mace. Beat until smooth. Add an additional 1 to 2 tablespoons milk, stirring until glaze is of spreading consistency.

MARZIPAN FROSTING FOR
FRUITCAKE

2 c. almond paste
2 egg whites
3 c. confectioners' sugar
  Few drops of rose water or lemon juice

Beat egg whites until fluffy. Gradually work in almond paste. Add sugar and blend until smooth. Add a few drops of rose water or lemon juice until frosting is of spreading consistency.

FRUITCAKE

Make several weeks ahead for a Christmas favorite.

1 c. golden raisins
1 c. dark raisins
1 c. *each* of candied citron, lemon peel and orange peel
½ c. *each* of candied pineapple and cherries, halved
1½ c. snipped figs
1 c. chopped dates
½ c. currants
1 c. almonds, pecan or walnut halves
4 c. flour
½ t. salt
2 t. baking powder
½ lb. butter or margarine
2 c. sugar
6 eggs
1 t. lemon extract
1 c. sherry

In a large bowl, combine all fruits and nuts. Combine flour, salt and baking powder and sprinkle over the fruit and nuts. Toss lightly until fruit and nuts are well coated. In a large bowl with electric mixer at medium speed, cream butter and sugar. Add eggs and lemon extract and beat until light and fluffy (about 4 minutes). Add to flour and fruit mixture along with sherry; stir until just mixed. Turn into a greased 10-inch tube pan or a 12-cup bundt cake pan and bake in a preheated 300° oven for 3 hours or until toothpick inserted in the center comes out clean. Cool in pan on cake rack for 1 hour. Loosen cake all around with a spatula and turn out of pan onto rack to cool completely. Wrap in foil and freeze. Thaw cake at room temperature, unwrapped. Serve frosted with a confectioners' sugar icing or just sprinkle with confectioners' sugar. Makes 16 servings.

*Pictured opposite:
Fruitcake*

SWISS MERINGUE DROPS WITH FUDGE FILLING

    2 egg whites
  ⅛ t. cream of tartar
  ⅛ t. salt
  ¼ c. sugar
  ¼ t. almond extract
    2 T. chopped pistachio nuts (optional)

Beat egg whites until foamy. Add cream of tartar and salt; beat until stiff peaks form. Add sugar, a tablespoonful at a time, and beat until smooth and satiny. Fold in almond extract. Cover ungreased cookie sheets with brown paper. Drop meringue by teaspoonfuls and shape into mounds the size of a small walnut. Make a depression in the center of each cookie with a spoon. Bake in a preheated 250° oven for about 30 to 45 minutes. Fill Meringues with a teaspoonful of cooled Fudge Filling. Sprinkle with nuts. Makes 5 dozen.

FUDGE FILLING

  ¼ c. butter
  ⅓ c. chocolate chips
    2 T. confectioners' sugar
    2 egg yolks

Melt butter and chocolate in a saucepan. Beat egg yolks slightly; stir in sugar; blend into chocolate. Cook at a very low heat 1 minute, stirring constantly. Remove from heat and stir until cool.

FILBERT DROPS

  ½ c. butter or margarine
    1 c. sugar
    1 egg yolk
    1 T. water
  ½ t. grated lemon peel
    1 t. grated orange peel
    1 c. flour
  ¼ t. salt
    1 egg white
  ⅔ c. finely ground filberts

Beat butter with sugar, egg yolk, water and peels until very light and fluffy. At low speed of mixer, beat in flour and salt just until mixed. Refrigerate until easy to handle. Form dough into 1-inch balls. Roll in unbeaten egg white and then in ground nuts. Place on a greased cookie sheet and bake in a 350° oven 15 minutes or until done. Store in a tightly covered container. Makes 2 dozen.

GLAZED PFEFFERNUESSE

  1¼ c. butter
  1¼ c. brown sugar, packed
  ¾ c. molasses
  ½ c. warm water
  ½ t. baking soda
     Dash pepper
  ½ t. cloves
  ½ t. allspice
  ¼ t. nutmeg
  ¼ t. mace
  1½ t. cinnamon
  ⅛ t. crushed cardamom
    6 c. sifted cake flour
  ½ t. salt
     Few drops anise oil or 1 t. anise extract
    2 c. chopped nuts
     Confectioners' sugar

Cream butter; add sugar and cream well. Blend in molasses and half the water. Dissolve soda in remaining water. Sift together dry ingredients. Add to creamed mixture with soda, water, anise and nuts. Mix well and chill. Shape dough into 1-inch balls. Place on greased cookie sheets and bake in a preheated 375° oven for 10 to 12 minutes. Dip top of hot cookie into glaze; coat with confectioners' sugar. Makes 12 dozen cookies.

GLAZE

    1 c. confectioners' sugar
    3 T. hot milk
  ¼ t. vanilla

Blend together confectioners' sugar, milk and vanilla.

RUSSIAN TEACAKES

    1 c. butter or margarine, softened
  ½ c. confectioners' sugar
    1 t. vanilla
  2¼ c. all-purpose flour
  ¼ t. salt
  ¾ c. finely chopped nuts
     Confectioners' sugar

Cream butter, sugar and vanilla. Work in flour, salt and nuts until dough holds together. Shape dough into 1-inch balls. Place on ungreased cookie sheets. Bake in a preheated 400° oven 10 to 12 minutes, until set but not brown. While warm, roll in confectioners' sugar. Cool; roll again in sugar. Makes 5 dozen.

EASY ROLLED SUGAR COOKIES

1 c. butter
1 c. sugar
2 egg yolks
1 t. vanilla
½ t. salt
3 c. sifted flour
1 t. baking powder
⅓ c. milk

Cream butter; add sugar gradually. Mix in egg yolks and vanilla. Blend in sifted dry ingredients and milk. Chill. Roll ⅛ inch thick on a well-floured surface. Cut with cookie cutters and place on greased cookie sheets. Decorate before baking with colored sugar or wait until baked and cooled, then frost. Bake in a preheated 350° oven 8 to 10 minutes. Makes 5 dozen.

SPRITZ

1 c. butter
½ c. plus 1 T. sugar
1 egg
¾ t. salt
1 t. vanilla
½ t. almond extract
2½ c. sifted flour

Cream butter and sugar. Blend egg, salt, extracts and flour. Knead dough in hands until soft and pliable. Force dough through a cookie press onto ungreased cookie sheets. Decorate and place in a 400° oven for 8 minutes. Makes 5 dozen.

MONDCHEN

1 c. butter
1 c. sugar
1¼ c. unblanched almonds, grated
1 c. sifted all-purpose flour
¼ t. salt
1 t. grated lemon rind
1½ c. confectioners' sugar
1 t. vanilla
2 T. hot water

Cream butter; add sugar gradually. Blend in almonds, flour, salt and lemon rind. Roll dough ¼ inch thick onto floured canvas or board. Cut with a crescent cutter and place on greased cookie sheets. Bake in a preheated 350° oven for 10 to 12 minutes. Blend confectioners' sugar, vanilla and water; spread on hot cookies. Makes 7 dozen.

CANDY CANES

1 c. shortening *or* ½ c. butter, softened
1 c. sifted confectioners' sugar
1 egg
1½ t. almond flavoring
2½ c. sifted flour
1 t. salt
½ t. red food coloring

Combine shortening, sugar, egg and flavoring, mixing well. Sift flour and salt together; stir into shortening mixture. Divide dough in half and blend red food coloring into one half. Take one teaspoon of each color dough. Roll each into a 4-inch long strip on a floured board. Place strips side by side, pressing together lightly. Twist into a rope. Place on ungreased cookie sheets and curve top of each piece to form a crook. Place in a preheated 375° oven for 9 minutes or until lightly browned. Remove while still warm. Makes 4 dozen.

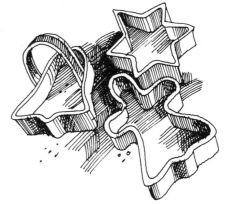

SWEDISH GINGER COOKIES

½ c. dark corn syrup
½ c. sugar
½ c. melted butter
6 T. light cream
½ t. ginger
½ t. cloves
½ t. cinnamon
½ t. baking soda
2 T. light cream
3 c. sifted all-purpose flour

Boil syrup 1 minute; cool slightly. Add sugar, butter, 6 tablespoons cream and spices. Dissolve soda in remaining cream and add to syrup mixture. Blend in flour. Refrigerate. Roll ⅛ inch thick on floured canvas and cut into desired shapes. Place on greased cookie sheets; decorate before baking. Bake in a 350° oven for 10 to 15 minutes, depending upon the size and thickness of cookies. Makes 4½ dozen.

ZUCCARINI
(ITALIAN SUGAR COOKIES)

½ c. butter
¼ c. sugar
3 eggs
3 c. sifted cake flour
½ t. salt
2 t. baking powder
½ t. almond extract
½ t. anise extract

Cream butter; gradually add sugar. Beat in eggs, one at a time. Sift together dry ingredients and blend in. Add flavorings and chill overnight. Roll rounded teaspoonfuls of dough on lightly floured board with palm of hand to the size of a 4½-inch pencil; tie loosely into a knot. Place on greased cookie sheets and bake in a 400° oven for 10 to 12 minutes. Cool and dip in glaze. Makes 8 dozen cookies.

GLAZE

1½ c. sugar
½ c. water
1 t. anise extract

Combine all ingredients, beating smooth.

CHOCOLATE MINT WAFERS

⅔ c. butter or margarine
1 c. sugar
1 egg
2 c. sifted flour
¾ c. cocoa
1 t. baking powder
½ t. salt
½ t. baking soda
¼ c. milk

Cream butter with sugar. Add egg and beat well. Sift dry ingredients; add alternately with milk. Mix thoroughly. Chill. Roll out ⅛ inch thick. Cut with floured 2½-inch cookie cutters. Place on a greased cookie sheet and bake in a 350° oven 8 minutes. Put 2 cookies together with Mint Filling. Makes about 2 dozen.

MINT FILLING

½ c. sifted confectioners' sugar
Dash salt
2 drops peppermint extract
3 to 4 t. light cream

Combine all ingredients. Beat until of spreading consistency.

Pictured Opposite:
Buttercream Bars
Speedy Chocolate Fudge, p. 63

HUNGARIAN POPPY SEED
NUT SLICES

Crispy and good.

1 c. butter or margarine, softened
1 c. sugar
1 egg
1 t. vanilla
½ t. cinnamon
1½ c. finely chopped nuts
½ c. poppy seeds
2 c. flour
¼ t. salt
2 T. sugar

Cream butter and sugar; add egg, vanilla, and cinnamon. Beat for 2 to 3 minutes. Add nuts and poppy seed and beat for another minute. Stir in flour and salt gradually. Shape dough into 2 rolls on waxed paper. Roll in sugar. Wrap and refrigerate for 2 to 3 hours. Cut into ¼-inch slices. Place cookies on ungreased cookie sheet and bake in a 325° oven about 20 minutes or just until cookies start to brown. Cool on racks. Makes 6 to 8 dozen cookies.

BUTTERCREAM BARS

Crunchy crust, satiny smooth chocolate, topped with toffee bars. Keep refrigerated until serving time.

½ c. butter or margarine
1 c. toasted bread crumbs
1 c. flour
¼ c. sugar
½ t. salt
2 toffee bars

Cream butter, blend in crumbs, flour, sugar and salt until smooth. Press into an 8 or 9-inch baking pan. Bake at 325° for 25 minutes. Cool and spread with Buttercream. Sprinkle with 2 toffee bars, chilled and crumbled. Chill until firm and cut into 1-inch squares.

BUTTERCREAM

2 1-oz. squares chocolate, melted
½ c. butter
¾ c. sugar
2 eggs
1 t. vanilla

Cream butter and sugar until smooth. Add chocolate and blend. Add eggs and vanilla. Beat 5 minutes until smooth.

MARZIPAN BARS

½ c. butter or margarine
½ c. brown sugar, packed
1 egg yolk
1 t. vanilla
2 c. flour
½ t. baking soda
¼ t. salt
¼ c. milk
1 c. raspberry jelly

Cream butter and brown sugar; beat in egg yolk and vanilla. Combine flour, soda and salt. Blend in alternately with milk. Spread in bottom of a greased 15 x 10 x 1-inch pan and cover with jelly. Pour Filling over jelly layer. Bake in a preheated 350° oven for 35 minutes. Cool on rack. Spread with Icing and cut into small bars.

FILLING

8 oz. almond paste, cut in small pieces
1 egg white
½ c. sugar
1 t. vanilla
3 T. butter or margarine, softened
3 eggs
   Drop green food coloring

Combine almond paste with egg white, sugar, vanilla and butter. Beat until smooth. Add eggs, one at a time, beating after each addition. Add food coloring to desired tint.

ICING

2 1-oz. squares unsweetened chocolate, melted
1 T. butter, softened
1 t. vanilla
2 c. confectioners' sugar
¼ c. hot milk

Combine all ingredients; beat until smooth.

MOUND BARS

2 c. graham cracker crumbs
¼ c. confectioners' sugar
½ c. melted butter or margarine
1 15-oz. can sweetened condensed milk
2⅓ c. flaked coconut
1 4-oz. bar semisweet or German sweet chocolate
2 T. butter

Mix together crumbs, sugar and butter. Firmly press into bottom of ungreased 13 x 9 x 2-inch pan. Bake in a preheated 350° oven for 10 minutes. Combine milk and coconut and spread over baked layer. Return to oven and bake an additional 15 minutes. Cool. Melt chocolate with butter over low heat. Spread evenly over coconut filling. Cool; cut into 2 x 1-inch bars. Refrigerate or freeze until served. Makes 4½ dozen bars.

DUTCH CHOCOLATE BARS

1 c. sifted flour
1½ c. sugar
½ t. salt
½ t. baking powder
½ c. butter, softened
1 egg, slightly beaten
2 1-oz. squares unsweetened chocolate, melted
1 t. vanilla
1 c. rolled oats

Sift together flour, sugar, salt and baking powder into mixing bowl. Add butter, egg, cooled chocolate and vanilla. Mix until smooth. Stir in oats. Spread into greased 13 x 9 x 2-inch pan. Bake in a preheated 350° oven for 25 minutes. Frost with Peppermint Frosting. Cut into small bars. Makes about 32 bars.

PEPPERMINT FROSTING

¼ c. butter, softened
2 c. confectioners' sugar
1 t. peppermint extract
   Few drops green food coloring
3 T. light cream (about)

Blend butter, sugar, extract and food coloring. Add enough cream to make frosting of spreading consistency, beating well.

CHOCO-NUT BARS

½ c. peanut butter
6 T. butter or margarine, softened
1 c. sugar
2 eggs
1 t. vanilla
1 c. whole wheat flour
1 t. baking powder
½ c. salted peanuts
½ c. chocolate chips

Cream together the peanut butter, butter and sugar. Beat in eggs and vanilla. Combine flour and baking powder and stir in. Add nuts and chocolate chips. Pour into an 11 x 7½ x 1½-inch pan and bake in a preheated 350° oven 25 to 30 minutes. Cool and cut into bars. Makes 24 bars.

APRICOT BARS

2¼ c. flour
½ lb. butter or margarine
½ c. sugar
2 t. lemon juice
3 egg yolks
1 12 to 16-oz. jar apricot preserves
3 egg whites
½ c. sugar
1 c. chopped nuts

Cut butter into flour as for a pie crust. Add sugar, lemon juice and egg yolks, blending well. Press firmly into an ungreased 13 x 9 x 2-inch pan. Spread preserves over. Beat egg whites until frothy. Add sugar a little at a time, beating until stiff, but not dry. Fold in nuts. Spread on top of preserves and bake in a 350° oven 40 minutes. Cool 10 minutes and cut into bars.

TOFFEE BARS

1 c. butter, softened
1 c. brown sugar
1 egg yolk
1 t. vanilla
2 c. flour
¼ t. salt
4 ⅞-oz. milk chocolate bars
½ c. chopped nuts

Grease a 13 x 9 x 2-inch baking pan. Cream butter, sugar, egg yolk and vanilla. Blend in flour and salt. Press evenly in bottom of pan. Bake in a 350° oven for 25 to 30 minutes or until very light brown. Remove from oven. Immediately place separated squares of chocolate candy on crust. As soon as chocolate is soft, spread evenly. Sprinkle on nuts. While warm, cut into 2-inch squares. Makes about 32 bars.

DATE-NUT BALLS

1 T. margarine
¼ c. light corn syrup
½ t. vanilla
3 T. instant nonfat dry milk
¼ t. salt
2 c. confectioners' sugar
1 c. chopped dates
1 t. grated orange or lemon rind
1 c. chopped nuts

Blend together all ingredients except the nuts. Knead until thoroughly mixed. Form into small balls and dip each ball into chopped nuts. Makes 3 to 4 dozen.

APPLE JACKS

Beginning bakers can make these with Mom.

1 c. brown sugar
½ c. butter or margarine
1 egg
1½ c. flour
½ t. baking soda
½ t. salt
½ t. nutmeg
½ t. cinnamon
¼ t. ground cloves
¼ t. ginger
1 c. chopped peeled apple
Sugar

Cream butter and sugar; beat in egg. Add dry ingredients and beat until well blended. Stir in apple. Drop by teaspoonfuls onto greased cookie sheet. Bake in a 375° oven 12 to 15 minutes. Remove from oven and sprinkle with sugar. Makes about 4½ dozen.

PUMPKIN COOKIES

Cookies for the kids.

1 c. shortening
½ c. sugar
1 c. pumpkin
½ c. chopped nuts
⅓ c. raisins
1 t. baking soda
1 t. baking powder
¼ t. nutmeg
1 t. cinnamon
¼ t. salt
2¼ c. flour
1 t. vanilla

Cream shortening and sugar. Add pumpkin, raisins and nuts. Mix together dry ingredients and stir in. Add vanilla. Drop by teaspoonfuls on a well-greased cookie sheet. Flatten slightly with the bottom of a glass dipped in sugar. Bake in a preheated 350° oven 10 minutes. When done, may be frosted with Icing. Makes about 5 dozen.

Icing

1 c. brown sugar
3 T. evaporated milk
1 t. butter
Confectioners' sugar

In a saucepan, add just enough milk to moisten brown sugar. Bring to a boil and cook for 3 minutes. Cool and add butter. Mix in enough confectioners' sugar until of spreading consistency.

BROWNIES

Old favorites; always good.

- 2 1-oz. squares unsweetened chocolate
- ⅓ c. butter or margarine
- 1 c. sugar
- 2 eggs
- ½ t. vanilla
- ½ c. flour
- ½ c. chopped nuts (optional)

Melt chocolate and butter in a saucepan over low heat. Remove and let cool. Beat in sugar, eggs and vanilla. Stir in flour and nuts. Spread in a greased 8 x 8 x 2-inch pan and bake in a preheated 350° oven for 25 minutes. Cool slightly and cut into squares or bars.

PEANUT BUTTER BROWNIES

- ⅓ c. melted butter or margarine
- 1⅓ c. brown sugar, firmly packed
- ½ c. peanut butter, smooth or chunky
- 3 eggs
- 1 t. vanilla
- 1 c. flour
- ¾ t. baking powder
- ¼ t. baking soda
- ½ t. salt
- ½ c. chopped peanuts

Melt butter in saucepan. Beat in brown sugar, peanut butter, vanilla and eggs until well blended. Add flour, baking powder, soda, salt and peanuts and blend well. Pour into an oiled 9 x 12-inch pan. Bake in a preheated 350° oven for 20 to 30 minutes until toothpick inserted in center comes out clean. If desired, frost with Broiled Frosting.

BROILED FROSTING

- 4 T. butter or margarine
- 1 3-oz. pkg. cream cheese
- 1½ c. brown sugar, firmly packed
- ½ c. chopped salted peanuts

Melt butter and cream cheese over low heat. Remove from heat and stir in brown sugar and peanuts. Spread over hot brownies when they come from the oven. Broil 3 inches from heat for a few seconds until frosting is bubbly. Watch carefully so as not to scorch. Cool and cut into bars. Makes 2 to 2½ dozen bars.

CHOCOLATE CREAMS

- 1 6-oz. pkg. semisweet chocolate chips
- ¼ c. milk
- 1 t. rum extract
- 1 t. vanilla
- 2 t. hot coffee
- ⅛ t. salt
- 4 c. confectioners' sugar
- ½ c. chocolate jimmies

In a saucepan, combine chocolate and milk. Blend and heat slowly, stirring constantly. Add rum extract, vanilla and coffee. Remove from heat and beat in sugar. When cool enough to handle, make into 1-inch balls; add more coffee if necessary. Roll in chocolate jimmies. Store in the refrigerator. Makes about 48.

SPEEDY CHOCOLATE FUDGE

- 1½ 12-oz. pkgs. semisweet chocolate chips
- 1 15-oz. can sweetened condensed milk
- ⅛ t. salt
- 1 t. vanilla
- ½ c. chopped nuts (optional)

Melt chocolate over low heat, stirring. Remove from heat and stir in sweetened condensed milk, salt, vanilla and nuts. Pour into a waxed paper lined 8-inch square pan; spread evenly, smoothing surface. Refrigerate until firm, about 2 hours. Turn candy out on board and peel off paper. With a sharp knife, cut fudge into desired size pieces and store in an airtight container.

MINT PATTIES

Tint these a pale pink for peppermint, pale green for wintergreen.

- 3 c. confectioners' sugar
- 1 c. boiling water
- 10 drops oil of peppermint or oil of wintergreen
  Food coloring

Boil sugar and water to a soft-ball stage (234° on a candy thermometer). Add flavoring. Remove from heat and beat until mixture begins to thicken. Beat in coloring. Drop from spoon onto waxed paper to form small thin patties. Keep mixture over hot water while dropping patties. Cool. Makes about 48 patties.

Index ... *all gifts to enjoy year round ... from our kitchen to yours!*

Christmas Kitchen
COOKBOOK

CONTENTS

Book I Christmas Cookbook

Book II Gourmet Christmas Cookbook

Book III Christmas Kitchen Cookbook

Nut Roll, page 4

CANDIES

NUT ROLL

1 7½-oz. jar marshmallow creme
1 t. vanilla
3½ c. confectioners' sugar
1 lb. caramels
9½ c. chopped nuts

Combine marshmallow creme and vanilla; add sugar gradually. Shape into rolls about 1 inch in diameter. Wrap in plastic wrap and freeze for at least 6 hours. Melt caramels over hot water; keep warm. Dip candy rolls in caramels, then roll in nuts until well coated. Store cooled candy in a covered container. Makes about 5 pounds.

CHOCOLATE FUDGE

4½ c. sugar
    Dash salt
1 14½-oz. can (1⅔ c.) evaporated milk (undiluted)
2 T. butter
1 12-oz. package semisweet chocolate chips
3 packages (¼ lb. each) sweet cooking chocolate
1 1-pint jar marshmallow creme
2 T. vanilla
2 c. nutmeats (optional)

In a large heavy saucepan stir together sugar, salt, evaporated milk and butter. Stirring constantly, bring to a boil. Boil 7 minutes, stirring occasionally. Pour boiling hot syrup over both kinds of chocolate and marshmallow creme. Stir vigorously until chocolate melts. Add vanilla. Stir in nutmeats. Turn into buttered pan (9 x 9 x 1¾). Let stand in cool place to set. Refrigerate if necessary to keep firm, or store in tightly covered metal box.

Mrs. Charles W. Bailey

'SWONDERFUL CANDY

2 1-lb. boxes confectioners' sugar
12 oz. cream cheese, softened
½ c. finely chopped candied cherries
½ c. finely chopped nuts
    Almond or vanilla extract

Sift sugar. Mash cream cheese. Combine all ingredients, using 1 small bottle of extract or as much as desired. Knead as bread. Pack mixture into a square tin and chill in freezer before cutting.

Alba M. Wahl

APRICOT ACORNS

1 8-oz. can almond paste, crumbled
½ c. wheat germ
1 c. honey
½ c. sesame seeds
2 c. instant nonfat dry milk
36 dried apricots (about 8 oz.)
36 whole cloves

In a bowl, mix almond paste, wheat germ, honey, sesame seeds and milk powder until the mixture is smooth and thoroughly combined. Shape into 36 balls. Place apricot half on one side of each ball. Fasten apricot in place with a whole clove. Pinch the other side of the ball into a point to resemble an acorn. Place acorns side by side in a single layer on waxed paper or foil and let dry at room temperature. Store in an airtight container in a cool dry place until ready to serve.

PEANUT BUTTER KISSES

⅓ c. corn syrup
⅓ c. peanut butter
½ c. nonfat dry milk
⅓ c. confectioners' sugar
    Chopped nuts (optional)

In a small mixing bowl, combine corn syrup with peanut butter. When well mixed, gradually add nonfat dry milk and sifted confectioners' sugar. Shape into a roll about ¾ inch in diameter; roll in chopped nuts if desired. Wrap in waxed paper and chill. Cut into 24 one-inch pieces.

Rev. Amos L. Seldomridge

SNOW-WHITE FUDGE

3 c. sugar
1½ c. milk
¾ t. salt
3 T. butter or margarine
2 t. vanilla
½ c. chopped dried California apricots
½ c. marshmallow creme
⅓ c. chopped walnuts

Butter sides of 3-quart saucepan. Mix sugar, milk and salt in saucepan. Stir and heat until sugar dissolves and mixture boils. Cook, without stirring, to soft ball stage (238°). Stir in butter and vanilla. Place in pan of cold water and cool to lukewarm without stirring. Add apricots and beat until mixture holds shape. Stir in marshmallow creme and walnuts; beat until glossy. Spread fudge in buttered 9-inch square pan. When fudge sets, cut into 32 bars.

ORANGE CARAMEL FUDGE

3 c. sugar
½ c. hot water
1 c. evaporated milk
¼ t. salt
4 T. butter or margarine
2 t. grated orange rind
1 c. chopped nuts

Put 1 cup sugar in heavy saucepan. Cook and stir over medium heat until sugar is melted and golden colored. Add water and stir until sugar is dissolved. Stir in remaining sugar, milk and salt. Cook over low heat, stirring occasionally, until mixture reaches 242° on a candy thermometer. Remove from heat. Add butter, orange rind and nuts. Beat until thick and creamy. Turn into greased aluminum foil pan. Cool; mark into squares. Makes 1½ pounds.

Orange Caramel Fudge, this page

APRICOT SNOWBALLS

See color photo, page 35

2 c. uncrushed cornflakes (or bran or wheat flakes)
⅓ c. diced pitted dates
⅔ c. diced dried California apricots
½ c. chopped pecans
¼ c. honey
3 T. butter or margarine
1 t. vanilla
Granulated sugar (optional)
Strips of dried California apricots, red glacé cherry halves

Using a rolling pin, crush cornflakes between 2 sheets of waxed paper. Stir crushed cornflakes, dates, apricots and pecans until well mixed in large bowl. Melt honey and butter in small pan; blend in vanilla. Pour over cornflake mixture; mix thoroughly. Chill 30 minutes. Use 1 tablespoon of mixture to form each ball. Roll balls in sugar, if desired. Garnish each with a strip of apricot or a cherry half. Serve immediately or cover and chill until needed.

MELT-IN-THE MOUTH CARAMELS

1 c. butter or margarine
1 lb. brown sugar
Dash of salt
1 c. light corn syrup
1 14-oz. can sweetened condensed milk
1 t. vanilla

Melt butter in a heavy 3-quart saucepan. Add brown sugar and salt. Stir until thoroughly combined. Stir in corn syrup; mix well. Gradually add milk, stirring constantly. Cook and stir over medium heat until candy reaches firm ball stage (245° on candy thermometer), about 12 to 15 minutes. Remove from heat. Stir in vanilla. Pour in buttered 9 x 9 x 2-inch pan. Cool and cut into squares. Makes about 2½ pounds.

Mrs. Curtiss Mueller

MARZIPAN

8 oz. almond paste
¼ c. corn syrup
¾ c. marshmallow creme
1 lb. confectioners' sugar

Combine ingredients; blend with hands. Form into fruit shapes. Paint with food coloring dissolved in water.

PUDDING CANDY

1 3-oz. package pudding mix, any flavor (not instant)
1 c. sugar
½ c. evaporated milk
1 T. butter or margarine
1 T. salted peanuts
¼ t. vanilla
1 c. nuts or raisins or coconut

Combine pudding and sugar in saucepan; add milk and butter. Cook and stir over medium heat until mixture boils. Lower heat and boil for 3 minutes, stirring constantly. Remove from heat; add vanilla and nuts. Beat until mixture becomes dull. Drop from spoon onto waxed paper. Makes 2 dozen. *Note*: Try chocolate pudding with nuts or raisins; vanilla or lemon with coconut or almonds, butterscotch with pecans.

PRALINES

1½ t. baking soda
4 c. sugar
2 c. light cream or half-and-half
3 T. butter
4 c. shelled pecans

Combine sugar and soda in large saucepan. Add cream; stir until sugar is dissolved. Bring to a boil over medium heat, stirring; reduce heat. Cook until candy reaches soft ball stage (234°). Remove from heat; add butter. Stir in pecans; beat until thick enough to drop from spoon. Drop onto waxed paper. If candy thickens, add a tablespoonful of hot water. Cool candy until firm.

Photo opposite
Caramel Turtles, page 8

COCONUT BALLS

¾ c. mashed potatoes
4 c. coconut
1 1-lb. package confectioners' sugar
1 t. almond extract
2 T. butter
2 T. corn syrup
3 T. water
1 package chocolate frosting mix

Combine first 4 ingredients. Roll into balls, using 1 heaping teaspoonful for each. Refrigerate for at least 1 hour. Combine remaining ingredients in top of double boiler. Heat, stirring, for 5 minutes. Keeping chocolate mixture over hot water, dip coconut balls until thoroughly coated. Remove from chocolate and place on waxed paper. Refrigerate until hardened. Makes 5 dozen.

SKILLET CANDIES

1 c. melted butter
1½ c. light brown sugar
2 c. cut-up dates
2 T. milk
2 eggs, beaten
½ t. salt
1 c. chopped nuts
1 t. vanilla
4 c. crisp rice cereal
Coconut

Melt butter; add sugar and dates. Cook over low heat. Add milk and slowly stir in beaten eggs. Bring to a boil and boil for 3 minutes. Remove from heat. When cool, add nuts, vanilla and cereal. Stir to mix well. Use a teaspoon to form candy into balls. Roll in coconut. Makes about 6 dozen.

PEANUT BRITTLE

2 c. sugar
1 c. white corn syrup
½ c. water
¼ t. salt
1 t. butter
2 c. raw Spanish peanuts
2 t. baking soda

Using a large kettle, boil first 4 ingredients together until mixture reaches thread stage (238°). Then add butter and peanuts. Stir, cook until golden brown (300°). Remove from heat and add baking soda. Mixture will bubble up. Mix well and pour onto a well-greased enamel tabletop to cool. As it cools, pull as thin as possible. When cool, break into pieces and store in an airtight container.

Mabel White Epling

CARAMEL TURTLES

See color photo, page 7

1 c. pecan halves
36 light caramels
½ c. sweet chocolate, melted

Grease cookie sheet. Arrange pecans (flat side down) in clusters of 4. Place 1 caramel on each cluster of pecans. Heat in 325° oven until caramels soften (4-8 minutes). Remove from the oven; flatten caramel with buttered spatula. Cool slightly and remove from pan to waxed paper. Swirl melted chocolate on top.

Terry Gibson

FRANCES' PECAN BALLS

1 7½-oz. jar marshmallow creme
3½ c. confectioners' sugar
1 t. vanilla
¼ t. almond extract
1 lb. caramels
10 c. chopped pecans

Combine marshmallow creme, sugar and flavorings. Knead until ingredients are blended and mixture is soft. Form into balls about the size of pecans or smaller. Cover with plastic wrap and chill thoroughly. Melt caramels in top of double boiler. Dip balls into melted caramels and then roll them in chopped nuts. Store covered with plastic wrap. Can be kept several weeks. Yield: 5 pounds or about 116 balls.

Mrs. Dwight K. Beam

OATMEAL SQUARES

1 c. flaked coconut
½ c. cocoa
3 c. rolled oats
½ c. chopped pecans
½ t. salt
2 c. sugar
½ c. milk
½ c. butter
1 t. vanilla

Combine coconut, oatmeal, pecans and salt in large mixing bowl. Place sugar, milk, butter and vanilla in a saucepan; heat to boiling point. Boil for 2 minutes. Pour over oatmeal mixture; blend well. Spread in foil-lined 11 x 7 x 1½-inch pan. Refrigerate. Cut into small squares. Makes about 5 dozen.

BOURBON BALLS

1 c. vanilla wafer crumbs
1 c. finely chopped pecans
1 c. confectioners' sugar
2 T. cocoa
¼ c. bourbon
1½ T. light corn syrup
Confectioners' sugar for rolling

Mix crumbs, pecans, sugar and cocoa. Blend bourbon and syrup. Combine mixtures. Shape into balls; roll in sugar. Refrigerate.

ENGLISH TOFFEE

1 c. sugar
1 c. butter
3 T. water
1 t. vanilla
1 c. semisweet chocolate bits
1 c. chopped nuts

Combine first 4 ingredients in a medium saucepan. Cook over low to medium heat, stirring constantly, to hard crack stage (300°-310°). Remove from heat and pour onto a greased cookie sheet. While hot cover with chocolate chips. Spread. Sprinkle with chopped nuts.

TAN FUDGE

2 c. sugar
1 c. milk
1 7-oz. jar marshmallow creme
1 12-oz. jar crunchy peanut butter
1 t. vanilla

Combine sugar and milk in a large, heavy saucepan. Slowly bring to a boil. Cook, stirring, to soft ball stage (238°). Remove from heat and add remaining ingredients. Beat until blended. Pour into a buttered 9-inch pan; cool. When fudge has set, cut into squares.

Mary Ida Hoffman

CANDY STICKS

2 c. sugar
½ c. water
½ c. light corn syrup
2 T. lemon juice
1½ T. lemon rind
1 t. flavoring
Food coloring

Combine sugar, water, corn syrup, lemon juice and lemon rind in a medium saucepan. Bring to a boil and continue boiling, without stirring, until mixture reaches crack stage (290°). Remove from heat and add flavoring and food coloring. Pour onto a buttered platter. When candy is cool enough to handle, pull and twist into canes or sticks. *Note:* Try peppermint extract with red food coloring, lemon with yellow and cinnamon with red or brown. (To color candy brown, combine red and yellow food coloring with a drop of blue.)

LOLLIPOPS

Follow directions for Candy Sticks. Immediately after removing candy from heat, pour into buttered molds. Insert stick; let harden.

LEMON FRUIT-JELL CANDY

See color photo, page 55

 1 6-oz. bottle liquid fruit pectin
 2 T. water
 ½ t. baking soda
 1 c. sugar
 1 c. light corn syrup
 2 t. lemon extract
10 drops yellow food coloring
   Granulated sugar

Combine fruit pectin and water in 2-quart saucepan. Stir in baking soda. (Mixture will foam slightly.) Mix sugar and corn syrup in a large saucepan. Place both saucepans over high heat and cook both mixtures, stirring alternately, until foam has thinned from fruit pectin mixture and sugar mixture is boiling rapidly, 3 to 5 minutes. Pour fruit pectin mixture in a slow steady stream into boiling sugar mixture, stirring constantly. Boil and stir 1 minute longer. Remove from heat. Stir in lemon extract and yellow food coloring. Pour immediately into a buttered 9-inch square pan. Let stand at room temperature until mixture is cool and firm— about 3 hours. Invert pan onto waxed paper which has been sprinkled with granulated sugar. Cut candy into ¾-inch squares or shapes and roll in sugar. Allow candy to stand awhile; roll again in sugar to prevent stickiness. Let stand overnight, uncovered, at room temperature before packing or storing. Makes about 1 pound. *Note:* Candies may also be rolled in confectioners' sugar, colored sprinkles or crystal sugar, or dipped in melted semisweet chocolate.

MOLASSES TAFFY

 ½ c. butter or margarine
 1 c. molasses
 2 c. granulated sugar
 ¼ c. light corn syrup
 1½ c. water

Combine all ingredients in large saucepan; cook and stir over medium heat until sugar dissolves. Continue cooking until mixture thickens; then lower heat and cook to hard ball stage (260°). Pour onto a greased baking sheet and cool slightly. Butter hands and pull candy until hard and light. Stretch into a rope; cut into pieces. Makes 1½ pounds.

CHERRY NUT FUDGE

See color photo opposite

 2 c. granulated sugar
 1 c. heavy cream
   Dash salt
 ⅛ t. salt
 ½ t. vanilla
 ½ c. chopped nuts
 ½ c. chopped maraschino cherries

Bring sugar, cream and dash of salt to a boil over moderate heat, stirring constantly. When boiling point is reached, add ⅛ teaspoon salt. Cook until mixture reaches softball stage. Remove from heat and let stand until almost cold. Beat until mixture is thick and creamy. Cover with a damp cloth and let stand for ½ hour. Add vanilla, nuts and cherries and work in with hands. Press into a shallow, waxed-paper-lined pan. Makes about 1 pound.

CRANBERRY JELLY CANDY

See color photo, page 55

 1 16-oz. can jellied cranberry sauce
 3 3-oz. packages cherry, raspberry or orange flavor gelatin
 1 c. sugar
 ½ bottle liquid fruit pectin (3 fl. oz.)
 1 c. chopped nuts or cookie coconut (optional)
   Additional sugar or flaked or cookie coconut

Beat cranberry sauce in a saucepan until smooth. Bring to a boil. Stir in gelatin and sugar; simmer 10 minutes, stirring frequently until gelatin is dissolved. Remove from heat. Stir in fruit pectin; then add nuts and stir 10 minutes to prevent nuts from floating. Pour into buttered 9-inch square pan. Chill until firm, about 2 hours. Invert onto waxed paper, which has been sprinkled with additional sugar. Cut candy into ¾-inch squares with spatula dipped in warm water; roll in sugar. After about an hour, roll in sugar again to prevent stickiness. Makes about 2 pounds candy.

SEAFOAM

2½ c. white sugar
½ c. dark corn syrup
½ c. water
2 egg whites
½ c. chopped nuts

Boil sugar, syrup and water until mixture reaches hard crack stage. Beat the egg whites until very stiff. Pour hot syrup slowly over egg whites with the mixer running at high speed. Then beat until stiff enough to drop. Add nuts and drop onto wax paper. Work quickly as mixture thickens rapidly.

Betty Bonkoski

HOLIDAY MINTS

3 egg whites
6 c. confectioners' sugar
Red and green food coloring
½ t. peppermint extract
½ t. spearmint extract

Beat egg whites until stiff, adding sugar gradually. Divide candy into 2 portions. Tint half green and half red. Add peppermint extract to red mixture and spearmint extract to green mixture. Roll candy between 2 pieces of waxed paper. Cut with small round cookie cutter. Let dry overnight.

CHOCOLATE-COVERED CHERRIES

1 8-oz. jar maraschino cherries with stems
½ recipe Chocolate Fudge (p. 3)

Drain cherries thoroughly. Prepare fudge according to directions, adding enough water to make dipping consistency. Put fudge in double boiler over hot water. Dip each cherry, leaving stem exposed. Place dipped cherries on waxed paper and cool until fudge sets. Store in a covered container in a cool place.

CANDIED ORANGE PEEL

7 large oranges
1½ c. water
2 c. sugar
3 T. honey
¼ t. salt
1 t. unflavored gelatin
Sugar

Cut oranges into fourths. Remove pulp and scrape away white membrane. Cut peel into strips. Place peel in saucepan, cover with water and simmer 15 minutes. Drain. Pour 1½ cups water over peel. Add 2 cups sugar, honey and salt. Cook over low heat for 45 minutes, stirring occasionally. Soften gelatin in ¼ cup water. Remove orange mixture from heat; add softened gelatin. Stir to dissolve. When cool, drain candy; roll in sugar. Let dry overnight on waxed paper. Store in a covered container. Makes about ¾ pound.

CARAMEL CORN

4 c. popped corn
½ c. almonds
½ c. pecans
½ c. butter or margarine
¼ c. light corn syrup
⅔ c. sugar

Combine popped corn and nuts; spread on an ungreased baking sheet. Melt margarine; stir in corn syrup and sugar. Bring to a boil over medium heat, stirring constantly. Continue boiling for 10 to 15 minutes, stirring occasionally. When mixture turns a light caramel color, remove from heat and stir in vanilla. Pour over corn and nuts and mix until all pieces are coated. Spread out to dry. Break into pieces and store in a covered container. Makes 1 pound.

GLAZED NUTS

2 T. cold water
1 egg white, slightly beaten
½ c. sugar
½ t. salt
¼ t. cinnamon
¼ t. cloves
¼ t. allspice
2 c. whole pecans

Add water to egg white. Stir in sugar, salt and spices. Mix well. Add nuts and stir until coated. Place nuts, flat side down, on a greased cookie sheet. Bake at 250° for 1 hour. Remove from pan immediately.

TOASTED ALMOND BALLS

1 c. semisweet chocolate bits
1 c. butterscotch bits
¾ c. confectioners' sugar
½ c. cultured sour cream
1½ t. grated orange rind
¼ t. salt
2 c. vanilla wafer crumbs
¾ c. finely chopped toasted almonds

Melt chocolate and butterscotch bits at a low heat. Mix in sugar, sour cream, orange rind, salt and crumbs; chill. Shape into ¾-inch balls; roll in almonds. Makes about 6½ dozen.

QUICK FONDANT WAFERS

1 6-oz. bottle liquid fruit pectin
3 lbs. confectioners' sugar
½ t. peppermint, rum, almond or orange extract (optional)
6 drops food coloring (optional)

Pour fruit pectin into a bowl. Gradually add 2 pounds confectioners' sugar, mixing well after each addition. (Mixture will be very stiff.) Divide into four parts; wrap in waxed paper or cover with a wet cloth. The remaining 1 pound confectioners' sugar will be used to dust board and rolling pin. Place ¼ of the fondant at a time on a pastry board, well dusted with sugar. Add flavoring and food coloring, if desired. Knead until smooth, adding sugar to board as needed and lifting with a spatula to prevent sticking. (Any unrolled portion may be wrapped in waxed paper or plastic wrap and stored at room temperature overnight.) Roll out with sugar-dusted rolling pin, about ¼ inch thick, turning often and dusting with sugar to prevent sticking. Cut out with cookie cutters dipped in confectioners' sugar. If desired, make a small hole at top of each wafer with a wooden pick. Place, top side down, onto waxed paper on baking sheets or trays. Press trimmings together; knead again until smooth, roll and cut, or shape into small balls. Allow to dry, uncovered, for 24 hours, turning once. Pack wafers in layers between waxed paper in a loosely covered box. Makes about 2¾ pounds. *Note:* To tint and flavor all the fondant the same, add 2 teaspoons extract and about 24 drops food coloring after cooling.

COCONUT CHRISTMAS COOKIE TREE

1½ c. butter or margarine
1 c. sugar
2 eggs
4½ c. sifted all-purpose flour
1 t. vanilla
1 t. almond extract
4 T. hot milk
1 lb. unsifted confectioners' sugar
Flaked coconut

Cut star-shaped patterns from heavy paper 9, 8, 7¼, 6½, 5½, 4¾, 4, and 3 inches in diameter, measuring from point to point. Cut two round patterns 2½ and 1½ inches in diameter.

Cream butter until soft. Gradually add sugar, beating until light and fluffy. Add eggs and beat well. Add flour, a small amount at a time, mixing thoroughly after each addition. Blend in vanilla, almond extract and 2 cups of the coconut (cut). Divide dough into 2 equal portions, wrap in waxed paper and chill at least 30 minutes or until firm enough to roll.

Roll dough ⅛-inch thick on a lightly floured board. Cut 2 cookies from each star pattern, making a total of 16 cookies. Cut 12 cookies from the 1½-inch round pattern and 20 cookies from the 2½-inch round pattern. With a large drinking straw, cut a hole in the center of each cookie. Place on ungreased baking sheets. Bake at 350° for about 8 minutes, or until edges are lightly browned. Cool.

Gradually add hot milk to the confectioners' sugar, using just enough milk for a spreading consistency. Tint green with food coloring if desired. Spread on each star-shaped cookie. Sprinkle flaked coconut near edges.

To Make Tree

Place a 12- to 15-inch stick or thin candle in a candle holder. Secure with short stub of a candle or with paper. Slip 2 of the larger round cookies over stick. Top with largest star cookie and decrease to smallest size, placing 2 round cookies between each star-shaped cookie. Top with a rosette of frosting or a small candle. Decorate with silver dragées or small candles if desired. Makes 1 cookie tree.

COOKIES

STRIPED COOKIES

2½ c. sifted cake flour
1 t. double-acting baking powder
½ t. salt
½ c. butter or margarine
⅔ c. sugar
1 egg
1 T. milk
1 square unsweetened chocolate, melted
Milk

Sift flour with baking powder and salt. Cream butter. Gradually add sugar. Beat until light and fluffy. Add egg and milk. Blend well. Add flour mixture, a small amount at a time, beating well after each addition. Divide dough in half. Blend chocolate into one half. If necessary chill or freeze both parts of dough until firm enough to roll.

Roll each portion of dough on a lightly floured board into a 9 x 4½-inch rectangle. Brush chocolate dough lightly with milk and top with plain dough. Using a long, sharp knife, cut rectangle lengthwise in 3 equal strips 1½ inches wide.

Stack strips, alternating colors, brushing each layer with milk and pressing together lightly. Carefully wrap in waxed paper. Freeze until firm enough to slice, or chill overnight in refrigerator.

Cut in ⅛-inch slices, using a very sharp knife. Place on greased baking sheets. Bake at 400° for 6 to 8 minutes or just until white portions begin to brown. Makes about 5½ dozen.

SISTER JOAN'S CHRISTMAS COOKIES

2 c. broken nutmeats (walnuts or pecans)
1 lb. pitted dates cut into large pieces
½ c. dark seedless raisins
1 10-12 oz. jar maraschino cherries, cut in half
1 lb. dark brown sugar (not granulated)
½ c. butter or margarine
½ c. shortening
4 eggs
1¼ t. nutmeg
1 t. allspice
1 t. cinnamon
1 t. salt
1 t. baking soda
2 t. warm water
3 to 4 c. flour

Dissolve baking soda in warm water. Melt butter and shortening in large pan. Cool slightly and add brown sugar. Stir until dissolved. Stir in the following, beating well after each addition: baking soda and water; salt and spices; eggs (mix them in very well); fruit and nuts which have been cut up and dusted lightly with flour. Add flour until dough is just stiff enough to hold shape on spoon (drop cookie consistency). Drop from teaspoon onto greased and floured baking sheet. Bake in 350° oven for about 12-15 minutes until cookies spring back when pressed lightly. Cool. Makes 100 cookies.

Mrs. C. M. Stearns

LEMON FROSTED PECAN COOKIES

1 c. butter or margarine	1½ c. sifted flour
¾ c. sifted powdered sugar	¾ c. sifted cornstarch
2 T. milk	¾ c. chopped pecans

Mix and drop on cookie sheets. Bake at 400° for about 10 minutes. Cool and frost with 2 cups sifted powdered sugar, 4 tablespoons soft butter, 3 tablespoons lemon juice. Add a few drops of yellow food coloring if desired. Makes 5 to 6 dozen cookies.

Mrs. Robert Durkee

PEPPERMINT DELIGHTS

1 c. butter or margarine
1 c. sifted confectioners' sugar
2 t. vanilla
1½ c. sifted flour
½ t. salt
1 c. quick-cooking rolled oats
¼ c. crushed peppermint candy

Cream butter, add sugar and cream until fluffy. Add vanilla. Sift flour and salt together; add to creamed mixture. Fold in rolled oats and candy, mixing until dough holds together. Tint with red or green food coloring if desired. Roll out ⅛ inch thick on a board sprinkled with confectioners' sugar. Cut out cookies, sprinkle lightly with sugar and place on ungreased cookie sheets. Bake at 325° for 15 minutes. Makes 3 dozen cookies.

Clarence Ciolek

STIR-AND-DROP COOKIES

2 eggs
⅔ c. cooking oil
2 t. vanilla
1 t. grated lemon rind *or* 1 t. almond flavoring
¾ c. granulated sugar
2 c. flour
2 t. baking powder
½ t. salt

Heat oven to 400°. Beat eggs until blended. Stir in oil and flavorings. Blend in sugar until mixture thickens. Sift dry ingredients and add to mixture. Drop by teaspoonfuls about 2 inches apart on ungreased cookie sheet. Stamp each cookie with bottom of glass dipped in sugar. Decorate as you wish. Bake until cookies get a very light brown around the edges. Makes 3 to 5 dozen cookies. *Decorating ideas:* Place pecan half on cookie before baking. Or after cookies cool, frost with confectioners' sugar icing and top with assorted colored sprinkles.

Mr. & Mrs. Richard Davis

JEWELED SPICE BARS

1 8-oz. package cream cheese
½ c. margarine
1½ c. brown sugar, packed
1 egg
¼ c. honey
2¼ c. sifted flour
1½ t. baking powder
1 t. salt
1 t. cinnamon
1 t. nutmeg
1 c. chopped nuts
1 c. chopped candied fruit
½ c. raisins

Combine softened cream cheese, margarine, sugar and egg. Mix well. Stir in honey. Sift together flour, baking powder, salt, cinnamon and nutmeg. Add nuts, candied fruit and raisins. Toss lightly to coat fruit. Gradually add to cream cheese mixture. Pour into greased and floured pan, 15 x 10½ inches. Bake at 350° for 30 to 35 minutes.

CONFECTIONERS' SUGAR ICING

1⅓ c. sifted confectioners' sugar
2 T. milk
¼ t. vanilla

Drizzle over warm bars. Cool. Cut into 3 x 1-inch bars. Makes 50.

Beth Green

WALNUT STRIPS

1 c. butter or margarine
1 c. sugar
1 egg, separated
2 c. flour
½ t. cinnamon
1 T. water
½ c. finely chopped walnuts

Mix butter, sugar and egg yolk; beat well. Combine flour and cinnamon; add to butter mixture. Pat dough into a pan, 15½ x 10½ inches. Beat egg white and water until foamy. Spread over dough. Sprinkle walnuts on top. Bake for 20 to 25 minutes at 350°. Cut into thin strips.

PACKING COOKIES FOR MAILING

Soft bar and drop cookies usually travel well. Rolled or pressed cookies break more easily—they may become crumbs before the recipient gets them. Pack cookies of the same variety together. Otherwise the flavors will mingle and the distinctive taste of each kind will be lost.

For best results, wrap cookies singly or in pairs with plastic wrap. Pack them in layers, cushioning each row of cookies with a generous layer of filler such as popped corn or crumpled newspaper. Use a heavy cardboard box that will not be crushed before it reaches its destination. Add enough filler so the box is very full—the cookies should not have room to bounce around inside.

Label the package clearly. As a safety precaution, enclose an extra address label inside the package. Be sure to use adequate postage and to label the package "FRAGILE." If you wish, decorate the outside of the box with bright holiday stickers.

GINGERBREAD COOKIE BOX

See color photo opposite

GINGERBREAD CUTOUTS

1 c. butter
1 c. sugar
1 egg
1 c. dark molasses
2 T. vinegar
5 c. sifted flour
1½ t. baking soda
½ t. salt
2 t. ginger
1 t. cinnamon
1 t. cloves

Cream butter; add sugar gradually. Beat in egg, molasses and vinegar. Blend in sifted dry ingredients. Chill. Roll ⅛ to ¼ inch thick on floured surface; cut into desired shapes. Place on greased cookie sheets. Bake at 375° for 5 to 15 minutes depending on size and thickness of cookie.

SYRUP

1½ c. sugar
½ c. water
¼ c. light corn syrup

Combine all ingredients in a saucepan. Cover; bring to a boil; boil 5 minutes. Remove cover. Cook to 300° or hard crack stage. Switch to a warm heat setting to keep syrup boiling hot while putting parts of Gingerbread Box together. Work as quickly as possible. If mixture gets too thick, add a small amount of light corn syrup, bring to boiling point.

DECORATING FROSTING

2 egg whites
2½ c. confectioners' sugar
¼ c. light corn syrup
Food coloring

Beat egg whites until they hold a soft peak. Add sugar gradually and beat until sugar is dissolved and frosting stands in peaks. Add syrup and beat one minute. Divide frosting into small portions. Color each amount as desired with food coloring. Add a few drops of water if a thinner frosting is needed. Keep well covered when not in use.

INSTRUCTIONS FOR MAKING GINGERBREAD BOX

Make cardboard patterns using the following dimensions.

Sides—8 x 2¼ inches
Ends—6 x 2¼ inches
Bottom—8 x 5¾ inches
Top—8½ x 6¼ inches

Use Gingerbread Cutouts recipe. Place patterns on dough; cut around patterns with a sharp knife. Cut 2 sides, 2 ends, 1 bottom and 1 top. Place on greased cookie sheets. Bake as directed in recipe. Trim edges that are not straight while cookies are hot; work carefully. Cool on cookie sheets. Join the sides and ends to bottom of box by applying syrup to the edges; hold in place a few minutes until syrup sets. Decorate edges of box with Decorating Frosting. Decorate cover of box as desired. Fill box with miniature cookies or small Gingerbread Cutout cookies. Place cover on box.

Make a show-off gift box for Christmas cookies from a greeting card box with a see-through lid. Cover the bottom of the box with Christmas wrapping paper.

Store soft cookies in tins, with a slice of apple added to keep them moist. Crisp cookies should be kept in boxes—or freeze them so they'll stay oven-fresh.

Give Sandbakels with a set of molds, Springerle with a Springerle rolling pin, or Spritz Butter Cookies with a cookie press. The lucky recipient will be able to recreate your gift time and time again.

For a special friend, give a cookie jar filled with home-made cookies. Or make your own jar: spray paint an empty coffee can and stencil on a holiday design or wish. For a lasting gift, use colors and designs that will harmonize with the recipient's kitchen.

When cookie recipes specify a varying amount of flour, add the minimum amount first. Then bake a test cookie. If the cookie spreads more than it should, add a few tablespoons of flour. If you've added too much flour, the cookie may crack. Soften the dough with a little cream.

Any rolled cookie can be made into a Christmas tree ornament. Cut a piece of string or thread for each cookie. Before baking the cookies, press each down onto both ends of a string.

APRICOT CALICO COOKIES
See color photo, page 42

2 16- to 17-oz. cans apricot halves, drained and pureed
½ c. apricot preserves
¼ c. cornstarch
2 T. lemon juice
2 18-oz. packages refrigerated oatmeal-raisin cookie dough *or* 2 16-oz. packages refrigerated chocolate chip cookie dough
1 3½-oz. container red candied cherries, halved
1 3½-oz. container green candied cherries, quartered

In medium saucepan, combine pureed apricots, preserves, cornstarch and lemon juice. Cook over medium heat, stirring constantly, until mixture thickens and begins to boil. Cover and chill. Meanwhile, pat cookie dough evenly on bottom and sides of an ungreased 15½ x 10½ x 1-inch baking sheet. Evenly spread with apricot mixture. Decorate tops of cookies with flowers, using 1 red cherry half for flower and 2 green cherry quarters for leaves. Arrange flowers in rows on apricot mixture, 9 on the 15-inch sides and 8 on the 10-inch sides. Bake at 350° for 40 minutes or until toothpick inserted in center comes out clean. Cool on wire rack. When cool, cut into 2 x 1-inch bars, one flower on each cookie. Makes 72 cookies.

BUTTERSCOTCH CRISPS

2 c. sifted flour
½ t. salt
¾ c. butter
1 c. brown sugar
1 egg
1 t. vanilla
½ c. chopped nuts

Cream butter. Gradually add brown sugar and cream well. Add egg, vanilla and nuts; blend thoroughly. Sift flour and salt together. Add to beaten mixture and blend well. Shape dough into balls, using about 1 teaspoonful of dough. (If necessary, chill dough first.) Place on ungreased cookie sheet. Flatten with glass dipped in sugar. Bake at 400° for 8-10 minutes. Makes about 4 dozen.

PECAN PIE BARS

1 c. sifted flour
½ c. rolled oats
¼ c. brown sugar, packed
½ c. butter
3 eggs
¾ c. light corn syrup
1 c. coarsely chopped pecans
1 t. vanilla
¼ t. salt
½ c. brown sugar, packed
1 T. flour

Combine 1 cup flour, oats and ¼ cup brown sugar; cut in butter with pastry blender until mixture resembles coarse crumbs. Press mixture into greased 9 x 9 x 2-inch pan. Bake at 350° about 15 minutes. Beat eggs slightly; add remaining ingredients; blend well. Pour over partially baked crust. Bake at 350° about 25 minutes. Cool to room temperature. Cut into bars. Makes about 3 dozen.

CHOCOLATE PIXIES

2 c. sifted flour
¾ t. salt
2 t. baking powder
½ c. salad oil
4 oz. unsweetened chocolate, melted and cooled
2 c. granulated sugar
4 eggs
2 t. vanilla
½ c. chopped nuts
1 c. confectioners' sugar

Combine and sift flour, salt and baking powder. Mix in oil, melted chocolate and granulated sugar. Add eggs one at a time and mix well after each. Add vanilla and nuts and mix just until ingredients are combined. Chill for 1 hour. Using a tablespoon, drop batter into confectioners' sugar and shape into a ball. Place cookies about 2 inches apart on lightly greased cookie sheet. Bake at 350° for about 12 minutes. Makes about 4 dozen cookies.

Terry Jo Gibson

HONEY COOKIES

1 qt. honey
2 c. sugar
4 c. flour
1 c. butter
1 c. water
1 t. cinnamon
½ t. pepper
1 t. crushed cardamom seed
2 eggs, beaten
½ lb. nutmeats, finely chopped
1¼ T. baking soda
1 t. vanilla
8 c. flour

Cook honey and sugar together for 1 minute. Pour mixture over flour. Beat well, then add butter and water. Cool overnight. Then add next 7 ingredients and mix well. Add half of remaining flour. Chill. Add last 4 cups of flour when ready to roll cookies out. Roll and bake at 400° just until cookies begin to brown.

Mrs. Carlton Mueller

DREAM BARS

½ c. butter
1½ c. brown sugar
1⅛ c. flour
2 eggs
1 t. vanilla
½ t. baking powder
¼ t. salt
1½ c. shredded coconut
1 c. nutmeats

Cream butter, add ½ cup of brown sugar and beat well. Blend in 1 cup of flour and spread mixture in a large pan, about 9 x 13 inches. Bake for 15 minutes at 325°. Beat eggs with remaining brown sugar; add vanilla. Add remaining flour, baking powder, salt, coconut and nuts. Spread over baked layer. Return to oven and bake 25 additional minutes. Cut into bars while warm.

SPRINGERLE

4 eggs
2 c. sugar
4½ c. flour
Anise seed

Beat eggs until light and creamy. Add sugar gradually, beating until dissolved. Stir in flour until well blended. Chill several hours or overnight. Roll out ⅛ inch thick. If desired, press a floured springerle rolling pin on dough to emboss designs. Cut into squares. Transfer cookies onto a board that has been sprinkled with anise seed and additional flour. Let dry for 12 hours. Place cookies on greased baking sheet. Bake at 325° for 12 to 15 minutes. Makes about 9 dozen cookies.

LIZZIES

1½ c. sifted flour
1½ t. baking soda
 1 t. cinnamon
 ¼ t. nutmeg
 ¼ t. cloves
 ¼ c. butter
 ½ c. brown sugar, packed
 2 eggs
1½ T. milk
 ⅓ c. bourbon
 1 lb. seeded raisins
 1 lb. walnuts or pecans
 ½ lb. citron, chopped
 1 lb. candied cherries

Sift flour, soda and spices together. Cream butter, add sugar gradually, and cream until fluffy. Add eggs and blend well. Add sifted dry ingredients and mix. Blend in combined milk and bourbon. Add remaining ingredients and mix well. Drop by spoonfuls on ungreased baking sheets. Bake in preheated 325° oven for 12 minutes. Makes about 10 dozen.

LEBKUCHEN

1½ c. light corn syrup
 ½ t. baking soda
 ¼ c. shortening
 2 c. sifted flour
 ½ c. butter
1½ c. sugar
 2 eggs
 ½ c. cultured sour cream
4½ c. sifted flour
 ¼ t. baking soda
1½ t. baking powder
 ½ t. cinnamon
 ⅛ t. cloves
1¼ t. salt
 ⅓ c. finely chopped blanched almonds
 ⅓ c. finely chopped citron
Blanched almonds

Combine syrup, ½ teaspoon soda and shortening; bring to a boil; remove from heat. Mix in 2 cups flour; cover; refrigerate for several days. Remove from refrigerator. Allow to come to room temperature. Cream butter; add sugar gradually; beat in eggs and sour cream. Mix in room-temperature syrup mixture. Stir in sifted dry ingredients, chopped almonds and citron. Cover; refrigerate for several days. Allow dough to soften at room temperature before rolling. Roll dough ¼ inch thick on floured surface. Cut in large oblong pieces about 3 x 2 inches or use cookie cutters. Place on greased cookie sheets; decorate with blanched almonds. Bake at 350° about 15 minutes or until delicately browned. Makes about 8 dozen, depending on size.

PRALINE STRIPS

24 whole graham crackers
 1 c. butter
 1 c. brown sugar, packed
 1 c. chopped pecans

Arrange graham crackers in ungreased 15 x 10 x 1-inch pan. Place butter and sugar in saucepan. Heat to boiling point; boil 2 minutes. Stir in pecans; spread evenly over crackers. Bake at 350° about 10 minutes. Cut each cracker in half while warm. Makes 48.

PEANUT TOFFEE DIAMONDS

½ c. butter
½ c. chunk-style peanut butter
1 c. brown sugar, packed
1 egg
1 t. vanilla
¼ t. salt
2 c. sifted flour
1 c. chocolate bits, melted
½ c. chunk-style peanut butter
Whole salted peanuts

Cream butter and ½ cup peanut butter; add sugar gradually; beat in egg and vanilla. Blend in salt and flour. Pat into greased 15 x 10 x 1-inch pan. Bake at 325° for about 25 minutes. Combine chocolate and ½ cup peanut butter; spread over hot baked surface. Cut into diamonds while warm; place a peanut in center of each diamond. Makes about 4 dozen.

AUSTRIAN PEACH COOKIES

1 c. sugar
¾ c. vegetable oil
½ c. milk
2 eggs
¾ t. baking powder
½ t. vanilla
3½ to 4 c. flour
   Apricot filling
   Red and Yellow-Orange Sugars

In large bowl, combine sugar, oil, milk, eggs, baking powder and vanilla; blend in enough flour to form a soft dough. Roll into walnut-size balls and bake on ungreased cookie sheets for 15 to 20 minutes (cookies will be pale); cool completely. Scrape out cookies by gently rotating tip of sharp knife against flat side of cookie, leaving shell. Fill cookies with apricot filling. Press two cookies together to form a "peach." Brush lightly with additional brandy or water and immediately dip one spot in Red Sugar for blush, then roll entire cookie in Yellow-Orange Sugar for peach color. If desired, insert a piece of cinnamon stick "stem" through a green gumdrop "leaf" into the seam of each peach. Makes about 2½ dozen. Bake at 325°.

APRICOT FILLING

2 c. reserved cookie crumbs
1 c. peach or apricot preserves
½ c. chopped almonds
1 3-oz. package cream cheese, softened
2 T. instant tea powder
2 to 3 T. peach, apricot or plain brandy
¾ t. ground cinnamon

In medium bowl, combine ingredients. Mix until blended.

RED AND YELLOW-ORANGE SUGAR

1 c. sugar
   Red food coloring
   Yellow food coloring

To make Red Sugar, blend ⅓ cup sugar with a few drops red food coloring. To make Yellow-Orange Sugar, blend ⅔ cup sugar with 2 to 3 drops red food coloring. Add enough yellow food coloring to make a peach color.

Austrian Peach Cookies

ORANGE WALNUT WAFERS

½ c. butter or margarine
1 c. brown sugar
1 egg
½ t. vanilla
1 T. grated orange rind
1¾ c. flour
½ t. baking soda
¼ t. salt
½ c. chopped walnuts

Beat together butter, sugar, egg, vanilla and orange rind. Combine flour, baking soda and salt; stir into butter mixture. Add walnuts and mix well. Form into rolls 2 inches in diameter. Wrap in waxed paper or plastic wrap. Chill. When firm, slice ⅛ inch thick. Place on ungreased cookie sheet and bake for 8 to 10 minutes at 400°.

LEMON REFRIGERATOR COOKIES

See photo, page 29

1½ c. sifted flour
½ t. baking soda
¾ t. salt
½ c. butter or margarine
1 c. sugar
1 egg
1 t. lemon juice
2 t. grated lemon rind

Sift together flour, soda and salt. Cream the butter, sugar, egg and lemon juice and rind. Beat until light. Gradually add dry ingredients, mixing well. Divide dough in half; tint one half pink if desired. Shape each half into a long smooth roll about 2 inches in diameter. Wrap rolls in aluminum foil. Chill or freeze until firm enough to slice easily. With sharp knife, slice cookies ⅛ inch thick. Place on ungreased, foil-covered cookie sheets. Bake at 400° for 6 to 8 minutes, until lightly browned. Makes about 5 dozen cookies.

LEMON BELLS

Make dough for Lemon Refrigerator Cookies. Shape about ½ cup of the dough into a long pencil-shaped roll and remaining dough into a large roll about 2 inches in diameter. Wrap both in foil and chill. Remove large roll from refrigerator and mold into a bell shape. Chill or freeze until needed. To bake, cut in ⅛-inch slices and arrange on foil-covered cookie sheet. Slice the tiny roll and place a small round at bottom of each cookie. Bake as above.

MELTAWAY MAPLE CRISPS

½ c. butter
¼ c. sugar
1 t. maple flavoring
2 c. sifted cake flour
¾ c. chopped pecans

Cream butter; add sugar gradually. Add flavoring and beat until fluffy. Stir in flour and mix until a dough forms. Fold in pecans and press into a ball. Pinch off small pieces of dough and place on ungreased cookie sheet. Flatten cookies with finger or glass dipped in sugar. Bake at 350° for 7 minutes.

CINNAMON STARS

3 egg whites
¼ t. salt
1½ c. confectioners' sugar
1 T. grated lemon rind
½ t. cinnamon
3 cups grated unblanched almonds

Beat egg whites and salt until stiff but not dry. Add powdered sugar gradually and blend thoroughly. Reserve ½ cup egg white mixture for topping. Add remaining ingredients; blend. Roll out dough, a small portion at a time, on a board that has been generously sprinkled with confectioners' sugar. Roll ¼ inch thick and cut with a small star cookie cutter. Place on a baking sheet that has been greased and covered with brown paper. Cover cookies with a thin layer of topping, spreading topping to the points of the stars. Bake for about 20 minutes at 300°. Remove from baking sheet immediately. If cookies stick, lift brown paper from baking sheet and place it on a moistened board. After about 1 minute, remove cookies from paper. Makes about 10 dozen.

HOLIDAY BON BONS

½ c. finely chopped walnuts
1 c. ground dates
½ t. vanilla
1 egg white
⅛ t. salt
⅓ c. sugar
½ t. vanilla
Red and green food coloring

Combine nuts, dates and vanilla. Form into balls, using a scant ½ teaspoon of the mixture for each. Refrigerate mixture thoroughly. Beat egg white and salt until stiff, adding sugar gradually. Add vanilla. Divide egg white mixture in half. Tint one portion pink and the other green. Use 1 or 2 teaspoons to roll balls in meringue. Swirl tops. Bake on greased cookie sheets in 250° oven for about ½ hour. Makes 4-5 dozen.

THIMBELINA COOKIES

½ c. butter, softened
¼ c. sugar
1 egg yolk, well beaten
1 t. vanilla

1 c. flour
½ t. salt
1 egg white, unbeaten
1 c. chopped walnuts

Cream together butter and sugar. Beat in egg yolk and vanilla. Blend in flour and salt, sifted together. Shape into 1-inch balls. Dip each ball into egg white; roll in nuts. Place on ungreased baking sheet. Dent center of each ball. Bake for 5 minutes at 350°. Remove from oven and dent again. Bake 12 to 15 additional minutes. Cool. Fill with Tinted Butter Frosting. Makes about 3 dozen.

TINTED BUTTER FROSTING

Combine 2 cups sifted confectioners' sugar, 6 tablespoons melted butter, 1 tablespoon cream and ½ teaspoon vanilla. Mix well. Tint with food coloring.

SWEDISH BUTTER COOKIES

1 c. butter
½ c. sugar
1 egg, separated
1 T. cream
1 t. vanilla
2 c. sifted flour
½ t. baking powder
½ c. chopped pecans

Cream butter and sugar. Add egg yolk, cream and vanilla and mix well. Sift flour with baking powder and add to butter mixture. Stir in nuts. Form dough into small balls and dip in egg white, then chopped pecans. Make a small indentation in the center of the balls of dough after placing them on an ungreased cookie sheet. Fill indentations with jelly or with a red or green maraschino cherry half. Bake at 350° for 20 minutes. Handle carefully when removing from cookie sheet as they are very fragile.

HONEY LACE WAFERS

½ c. cake flour
¼ t. baking powder
⅛ t. baking soda
¼ c. honey
2 T. sugar
¼ c. butter
½ c. shredded coconut
1¾ t. grated orange rind (optional)

Sift flour once, measure, add baking powder and soda and sift again. Combine honey, sugar and butter in saucepan. Bring to a full boil and cook one minute. Remove from heat. Add sifted dry ingredients. Then add coconut and rind and mix well. Drop by ¼ teaspoonfuls onto greased and floured baking sheet. Bake a few at a time at 350° for 8-10 minutes. Let cool on sheet for about ½ minute; remove with spatula while still hot and immediately wrap cookies around a pencil, pressing edges together to seal. Makes about 3 dozen cookies.

PECAN FINGERS

1 c. butter
¼ c. confectioners' sugar
1 t. vanilla
1 T. water
2 c. flour
¼ t. salt
2 c. ground pecans
Confectioners' sugar

Cream butter; add sugar, vanilla and water. Beat well. Add flour and pecans. Chill for about 1 hour. Shape dough into small, fingerlike rolls. Bake for 1 hour at 250°. While cookies are still warm, roll them in confectioners' sugar. Makes about 5 dozen. *Note:* If you wish, form cookies into crescents, balls or other shapes. Always roll baked cookies in confectioners' sugar.

CRISP BUTTER WAFERS

1 c. butter	1 t. vanilla
⅔ c. sugar	1½ c. flour
1 egg	¼ t. salt

Beat butter, sugar, egg and vanilla until fluffy. Add flour and salt and mix well. Drop from teaspoon onto ungreased cookie sheets. Bake at 350° for 8-10 minutes or until cookies begin to brown around the edges. Makes about 4 dozen.

ANISE DROPS

1¾ c. flour
½ t. baking powder
3 eggs
1 c. sugar
Anise oil

Sift flour and baking powder together; set aside. Combine eggs and sugar in large mixing bowl. Beat for 30 minutes on medium speed. Add flour; blend thoroughly. Beat for 3 additional minutes. Add anise oil to taste. Drop cookies from teaspoon onto greased baking sheets. Let stand overnight in a cool, dry place. Bake at 325° for about 12 minutes. Cookies should form a creamy white "cap." Makes 8-10 dozen cookies.

OLD-FASHIONED BROWNIES

2 oz. baking chocolate
½ c. shortening
1 c. sugar
2 eggs, well beaten
1 t. vanilla
½ c. sifted flour
¼ t. salt
½ c. chopped pecans

Melt chocolate and shortening in top part of double boiler over hot water. Remove from heat. Add sugar, eggs and vanilla. Mix well. Add flour and salt and mix well. Stir in nuts. Pour into greased 9 x 9-inch pan. Bake at 375° for 15 to 18 minutes. Cut into squares or bars.

CHOCOLATE MINT WAFERS

⅔ c. butter
1 c. sugar
1 egg
2 c. flour
¾ c. cocoa
½ t. salt
1 t. baking powder
¼ c. milk

Cream butter and sugar thoroughly. Add egg and beat well. Add sifted dry ingredients alternately with milk. Mix thoroughly; chill. Roll ⅛ inch thick on lightly floured surface. Cut with floured 2 to 2½ inch cookie cutter. Bake on greased sheet 350° for 8 minutes. When cool, put together with Mint Filling.

MINT FILLING

½ c. confectioners' sugar
2 drops peppermint oil
3 to 4 T. light cream or milk
Salt

Beat until of spreading consistency.

Gladys Eborall

PEANUT BUTTER REFRIGERATOR COOKIES

See photo opposite

2 c. sifted flour
1 t. baking soda
½ t. salt
1 c. soft butter or margarine
1 c. light brown sugar, firmly packed
1 c. chunk style peanut butter
1 egg
1 t. vanilla

Sift together flour, soda and salt. Cream the butter and sugar until light, then beat in peanut butter, egg and vanilla. Mix in the dry ingredients, blending thoroughly. Form the mixture into two long rolls, about 2 inches in diameter. Wrap in foil and chill or freeze until needed. To bake, slice cookies with a very sharp knife about ⅛ inch thick and place on an ungreased foil-covered cookie sheet. Bake at 375° about 6 to 8 minutes or until lightly browned. Makes about 8 dozen cookies.

Note: It's easy to form refrigerator cookies into holiday shapes. After making rolls of dough, gently press them into the desired shapes. Then chill as usual.

VANILLA REFRIGERATOR WAFERS

½ c. butter
½ c. margarine
1¼ c. confectioners' sugar
1 egg
1 t. vanilla
2 c. flour
1 t. baking soda
1 t. cream of tartar
⅛ t. salt

Cream together butter, margarine and sugar. Beat in egg and vanilla. Combine dry ingredients and add to creamed mixture. Mix well. Divide dough in half. Form each half into a roll 2 inches in diameter. Wrap in waxed paper or aluminum foil. Chill in refrigerator or freezer until ready to bake. Slice ⅜ inch thick. Bake on ungreased cookie sheet in 350° oven for 8 to 10 minutes. Cool on rack. Makes about 7 dozen.

CHERRY-COCONUT BARS

1 c. sifted flour
½ c. butter or margarine
3 T. confectioners' sugar
2 eggs, slightly beaten
1 c. sugar
¼ c. flour
½ t. baking powder
¼ t. salt
1 t. vanilla
¾ c. chopped nuts
½ c. coconut
½ c. quartered maraschino cherries

Mix butter, flour, and sugar until smooth. Spread thin with fingers in an 8 or 9-inch square pan. Bake at 350° about 25 minutes. Stir rest of ingredients into eggs. Spread over top of baked pastry. Bake about 25 minutes at 350°. Cool and cut into bars.

Pauline Follin

CHRISTMAS FRUIT BARS
See photo below

1¼ c. sifted flour
1½ t. baking powder
1 t. salt
3 eggs
1 c. sugar
1 t. vanilla
1½ c. chopped mixed candied fruits
½ c. chopped dates
1 c. chopped walnuts

Line two 8-inch square pans with aluminum foil and grease lightly. Sift together flour, baking powder and salt. Beat eggs until light; add sugar, a little at a time, beating after each addition. Add vanilla. Stir in dry ingredients. Fold in fruits and nuts. Spread dough in foil-lined pans. Bake at 350° for 25 to 30 minutes. Cool; cut into bars. Makes two 8-inch pans; 18 bars each pan.

Lemon Refrigerator Cookies, page 25   *Peanut Butter Refrigerator Cookies, opposite*   *Christmas Fruit Bars, this page*

CAKES

ALMOND CHIFFON CAKE

2 c. sifted all-purpose flour
1½ c. sugar
1 T. baking powder
1 t. salt
7 egg yolks
½ c. salad oil
1 t. lemon extract
1 t. almond extract
¾ c. ice water
7 egg whites (1 c.)
½ t. cream of tartar

Sift first 4 ingredients 4 times. Set aside. Combine egg yolks, salad oil, extracts and ice water. Add dry ingredients. Beat 30 seconds and set aside. Beat egg whites and cream of tartar until stiff peaks form (about 5 minutes). Gradually pour egg yolk mixture over beaten egg whites. Pour into ungreased 10" tube pan. Bake at 325° for 55 minutes, increase temperature to 350° and bake 10 minutes longer. Invert to cool for 1½-2 hours. Ice with Double Boiler Frosting.

DOUBLE BOILER FROSTING

2 egg whites
1½ c. sugar
¼ t. cream of tartar
⅓ c. water
1 t. vanilla

Combine egg whites, sugar, cream of tartar and water in top of double boiler. Beat on high for 1 minute with electric mixer. Place over boiling water and beat on high speed for 7 minutes. Remove pan from boiling water. Add vanilla. Beat 2 minutes longer on high speed. Spread on cake and sprinkle sliced almonds on top.

Geneva Bratton

HOLIDAY MINT ANGEL CAKE

See color photo opposite

8 egg whites (about 1 cup)
¼ t. salt
1 t. cream of tartar
1 t. almond extract
1 t. vanilla
1¼ c. granulated sugar
1 c. cake flour
3½ c. whipped topping
½ c. hard mint candies, coarsely crushed

Preheat oven to 325°. Place egg whites in a small mixing bowl and beat until foamy. Add salt and cream of tartar and beat until soft peaks form. Fold in almond extract and vanilla. Gradually beat in sugar and continue beating until stiff. Sift flour into egg whites and gently fold in. Bake in an ungreased 10-inch tube pan for 50 to 60 minutes. Invert pan on a rack or place center over a soft drink bottle. Cool thoroughly. Remove from pan and slice into 3 layers. Place layer on a cake plate. Drizzle about 2 tablespoons Mint Syrup over the bottom layer. Spread on ½ cup of the whipped topping. Sprinkle on about 1 tablespoon crushed mints. Add second layer and repeat above procedure. Invert the top layer and sprinkle with remaining syrup. Place right side up on second layer. Spread entire cake with remaining whipped topping. Sprinkle with remaining crushed mints. If desired, place scoops of vanilla ice cream on top. Place in freezer until ready to serve.

MINT SYRUP

¼ c. hard mint candies
¼ c. water

Place mints in a blender and blend at high speed until coarsely crushed. Add water and blend until thick.

POPPY SEED CAKE

½ c. shortening
1½ c. sugar
⅔ c. poppy seeds
¼ t. salt
1¼ c. milk
1 t. almond extract
2 c. flour
3 egg whites
3½ t. baking powder

Cream shortening and sugar well. Add poppy seeds and mix thoroughly. Sift flour, salt and baking powder in separate bowl. Add dry ingredients and milk alternately, making sure to combine thoroughly after each addition. Add almond extract. Beat egg whites until perfect peaks form. Then fold into batter. Bake at 360° in 2 greased and floured layer cake pans (or a bundt pan) for 25 to 30 minutes, or until done. Cool completely and ice.

CREAM CHEESE ICING

1 3-oz. package cream cheese
1 T. milk
2½ c. confectioners' sugar
½ T. vanilla

Soften cheese with milk; add sugar and vanilla. Mix until smooth. If making a 2-layer cake, ice just center and top. If using a bundt pan ice the cake completely.

Patricia Dodson

APRICOT MINI SEVEN-LAYER CAKES

1 11¾-oz. package frozen pound cake
1 16-oz. can apricot halves, undrained
1 t. grated lemon peel
1 16½-oz. can vanilla frosting
2 T. minced maraschino cherries, well drained on paper towels
1 oz. semisweet chocolate, melted
¼ c. smooth peanut butter

Cut frozen cake in 21 vertical slices using a serrated knife with a sawing motion; set aside. Reserve 6 of the apricot halves for garnishing top of cakes. Whirl remaining undrained apricots and lemon peel in a blender until smooth. Spread some of the pureed apricots on a cake slice to within ⅛ inch of edge. Top with a second slice. Continue layering to make 7-layer "mini" cake. Place cake on its side on a serving platter with remaining cake slices until you have three separate "mini" cakes. Divide frosting into three small bowls. Stir cherries into one bowl, stir chocolate into second bowl, stir peanut butter into third bowl. If frostings thicken, thin to spreading consistency with a few drops of milk. Spread the sides and top of each cake with a different flavored frosting. Cut reserved apricots into slices. Decorate top of each cake with apricot slices. Chill until ready to serve.

EASY CHOCOLATE CAKE

½ c. butter or margarine
1¼ c. sugar
2 oz. unsweetened chocolate
2 eggs
½ t. baking powder
2 c. sifted flour
1 c. cold water
1 t. baking soda
¼ t. salt
1 t. vanilla
1 6-oz. package semisweet chocolate bits

Cream butter and sugar; add melted chocolate and beat thoroughly. Add well-beaten eggs. Sift baking powder, flour and salt together; add to mixture alternately with soda and water combined, beating well after each addition. Add vanilla and pour into greased baking pan, 9 x 13 inches. Sprinkle chocolate bits evenly over batter. Bake at 350° for 20 minutes or until done. Cool. Sprinkle with confectioners' sugar if desired.

Millicent Sprtel

VANILLA WAFER CAKE

¾ c. margarine
1½ c. sugar
6 eggs
3 c. vanilla wafer crumbs
½ c. milk
1 c. chopped pecans
1⅓ c. flaked coconut

Cream margarine. Gradually add sugar; cream until light and fluffy. Add eggs one at a time. Beat well after each addition. Alternately fold in crumbs and milk. Stir in nuts and coconut. Batter may appear curdled. Spoon into 9-inch tube pan which has been greased, floured and lined on bottom with waxed paper. Evenly spread batter in pan. Bake at 350° for 1 hour 10 minutes. Cool cake in pan 10 minutes; remove from pan; remove waxed paper and finish cooling on rack. Frost or glaze as desired.

Estella Long Black

MORAVIAN SUGAR CAKE

6 T. melted margarine
½ c. seasoned mashed potatoes
½ c. sugar
1 pkg. dry yeast
1 egg
½ t. salt
2½ c. flour

Dissolve yeast in ½ cup warm water for 5 minutes. Beat all ingredients well with an electric mixer except 1 cup of the flour. Then add the 1 cup of flour and mix with a spoon. Put dough into a greased bowl and let rise 2 hours or until double in bulk (it can be put in an 85° oven to rise). Punch down and spread in a 9 x 13-inch pan. Let rise ½ hour.

Sift ½ cup brown sugar and ½ teaspoon cinnamon. Make about 24 holes with little pats of cold margarine in the dough. Sprinkle with sugar and cinnamon mixture. Bake about 20 minutes at 400°.

Mrs. Edward L. Fischer

APPLESAUCE CAKE

1 c. brown sugar
1 c. white sugar
1 c. butter or margarine
2 eggs
3 c. flour
½ t. salt
1½ t. baking soda
1 t. cloves
1 t. nutmeg
1 t. cinnamon
1 c. applesauce
1 c. chocolate chips
½ c. raisins
1 c. coconut
1 c. chopped pecans

Blend together sugars and butter; add eggs. Combine flour with spices, salt and soda. Mix well and add to sugar and egg mixture. Add applesauce, chocolate chips, raisins, coconut and pecans. Pour into a 10-inch tube pan which has been lined with brown paper. Bake at 350° for 1½ hours. If cake browns too quickly, cover with an extra piece of brown paper. Keeps well.

Alice Leedy Mason

NUT DELIGHT CAKE

3 c. flour
2 c. sugar
1½ c. salad oil
1 t. vanilla
4 eggs, beaten
½ t. salt
1½ t. baking soda
1 large can evaporated milk
½ c. raisins (optional)
½ c. chopped walnuts
1 can nut filling

Combine all ingredients except nut filling. Beat until smooth. Add nut filling and beat at medium speed for about 3 minutes. Bake at 350° for about 1 hour and 10 minutes in an ungreased tube pan. Cool cake for at least ½ hour before removing from pan. Cake can be eaten same day, but its flavor improves with age.

Doris K. Finck

MINI-FRUITCAKES
See color photo opposite

3 c. unsifted flour
1⅓ c. sugar
1 t. salt
1 t. baking powder
2 t. ground cinnamon
1 t. ground nutmeg
½ c. orange juice
½ c. brandy or water
1 c. salad oil
4 eggs
¼ c. light corn syrup
1 c. dark seedless raisins
2 c. diced dried California apricots
2 c. mixed candied fruits (1 lb.)
2 c. pecan halves
⅓ c. light corn syrup

In large mixing bowl, combine all ingredients except fruits, nuts, and ⅓ cup corn syrup. Blend for ½ minute on low speed, scraping bowl constantly. Beat 3 minutes on high speed, scraping bowl occasionally. Stir in fruits and nuts. Spoon batter into 3 dozen 2½-inch muffin pans lined with paper baking cups. Bake in 275° oven for 65 to 70 minutes or until toothpick comes out clean when inserted in center of fruitcake. Cool fruitcakes in pans for 5 minutes; remove to cooling rack. Cool thoroughly. Heat corn syrup in small pan; brush over tops of cakes. Place cupcakes in container; cover with cheesecloth soaked in brandy. Cover tightly and store in a cool place for up to 2 weeks. For longer storage, freeze in tightly covered containers. Makes about 3 dozen.

CHEESECAKE

¾ stick butter, melted
9 whole graham crackers
2 T. sugar

Mix together and press in greased 9-inch round pan lined with aluminum foil.

CHEESE FILLING

3 8-oz. packages cream cheese
¾ c. sugar
3 eggs
Pinch of salt

Mix above ingredients and pour into crust. Bake 20 minutes at 375°.

SOUR CREAM TOPPING

1 pt. sour cream
1 T. sugar
1 t. vanilla

Mix and pour on top of pie. Bake 5 minutes at 475°. Cool in refrigerator several hours before serving.

Jackie Gray

POUND CAKE DELIGHT

½ c. shortening
1 c. butter
3 c. sugar
1 c. sweet milk
3½ c. sifted flour
6 eggs
1 t. baking powder
½ t. salt
1 t. rum extract
1 t. coconut extract
1 t. lemon extract

Cream the first 3 ingredients. Add eggs one at a time. Add sifted dry ingredients alternately with milk and flavorings. Bake at 325° for 1 hour 20 minutes to 1 hour 30 minutes in 10-inch greased and floured tube pan.

ALMOND ICING

1 c. sugar
½ c. water
1 t. almond extract

Boil ingredients together for about 2 minutes. Pour over warm cake which has been poked with holes with a meat fork.

Geneva Bratton

*Photo opposite
Mini-Fruitcakes, this page
Brandied Apricots, page 52
Apricot Snowballs, page 6*

DECORATING, GLAZING AND STORING FRUITCAKES

Let baked fruitcakes stand in pans until almost cold. Remove from pans; cool on racks until the following day. Cover loosely with clean towels.

Wrap cold fruitcakes in 2 thicknesses of waxed paper and store in a tightly covered container. Or wrap in a cloth moistened with wine or brandy, or pour about ¼ cup wine or brandy over each cake. Then wrap cakes in waxed paper and place in a tightly covered container; moisten the cloth or pour liquor over cakes 2 or 3 times during aging period.

To make Apricot Glaze, force 1 cup stewed or canned apricots through a fine sieve. Add ¾ cup sugar and ⅓ cup boiling water; cook uncovered until mixture is as thick as jam. Cool.

Allow fruitcakes to ripen for several weeks before glazing or serving. Then arrange nuts and candied fruits on cakes in the designs desired. Cover fruitcakes and decorations with Apricot Glaze. Before packing or serving cakes, let glaze dry for several hours.

DARK FRUITCAKE

1 c. light molasses	2¼ c. sifted flour
½ c. water	¼ t. baking soda
2 lbs. seedless raisins	1 t. salt
2 lbs. mixed candied fruit, diced	1½ t. cinnamon
	1¼ t. nutmeg
1 c. butter	¾ t. allspice
1¼ c. sugar	½ t. cloves
6 eggs	½ c. orange juice
1 T. grated orange rind	3 c. coarsely chopped nuts

Blend molasses and water together in a large saucepan. Bring to a boil at a medium heat; stir constantly. Add raisins; bring to a boil again; stir well. Reduce heat to low; simmer for 5 minutes. Remove from heat; mix in candied fruit; set aside to cool. Cream butter; add sugar gradually; beat in eggs one at a time; add orange rind. Add sifted dry ingredients alternately with orange juice to creamed mixture. Stir in fruit mixture and nuts. Pour into 2 greased 9 x 5 x 3-inch pans lined with waxed paper; grease paper. Bake in 275° oven for about 3 hours. Makes two 3½-pound fruitcakes.

WHITE FRUITCAKE

1 c. butter or margarine
1 c. sugar
2 c. flour (more if needed)
5 eggs
2 t. baking powder
½ t. salt
1 lb. pecans or walnuts
1 lb. white raisins
1 lb. fruit mix
½ lb. coconut
1 small can crushed pineapple
1 12-oz. jar maraschino cherries, drained (optional)
1 12-oz. package dried apricots (optional)

Cream the butter or margarine; add the sugar and mix. Beat in eggs. Sift dry ingredients together; add to creamed mixture alternately with fruit. Mix all very thoroughly. The mixture will be thick but do not add any additional liquid. Spoon into small baking tins and bake for ½ hour at 275°, then 1 hour at 300°. Makes 3 small cakes.

Barbara T. Price

36

NO-BAKE HOLIDAY FRUITCAKE

  1 qt. paperboard milk carton, empty
  4 c. pound cake crumbs (11¼-oz. cake)
1½ c. miniature marshmallows
1¼ c. cut-up mixed candied fruits
  1 c. seedless raisins
  ¾ c. finely cut dates
  ¾ c. chopped walnuts
  ½ t. cinnamon
  ½ t. nutmeg
  ¼ t. cloves
  ⅓ c. milk
  2 T. frozen orange juice concentrate,
     undiluted

Rinse out milk carton and let dry. Cut out one side of carton (see photo); set carton on side to form a pan and place cut-out piece in bottom of pan to make a sliding base for cake. Flatten pouring end of carton and secure with tape. Break pound cake into crumbs by hand or in blender. In large bowl combine pound cake crumbs with marshmallows, fruits, nuts and spices. Add milk and orange juice concentrate; mix with spoon, then with hands until crumbs are evenly moistened. Pack into prepared milk carton. If desired, garnish with additional fruits and nuts. Cover with plastic wrap and chill at least 2 days before slicing. Makes one 2-pound fruitcake.

Note: For 4-pound fruitcake, double above recipe and pack into ½-gallon milk carton. During chilling, turn carton on its side with weight on top to keep sides of cake straight. For two 1-pound fruitcakes, pack half of above mixture into each of two 1-pint milk cartons. For four ½-pound fruitcakes, pack ¼ of above mixture into each of four ½-pint milk cartons. To prepare ½-pint cartons, cut off entire top to make a square container.

BREADS AND COFFEE CAKES

CHRISTMAS APRICOT WREATH
See color photo opposite

1 13¾-oz. package hot roll mix
¼ c. butter or margarine, softened
1 egg, beaten
   Fruit-Nut Filling
   Confectioners' Sugar Glaze
6 dried California apricots

Prepare hot roll mix according to directions; allow to rise for 35 minutes or until doubled in bulk. Roll out dough to an 18 x 15-inch rectangle. Spread with butter. Sprinkle Fruit-Nut Filling evenly over dough. Roll up, jelly roll fashion, starting with the long end. Place dough on ungreased baking sheet; form into a wreath. Allow to rise about 30 minutes. Brush ring with beaten egg. Bake in 325° oven 35 to 40 minutes or until lightly browned. Cool on sheet for 5 minutes. Loosen bottom of coffee cake with a long metal spatula. Carefully remove to rack. Cool to lukewarm. Drizzle glaze over surface of warm coffee cake. To garnish, form "flowers" by arranging apricot halves in ring around top of coffee cake. Cut red cherries reserved from filling into halves; place one in the center of each apricot flower. Cut each reserved green cherry into 5 wedges and use to garnish apricot flowers.

FRUIT-NUT FILLING

1 4-oz. jar red glacé cherries
1 4-oz. jar green glacé cherries
1 c. diced dried California apricots
⅔ c. chopped toasted blanched almonds
¼ c. sugar
2 T. brandy

Set 3 red and 6 green cherries aside for garnish; chop remaining cherries. Combine all ingredients in bowl. Mix together thoroughly.

CONFECTIONERS' SUGAR GLAZE

1 c. confectioners' sugar
4 t. milk
1 T. brandy

Stir ingredients together in a small bowl until well mixed and of spreading consistency.

Note: Coffee cake may be prepared, completely baked, then frozen until serving day. Instead of glazing cooled cake, wrap in foil and freeze. To serve, thaw in foil at room temperature for 3 hours, then heat for 20 minutes in 300° oven. Glaze as directed.

APRICOT-CRANBERRY LOAF
See color photo opposite

2 c. unsifted flour
¾ c. sugar
1 T. baking powder
½ t. salt
1 c. diced dried California apricots
1 c. chopped fresh or frozen cranberries
½ c. chopped toasted almonds
2 eggs
1 c. milk
¼ c. butter or margarine, melted
1 t. grated lemon peel

Stir flour, sugar, baking powder and salt together in large bowl; add apricots, cranberries and almonds. Toss lightly until fruits are coated. Beat eggs, milk, butter and peel in small bowl; pour over dry ingredients. Stir just until dry ingredients are moistened. Pour into a greased 9 x 5-inch loaf pan. Bake at 350° for 60 to 65 minutes or until cake tester inserted in center comes out clean. Cool in pan for 10 minutes; finish cooling on rack. Makes 1 loaf.

Photo opposite
Apricot-Cranberry Loaf, this page
Christmas Apricot Wreath, this page
Apricot Sticky Buns, page 45

RUSSIAN KULICH
See photo opposite

5 c. flour
2 packages dry yeast
1 c. milk
½ c. sugar
¼ c. vegetable oil
2 t. salt
2 eggs
2 t. grated lemon peel
½ c. chopped blanched almonds
¼ c. raisins
¼ c. chopped candied citron
¼ c. chopped candied orange peel
¼ c. chopped candied cherries
½ c. confectioners' sugar
1 T. milk
Candied fruit (optional)

Stir together 1 cup flour and yeast. Heat 1 cup milk, sugar, oil and salt over low heat to 120° to 130°, stirring to blend. Add to flour-yeast mixture; beat until smooth, about 2 minutes on medium speed of mixer. Beat in eggs, lemon peel, almonds, raisins and candied fruit. Add 1 cup flour; beat 1 minute on medium speed. Stir in more flour to make a soft dough. Turn out onto lightly floured board or pastry cloth; knead until smooth and satiny, about 8 to 10 minutes. Shape into ball and place in lightly greased bowl; turn to grease surface of ball. Cover; let rise in warm place (80 to 85°) until doubled, about 1½ hours. Punch down. Divide dough into 2 or 3 equal portions and shape into balls. Let rest 10 minutes. Generously grease two 46-ounce juice cans or three 1-pound coffee cans. Place dough in cans, filling about half full; brush with oil. Let rise until doubled, about 1 hour. Bake in preheated 350° oven for 30 to 35 minutes or until golden brown. Immediately remove from cans and cool. Blend confectioners' sugar and 1 tablespoon milk until smooth; ice top of loaves. Decorate with candied fruit if desired. 3 medium or 2 large loaves.

KUGELHUPF
See photo opposite

3 to 4 c. flour
2 packages dry yeast
1 c. milk
1 c. raisins
½ c. water
½ c. sugar
½ c. butter
1 t. salt
3 eggs, room temperature
2 t. rum extract
Butter, softened
⅓ c. ground almonds
Sifted confectioners' sugar
Candied fruits
Nuts
Light corn syrup

Stir together 2 cups flour and yeast. Heat milk, raisins, water, sugar, ½ cup butter and salt over low heat to 120° to 130°, stirring to blend; add to flour-yeast mixture and beat until smooth, about 3 minutes on medium speed of mixer. Blend in eggs and extract; add ½ cup flour and continue to beat 2 minutes. Add enough flour to make a thick batter. Cover; let rise in a warm place (80 to 85°) until doubled in volume and batter is bubbly, about 1 hour. Stir down. Spoon into two 1½-quarts or three 1-quart ram's head or other fancy molds that have been buttered and dusted with ground almonds. Cover; let rise in warm place until doubled, about 30 minutes. Bake in preheated 325° oven 1 hour for 1½-quart loaves or 45 minutes for 1-quart loaves. If necessary to prevent excessive browning, cover during the last 10 minutes of baking. Unmold on wire racks. Dust with confectioners' sugar. Decorate with candied fruits and nuts that have been dipped in corn syrup. 2 large or 3 small loaves.

BANANA-NUT BREAD

2 eggs
2 c. brown sugar
2 c. sour milk or buttermilk
1 t. baking soda
1 t. baking powder
3 c. sifted flour
1 c. wheat germ
1 t. salt
1 c. nuts
1 c. mashed bananas

Beat eggs until light. Add sugar and beat slightly. Add milk. Sift together flour, soda, baking powder and salt and add to eggs and sugar. Then add wheat germ, nuts and bananas. Bake in two loaves at 350° for 1 hour.

Ginny Muente

Russian Kulich, opposite
Kugelhupf, opposite
Austrian Almond Braid, this page

AUSTRIAN ALMOND BRAID

See photo at left

5 to 5½ c. flour
2 packages dry yeast
1 c. milk
½ c. sugar
½ c. shortening or butter
¼ c. water
2 t. salt
2 eggs, room temperature
½ c. golden raisins
½ c. candied mixed fruit, chopped
½ c. chopped blanched almonds
  Vegetable oil
  Almond Icing

Stir together 2 cups flour and yeast. Heat milk, sugar, shortening, water and salt in saucepan over low heat to 120° to 130°, stirring to blend. Add liquid ingredients to flour-yeast mixture and beat until smooth, about 3 minutes on medium speed of mixer. Blend in eggs. Add 1 cup flour and beat 1 minute. Stir in fruit and almonds; add more flour to make a soft dough. Turn out on lightly floured board and knead until smooth and satiny, about 5 to 10 minutes. Cover dough; let rest 20 minutes. Divide dough in half. For each braid, take two-thirds of 1 portion of dough and divide into thirds. Roll each piece with hands into a 15-inch strand. Braid strands on lightly greased baking sheet. Divide remaining third into thirds; form three 18-inch strands. Braid strands loosely; place on first braid, pressing in lightly. Tuck ends of top braid under ends of bottom braid. Brush with oil and let rise in warm place (80 to 85°) until doubled, about 45 minutes. Bake in preheated 350° oven for 25 to 30 minutes, or until golden brown. Remove from baking sheets to cooling rack. Ice braids with Almond Icing while still slightly warm. Decorate with candied fruit and nuts, if desired. 2 large loaves.

ALMOND ICING

1½ c. confectioners' sugar
2 T. milk
1 t. almond extract

In small bowl, stir together all ingredients until smooth.

DATE & NUT LOAF

1¾ c. whole nuts
13 oz. whole dates
¾ c. flour
2 t. baking powder
2 eggs, separated
½ c. sugar
1 t. vanilla

Mix together all ingredients except egg whites. Fold in stiffly beaten egg whites last. Batter will be stiff. Press into loaf pan. Bake at 325° for 1 hour. Cool before slicing.

Hazel I. Dalton

CHEESE BISCUITS

½ lb. sharp cheese
½ c. butter
1 c. flour
¼ t. red pepper
¼ t. salt

All ingredients should be at room temperature. Grate cheese into a large bowl. Add remaining ingredients and blend thoroughly. Roll out ⅓ to ½ inch thick. Cut in small rounds. Place on ungreased baking sheet and brush tops with milk. Bake at 400° until lightly browned.

APRICOT CAROLING TREE
See color photo opposite

1 13¾-oz. package hot roll mix
¼ c. butter or margarine, softened
9 jumbo green gumdrops, cut in halves crosswise
18 whole candied red cherries
6 canned apricot halves, well drained
6 small green birthday candles
Apricot Filling

Prepare hot roll mix according to package directions for rolls. Cover; let rise in warm place, free from draft, until doubled in bulk, about 30 to 45 minutes. Turn dough onto floured surface and knead lightly until not sticky. Roll dough into a 16 x 12-inch rectangle; spread with butter. Spread cooled filling evenly on dough to within ½ inch of edges. Starting with 16-inch side, roll up jelly roll fashion; seal edges. Cut into sixteen 1-inch slices. Grease a large (17 x 14-inch) baking sheet. Using a spatula, arrange the 16 slices, cut side down, in a triangle shape in 5 rows. For first row, place 1 slice at top of 14-inch side of cookie sheet. Increase by 1 slice for each additional row, with slices touching; last row will contain 5 slices. Place remaining slice under last row to form base of Christmas tree. Cover; let rise in warm place, free from drafts, until doubled in bulk, about 30 to 45 minutes. Bake at 375° for 20 to 25 minutes or until lightly browned. Carefully remove from baking sheet to cool on wire rack. To decorate tree, make 6 apricot cluster flowers: arrange 3 gumdrop halves, cut side up, alternately with 3 whole cherries in a 3-inch circle. Top with well-drained apricot half, cut side down. Place candle in center of apricot. Decorate tree by arranging 3 apricot clusters in a row near the bottom, 2 in the middle and 1 near the top of tree.

APRICOT FILLING

1 16- or 17-oz. can apricot halves, drained
¾ c. apricot preserves
3 T. cornstarch
1½ t. grated orange peel
½ c. chopped walnuts

Cut each apricot into quarters. In a medium saucepan, combine apricots, preserves, cornstarch and orange peel. Cook over medium heat, stirring constantly, until mixture thickens and begins to boil. Cover and chill until cool; stir in walnuts.

Photo opposite
Apricot Caroling Tree, this page
Apricot Calico Cookies, page 20

PANETONE

2 packages dry yeast
4¼ to 4¾ c. all-purpose flour
½ c. milk, scalded
½ c. warm water (110°-115°)
1½ t. anise seed
¼ c. soft butter
½ c. sugar
1 t. salt
2 eggs, room temperature
¾ t. vanilla
⅓ c. cut-up candied fruit
½ c. chopped nuts
2 T. pine nuts, if desired
½ c. raisins, dark or golden
1 egg, beaten
1 T. water

Stir yeast into 1½ cups flour in large mixing bowl. Measure milk, water, anise seed, butter, sugar and salt into a saucepan. Heat until warm (120°-130°), stirring constantly.

Pour into bowl. Add eggs and vanilla. Beat ½ minute at low speed, scraping bowl constantly. Beat 3 more minutes at high speed. Add candied fruit, nuts and raisins. Gradually add enough additional flour to form a soft dough. Turn onto lightly floured board. Knead until smooth. Place dough in greased bowl. Turn over. Cover. Let rise on a rack over hot water for 1 to 1½ hours, until doubled and a dent is left when finger is pressed deep into side of dough. Punch down dough. Let rest 10 minutes. Divide dough into 2 pieces and shape each into a ball. Place on opposite corners of a large greased baking sheet. Flatten tops of balls slightly with knuckles. Let loaves rise again until doubled, 45 to 60 minutes. Just before baking, brush loaves with 1 beaten egg mixed with 1 tablespoon water. Bake in preheated 375° oven 30 to 40 minutes or until well browned. Remove from pan; cool on racks. Makes 2 loaves.

APRICOT STICKY BUNS

See color photo, page 39

1 13¾-oz. package hot roll mix
½ c. finely diced dried apricots
¼ c. water
¼ c. sugar
2 T. butter or margarine, softened
¼ c. blanched almonds
Confectioners' Sugar Glaze (optional)

Prepare hot roll mix according to package directions; let rise as directed. While dough is rising, combine dried apricots, water and sugar in saucepan. Bring to a boil and simmer for 15 minutes, uncovered, until most of liquid has evaporated and apricots are tender. Remove from heat and stir in butter and chopped almonds. Set aside to cool. Punch dough down and roll out on lightly floured board to form a 12 x 10-inch rectangle. Spread dough with cooled apricot mixture. Beginning at long side, roll up jelly roll fashion. Seal edge tightly. Cut into 12 rolls, each 1 inch thick. Transfer to well-greased muffin tins. Cover and let rise until a finger pushed into the dough leaves a dent. Bake at 350° for 30 minutes or until browned. Remove from pan immediately. If desired, drizzle Confectioners' Sugar Glaze over warm buns.

CONFECTIONERS' SUGAR GLAZE

1 T. butter or margarine, softened
1 c. confectioners' sugar
3 T. milk

Combine ingredients and blend thoroughly.

RAISIN BREAD

2 c. raisins   1½ c. sugar
2 c. water   Dash of salt
2 t. baking soda   1½ t. vanilla
2 eggs   3 c. flour
1 c. nutmeats

Combine raisins, water and soda; bring to a boil. Cool completely. Beat together eggs, sugar, salt and vanilla. Add raisin mixture with flour and eggs. Fold in nuts. Bake at 350° for 1 hour.

Gladys Daniels

Make your favorite sweet bread dough into a special holiday treat by forming it into a star, wreath or cane shape. If you feel particularly ambitious, try shaping an angel or Christmas tree. Decorate with colored icing.

Yeast breads usually have the best flavor the day they are baked, so make them as close to the gift day as possible.

Stiff raised breads can be baked on cookie sheets instead of in pans. This allows more variety in shaping the bread. For a rich golden crust, brush with an egg wash made by lightly beating together one egg yolk and a tablespoon of water.

Give a loaf of homemade bread on a breadboard. Wrap it in clear plastic, decorate with ribbon and a sprig of evergreen.

Make breads in fancy shapes by baking them in cans, molds or other unusual containers. Let your imagination be your guide. You can use any oven-proof container that is open on the top so the bread has room to rise.

MARMALADE-NUT BREAD

2½ c. unsifted flour, stirred before
   measuring
⅓ c. sugar
3½ t. baking powder
 1 t. salt
 1 c. coarsely chopped walnuts
 1 egg
 1 c. sweet orange marmalade
 1 c. orange juice
 3 T. vegetable oil

In large mixing bowl, thoroughly stir together flour, sugar, baking powder and salt.

Add walnuts; toss to coat evenly. In medium bowl, beat egg slightly; stir in marmalade, orange juice and vegetable oil. Add to flour mixture; stir only until dry ingredients are moistened. Divide batter evenly between 2 well-greased loaf pans, 8½ x 4½ x 2½-inches. Bake in preheated 350° oven 1 hour or until wooden pick inserted in center comes out clean. Cool in pans on rack 10 minutes; remove from pans; cool thoroughly on rack. Wrap tightly in foil. Allow flavors to mellow overnight before serving.

STOLLEN

2 packages active dry yeast
¼ c. warm water
1½ c. milk
½ c. sugar
1½ t. salt
¾ c. butter
2 c. sifted flour
3 eggs, beaten
½ t. ground cardamom
½ c. seedless raisins
1 c. sliced candied red and green cherries
4 c. sifted flour (about)
  Melted butter

Soften active dry yeast in warm water. Scald milk; stir in sugar, salt and butter; cool to lukewarm. Mix in 2 cups flour, yeast, eggs, cardamom and fruit. Add enough remaining flour to make a stiff dough. Knead on floured surface; place in greased bowl; grease top of dough; cover. Let rise until doubled. Punch dough down; cover; let rest 10 minutes. Divide into three equal parts. Shape each piece into a 10 x 8-inch oval; fold lengthwise. Place in greased shallow pans. Let rise until almost doubled. Bake at 350° about 30 minutes. Frost and decorate if desired. Makes 3 stollen.

HONEY WHEAT BREAD

1 package dry yeast
1 c. warm water
½ c. honey
1 T. salt
2 T. shortening
1 c. milk, scalded
3 c. whole wheat flour
3 c. white flour

Dissolve yeast in warm water. Combine honey, salt, shortening and hot milk; stir until shortening melts. Cool to lukewarm. Add yeast mixture. Gradually add flours. Knead until satiny, 8-10 minutes. Place in greased bowl; cover. Let rise in warm place for 2-2½ hours. Punch down; let rise again. Shape into 2 loaves. Put in greased pans, 9 x 5 inches. Let rise until tops of loaves are above pan edges. Bake at 350° for 50 to 60 minutes.

DANISH COFFEE CAKE

2 c. sugar
1 T. cinnamon
1 c. shortening
4 eggs, separated
¼ t. salt
3 c. flour
3 t. baking powder
1 c. milk
1 t. vanilla or almond extract

Make a mixture of ½ cup sugar and cinnamon. Mix well and set aside. Cream shortening, gradually add 1½ cups sugar and cream well. Add the egg yolks singly and beat. Combine flour and baking powder; add to creamed mixture alternately with milk. Combine salt and egg whites and beat until stiff. Add flavoring and mix well. Then fold the 2 mixtures together. Spoon layers of batter into a well-oiled bundt pan, with cinnamon mixture on top of each layer of batter. Try to use all the cinnamon mixture. Bake 1 hour in a 375° oven. Let cool 10 minutes. Loosen sides with a knife and turn out on rack to cool completely. Sift confectioners' sugar over top and sides of cake.

Edna M. Wagner

SAFFRON BREAD

2½ c. milk
½ lb. butter
1 package saffron
1 t. salt
2 oz. yeast
1 c. sugar
2 eggs
8 c. flour
1½ c. seeded raisins

Heat milk, add butter to melt and cool to lukewarm. Dissolve saffron and yeast in 1 teaspoon milk. Add to milk—blend in beaten eggs. Stir in flour until sticky and knead in rest of flour along with raisins. Keep kneading until smooth, firm and glossy. Let rise in greased bowl until double in size. Place on board and shape into braided loaves. Let rise 1 hour after placing in bread tins. Bake at 375° for 45 minutes. Makes 2 loaves.

Jill Susan Dalbey

Mexican Fiesta Bread

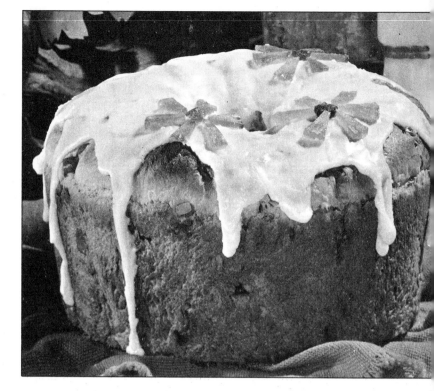

MEXICAN FIESTA BREAD

4½ to 5½ c. flour
2 packages dry yeast
⅔ c. milk
½ c. water
½ c. butter
⅓ c. sugar
1 t. salt
3 eggs, room temperature
1 c. candied fruit
1 c. chopped nuts
   Vegetable oil
   Powdered Sugar Frosting
   Candied fruit or nuts

Stir together 1¾ cups flour and yeast. Heat milk, water, butter, sugar and salt over low heat to 120 to 130°, stirring to blend. Add liquid ingredients to flour-yeast mixture and beat until smooth, about 3 minutes on medium speed of mixer. Blend in eggs. Add 1 cup flour and beat 1 minute on medium speed. Stir in fruit, nuts and more flour to make a moderately soft dough. (Dough will be sticky.) Turn onto lightly floured surface and knead until smooth and satiny, about 5 to 10 minutes. Cover dough; let rest 20 minutes. Roll into 22 x 12-inch rectangle. Roll up jelly roll fashion, starting at 22-inch end. Seal bottom; pinch ends together to form a ring. Place seam down in greased 10-inch tube pan. Brush with oil; let rise in warm place (80 to 85°) until doubled, about 1 hour. Bake in preheated 375° oven 50 to 60 minutes, or until done. Remove from pan immediately. Cool. Frost with Confectioners' Sugar Frosting; decorate with candied fruit or nuts. One 10-inch tube.

CONFECTIONERS' SUGAR FROSTING

1 c. confectioners' sugar, sifted
5 t. milk

Blend together sugar and milk.

QUICK COFFEE CAKE

¼ c. shortening
½ c. sugar
1 egg
½ c. milk
1½ c. flour
1½ t. baking powder
½ t. nutmeg
½ t. salt
½ t. vanilla

Beat egg slightly; add shortening, and sugar and mix well. Stir in milk. Sift together flour, baking powder, nutmeg and salt. Add to egg mixture. Stir in vanilla. Pour into greased and floured 9-inch square pan. Sprinkle with Brown Sugar Topping. Bake at 375° for 25-30 minutes.

BROWN SUGAR TOPPING

½ c. brown sugar
1½ T. butter, melted
1 T. flour
½ t. cinnamon

Combine ingredients until well blended.

48

HUNGARIAN CHRISTMAS BREAD

4½ to 5 c. flour
2 packages dry yeast
½ c. milk
½ c. water
½ c. sugar
¼ c. oil
2 t. salt
2 eggs
1 12-oz. can poppy-seed cake and pastry filling
1 c. golden raisins
1 egg, room temperature
Poppy seeds

Stir together 2 cups flour and yeast. Heat milk, water, sugar, oil and salt over low heat to 120° to 130°, stirring to blend. Add liquid ingredients to flour mixture and beat until smooth, about 2 minutes on medium speed of electric mixer. Blend in 2 eggs. Add 1 cup flour and beat 1 minute. Stir in enough additional flour to make a moderately stiff dough. Turn onto lightly floured board and knead until smooth and satiny, 5 to 8 minutes. Cover with pan or bowl; let rest 30 minutes. Divide in half. Roll each half into 10 x 12-inch rectangle. Spread with poppy-seed filling, leaving 1-inch margin on all sides; sprinkle with raisins. Roll up jelly roll fashion. Seal bottom and ends securely. Place on greased baking sheet, seam side down. Make shallow, diagonal cuts across top. Beat egg; brush tops and side of dough. Sprinkle generously with poppy seeds. Let rise in warm place (80 to 85°) until doubled, about 45 minutes. Bake in preheated 350° oven 30 to 40 minutes. 2 loaves.

CHRISTMAS CANE COFFEECAKE

1 package active dry yeast
¼ c. warm water
1 c. milk
2 eggs, beaten
4¼ c. sifted flour
½ c. sugar
1 t. salt
1 t. grated lemon rind
1 c. cold butter

Soften yeast in warm water. Scald milk; cool to lukewarm; blend in softened yeast and eggs. Combine flour, sugar, salt and lemon rind. Cut in butter until mixture resembles coarse crumbs. Add yeast mixture; mix well. Dough is soft. Place in greased bowl; cover; refrigerate overnight. Divide dough into thirds. Roll each third on floured surface into a 6 x 15-inch rectangle. Spread ⅓ of Cranberry Filling lengthwise down center of dough in a strip 2 inches wide. Cut dough with scissors from both outer edges toward filling. Make cuts every ½ inch. Do not cut too close to filling. Crisscross pieces of dough over filling. Place on greased cookie sheet. Stretch shaped dough to about 20 inches; curve top to form a cane. Let rise about ½ hour. Bake at 375° about 25 minutes. Frost with thin confectioners' sugar glaze and decorate if desired. Makes 3 canes.

CRANBERRY FILLING

1½ c. finely chopped cranberries
¾ c. sugar
½ c. raisins
⅓ c. chopped pecans
⅓ c. honey
1 t. grated orange rind

Combine all ingredients. Cook over medium heat about 5 minutes. Stir. Cool.

SNACKS

BLUE CHEESE BALL
See color photo opposite

1 8-oz. package cream cheese, softened
4 oz. blue cheese, crumbled
¼ c. chopped green onion
1 t. lemon juice
1 clove garlic, minced
¼ t. pepper
¼ t. salt
½ c. chopped parsley

Combine all ingredients except parsley; blend well. Form mixture into a ball. Roll in chopped parsley. Chill thoroughly.

CHEDDAR CHEESE BALL

1 8-oz. package cream cheese, softened
4 oz. sharp cheddar cheese, grated
1 T. chopped pimiento
¼ t. cayenne pepper
¼ t. salt
1 T. chopped green pepper
1 t. chopped onion
1½ t. Worcestershire sauce
Red Walnuts

Put cream cheese into small mixing bowl; beat until smooth and creamy. Add remaining ingredients except Red Walnuts. Blend well. Shape into a ball, roll in nuts and chill.

RED WALNUTS

½ t. red food coloring
1½ T. warm water
1 c. finely chopped walnuts

Dissolve food coloring in water. Sprinkle over walnuts and stir until all nuts are red. Spread nuts on an ungreased cookie sheet and bake at 250° for 10-15 minutes. Do not allow nuts to brown. If walnuts are not completely dry, turn off oven and allow nuts to remain inside until dry. Cool thoroughly.

SMOKED BEEF DIP

1 t. minced onion
1 T. sherry
1 8-oz. package cream cheese
2 T. mayonnaise
¼ c. stuffed olives, minced
1 3-oz. package smoked beef, minced

Soak onion in sherry until soft. Add remaining ingredients.

Mrs. Roger C. Wilder

CHEESE POPCORN

Vegetable oil
Popcorn
1 t. paprika
1 t. salt or onion or garlic salt
⅓ c. grated cheese

Pour oil to depth of about ⅛ inch in pan. Pour in enough popcorn to cover bottom of pan 1 kernel deep. Cover tightly and place over high heat, shaking until corn stops popping. Combine paprika, salt and grated cheese. Sprinkle over hot corn, mixing so that all kernels are coated.

Edith Pikelny

NIBBLE MIX

1 lb. butter, melted
6 T. Worcestershire sauce
2 t. garlic salt
2 t. onion salt

Place butter in a baking dish and put in roaster or oven to melt. Stir in Worcestershire sauce. Add small boxes of the following.

Rice Chex	Wheat Chex
Cheerios	Pretzel sticks

1 can mixed nuts

Sprinkle with the garlic and onion salts. Mix. Bake at 225° for 1 hour, stirring occasionally.

Edith Shaska

RELISHES, JELLIES AND PRESERVES

HAPPY HOLIDAYS CONSERVE

2 30-oz. cans apricot halves
1 c. glacé mixed fruits
½ c. quartered red glacé cherries
1½ c. sugar
¼ t. salt
¼ t. nutmeg
1 T. grated lemon peel
1 T. grated orange peel
1½ c. finely chopped pecans

Drain apricots, reserving 1½ cups syrup. Coarsely chop the apricots. Place apricots, the 1½ cups apricot syrup and all remaining ingredients except pecans in 6-quart pot. Bring to a boil, stirring occasionally. Reduce heat; simmer uncovered about 25 minutes or until thickened and of desired consistency. Stir in pecans; ladle into hot sterilized jars and seal and lid or cover with paraffin according to manufacturer's directions. Makes about 6 cups.

TILLIE'S WATERMELON PICKLES

7 lbs. watermelon rinds
7 c. sugar
2 c. vinegar
  Cinnamon sticks
  Whole cloves
  Maraschino cherries

Put melon rinds in a large kettle; cover with water. Boil until tender. Combine sugar and vinegar; bring to a boil and pour over rinds. Add cinnamon and cloves to taste. The next morning, drain and bring syrup to a boil again; pour over rinds. On the third morning, drain again. Cut rind into desired shapes. Pack in jars and pour hot syrup over. If desired, add a few maraschino cherries. Seal. *Note:* The cherries will fade if pickles are not used for a long time.

Dorothy Benson

APPLE JELLY

3 lbs. ripe, tart apples
3 c. water
2 T. lemon juice
3 c. sugar

Cut washed, unpeeled, uncored apples into small pieces. Add water, cover and bring to a boil. Simmer for 20 to 25 minutes, until apples are soft. Extract juice; measure. Combine 4 cups apple juice, lemon juice and sugar in a large kettle; stir well. Boil over high heat until mixture reaches 220° and jelly forms a sheet on a metal spoon. Skim off foam; pour jelly immediately into hot sterilized glasses. Seal.

MINT JELLY

1 c. firmly packed mint leaves
1 c. boiling water
3 lbs. ripe, tart apples
3 c. water
2 T. lemon juice
3 c. sugar
  Green food coloring

Pour boiling water over mint leaves and let stand for 1 hour. Press the juice from the leaves. Measure 8 tablespoons of mint extract into a large saucepan. Proceed as for Apple Jelly (above). Before pouring jelly into glasses, tint with food coloring.

BRANDIED APRICOTS
See color photo, page 35

2 30-oz. cans whole apricots
¾ c. brandy
2 cinnamon sticks, broken
6 whole cloves

Drain apricots, reserving 2 cups syrup. In medium saucepan combine syrup with brandy and spices. Bring to a boil, reduce heat and simmer uncovered for 15 minutes. Pour hot syrup over drained apricots in bowl. Cover and chill for 3 to 4 hours or until serving time, or pack into jars immediately.

CHERRY JAM

4 c. pitted sour cherries
¼ c. water
5 c. sugar
1 6-oz. bottle liquid pectin

Combine cherries and water in large kettle. Bring to a boil, then simmer for 15 minutes. Stir in sugar. Bring mixture to a boil; then boil, stirring, for 3 minutes. Stir in pectin. Remove from heat; stir and skim for 5 minutes. Pour into hot sterilized jars. Seal at once.

SWEET ONION RINGS

8 c. sliced onions (about 3 lbs.)
  Boiling water
1 c. distilled white vinegar
1 c. granulated sugar
2 t. salt
½ t. mustard seed

Cook onions in boiling water for 4 minutes; drain. Combine vinegar and remaining ingredients in large saucepan; bring to boil. Add onions; simmer 4 minutes. Continue simmering while quickly packing one clean, hot jar at a time. Fill to within ½ inch of top, making sure vinegar solution covers onions. Cap each jar at once. Process 5 minutes in boiling water bath. Makes 2 to 3 pints.

Sweet Onion Rings, this page

Pack an assortment of jellies in a small wooden crate. Attach a wire handle and, if you wish, stencil a Christmas greeting on the side slats.

Give jellies in decorative heat-proof jars or glasses. Be sure to label with variety, date and your name. If you wish, decorate the jar with colorful stickers or photographs of the kind of fruit used in the jelly.

For a lasting remembrance, give pepper relish with a pepper plant, mint jelly with a mint plant, etc. Long after the cooked gift is gone, the plant will be a reminder of your thoughtfulness. And if you attach the recipe, the recipient will be doubly pleased: she'll be able to make her own relish or jelly from the plant when it matures.

A mouthwatering gift combination is a jar of homemade preserves with a loaf of homemade bread. This is one gift that probably won't last through the holidays, so pack the preserves in an especially pretty jar.

GRAPE BURGUNDY JELLY

See color photo opposite

1½ lbs. fully ripe Concord grapes
¼ c. water
5 c. sugar
1 c. Burgundy wine
½ bottle liquid fruit pectin (3 fl. oz.)

Thoroughly crush the grapes, one layer at a time. Add ¼ cup water; bring to a boil and simmer, covered, for 10 minutes. Place in jelly cloth or bag and squeeze out juice. Measure 2 cups into a large saucepan. Thoroughly mix sugar and wine into juice in saucepan. Place over high heat and bring just to a boil, stirring constantly. Remove from heat. Stir in fruit pectin at once. Skim off foam with metal spoon; pour jelly quickly into glasses. Cover at once with ⅛ inch hot paraffin. Makes about 5½ cups or 7 glasses, 6 fluid ounces each.

CRANBERRY CLARET JELLY

See color photo opposite

3½ c. sugar
1 c. cranberry juice cocktail
1 c. claret wine
½ bottle liquid fruit pectin (3 fl. oz.)

Measure sugar, cranberry juice cocktail and wine into a large saucepan. Stir over medium heat, bringing mixture to just below the boiling point. Continue stirring until the sugar is dissolved, about 5 minutes. Remove from heat. At once stir in fruit pectin and mix well. Skim off foam with metal spoon and pour quickly into glasses. Cover at once with ⅛ inch hot paraffin. Makes about 4 cups or 5 glasses, 6 fluid ounces each.

ORANGE MARMALADE

5 oranges
2 grapefruit
12 c. cold water
8½ c. sugar
Juice of 2 lemons

Slice fruit thin and cut in small pieces. Add water and boil for 1 hour or until fruit is soft. Add sugar and boil for 45 minutes. Add lemon juice. Boil until thick and 2 drops fall from spoon when tested. Pour into glasses and seal with paraffin.

Bina Sterling

APRICOT MUSCATEL JELLY

See color photo opposite

3½ c. sugar
1 c. muscatel wine
1 c. apricot nectar
2 T. lemon juice
½ bottle liquid fruit pectin (3 fl. oz.)

Measure sugar, wine, nectar and juice into large saucepan. Stir over medium heat, bringing mixture to just below the boiling point. Continue stirring until the sugar is dissolved, about 5 minutes. Remove from heat. At once stir in fruit pectin and mix well. Skim off foam with metal spoon and pour quickly into glasses. Cover at once with ⅛ inch hot paraffin. Makes about 4 cups or 5 glasses, 6 fluid ounces each.

BAKED APPLE BUTTER

10 lbs. apples
1½ qts. cider
1 T. cloves
1 T. cinnamon
1 T. nutmeg
5 lbs. sugar

Peel, core and quarter apples, adding enough water to cover. Simmer in a large pot until they reach sauce consistency. Stir in the cider, cloves, cinnamon, nutmeg and sugar. Pour the mixture into an enameled roasting pan. Cover. Place in a 350° oven. Stir occasionally, until the mixture boils. Then turn down the oven to 250° and bake 5 hours, or overnight. Ladle the thick apple butter into sterilized jars and seal for storage.

Rosalie L. Kennedy

RED PEPPER RELISH

1 peck red peppers
3 lbs. white sugar
3 pts. white vinegar
2 oz. mustard seeds

Remove seeds from peppers and grind peppers with a fine cutter. Wash mustard seeds and soak in hot water about 2 to 3 hours. Place all ingredients together and cook slowly until mixture jellies from a spoon. Watch carefully and stir often so it does not scorch. Use low heat.

Eleanore B. Malec

Photo opposite
Apricot Muscatel Jelly, this page
Cranberry Claret Jelly, this page
Grape Burgundy Jelly, this page
Lemon Fruit-Jell Candy, page 11
Cranberry Jelly Candy, page 11

From our house
to your house
for this
holiday season
B.

BEVERAGES

HOT CRANBERRY PUNCH

4 c. water
½ lb. cranberries
2 c. sugar
1 large orange
1½ inches stick cinnamon
1 t. whole cloves
1 qt. apple juice
1 pt. apple wine

Combine water, cranberries and sugar in a saucepan. Cut orange into quarters and add. Combine spices in a cheesecloth bag; add. Bring mixture to a boil and simmer for 5 minutes, constantly crushing berries with a spoon. Remove spices and orange sections. Strain cranberry mixture. Set berries aside for use as a relish. Combine liquid and apple juice; heat to boiling. Add apple wine and heat but do not boil. Serve immediately in a heated bowl. *Note:* When making this punch as a gift, prepare as above except do not add wine. Give punch and wine in separate bottles; include directions for heating and serving.

SPARKLING PUNCH

½ c. sugar
1 c. water
4 cinnamon sticks
6 whole cloves
1 c. lemon juice, chilled
½ c. lime juice, chilled
2 c. orange juice, chilled
1 46-oz. can apricot nectar, chilled
6 7-oz. bottles 7-Up, chilled
1 lemon
1 lime

Combine sugar, water, cinnamon and cloves in saucepan, simmer for 5 minutes. Set aside for several hours or longer. Strain syrup; discard spices. At serving time, combine syrup and chilled juices in a large punch bowl. Slowly pour in 7-Up. Add ice if desired. Garnish with slices of lemon and lime.

MINT PUNCH

½ c. fresh mint
1 qt. water
4 c. sugar
¼ t. salt
¼ t. green food coloring
1 qt. lemon juice
4 16-oz. bottles ginger ale

Reserve a few sprigs of mint for garnish. Combine remaining mint with 1 cup water in blender. Blend for 30 seconds. Combine mint mixture with sugar and remaining water; simmer for 5 minutes. Strain; add salt, food coloring and lemon juice. Chill thoroughly. To serve, mix mint mixture gently with chilled ginger ale. Garnish with reserved mint.

CHRISTMAS PUNCH

2 c. boiling water
¾ c. sugar
½ t. cinnamon
¼ t. nutmeg
¼ t. salt
2 16-oz. bottles cranberry juice cocktail
1 6-oz. can frozen pineapple concentrate
1 c. cold water
2 12-oz. bottles carbonated water

Pour boiling water over sugar, cinnamon, nutmeg and salt; stir to dissolve. Chill thoroughly. To serve, combine with remaining ingredients in punch bowl. Add ice if desired.

PINK FRUIT PUNCH

6 c. sugar
6 c. water
2 packages strawberry Kool-Aid
1 12-oz. can frozen lemon juice
1 12-oz. can frozen orange juice
1 46-oz. can pineapple juice

Combine sugar and water. Boil for 5 minutes. Cool. Add remaining ingredients. When ready to serve the punch add 2 quarts of ginger ale plus enough water to make three gallons.

Mrs. Robert E. O'Leary

BLOSSOM BOUQUET

1 qt. elderberry blossoms
1 gallon boiling water
3 lbs. sugar
½ c. yeast
1 lb. raisins
1 orange
1 lemon

Soak blossoms in boiling water for 1½ hours. Then strain and boil for 10 minutes with sugar. Cool to lukewarm. Add yeast, raisins and cut up orange and lemon. Pour into a 5-gallon crock and allow to ferment for at least 24 hours. Mixture may take up to 6 days to clarify. When fermenting stage is done, wine can be bottled, but do not cap immediately. Place in a cool basement. The longer the wine is stored, the more delicious and clear it becomes.

Marie De Amhoggi

GRAPE WINE

3 6-oz. cans frozen grape juice
5 c. sugar
1 t. dry yeast

Combine ingredients; mix until dissolved. Pour into a gallon jug; fill with water to near top. Tie a balloon tightly onto the top of jug. Let mixture stand 21 days, then bottle.

Gertrude Hogate

GRAPEFRUIT WINE

2 qts. grapefruit juice
1 lb. sugar

Combine juice and sugar. Pour mixture into jug; cover with 2 layers or cheesecloth. Place jug in a small pan to catch overflow. Let stand at room temperature for 4 weeks or until fermenting has stopped. Strain wine through cheesecloth, avoiding the sediment. Strain again through filter paper. Pour into bottles; cork.

Homemade wine is a Christmas gift that's sure to be appreciated. But it needs sufficient time to ferment, so don't try to make wine as a last-minute Christmas gift.

An attractive and lasting gift to complement a bottle of homemade wine is an ice bucket.

Wines or punches can be decorated with pieces of the same fruit used in making them. If it's a small fruit, like grapes or cranberries, attach a few pieces to the ribbon you use to tie the gift. If it's a large fruit, you may prefer to decorate the label with colorful photographs of the fruit instead.

A decanter is a lovely, lasting gift to go with a bottle of homemade wine. If you're giving punch to a special friend, give a punchbowl too.

Punches that do not include carbonated beverages can be prepared in advance and given in a decorative bottle. For punches with carbonated ingredients, prepare the rest of the punch, bottle it and give it along with unopened bottles of carbonated beverages. Be sure to include directions for mixing and serving.

DECORATING WITH FOOD

FESTIVE APRICOT ORNAMENT

See color photo opposite

1 Styrofoam ball, about 4 inches in diameter
  Round toothpicks
  White glue
7 inches orange cord for hanging-loop
  Straight pins
  Dark raisins
1 10½-oz. package miniature marshmallows
1 8-oz. package California dried apricot halves
½ yard ribbon, ½ inch in diameter (green or orange)

Make tiny hole in top of ball with toothpick; fill with glue. Tie cord to make 3½-inch loop; push straight pin through knot and into hole in top of ball with toothpick half. Leave toothpick in ball to secure loop; let dry thoroughly. Attach a row of dark raisins around center of ball with straight pins. You will need about 2 dozen raisins. On both sides of raisin row, make a row of miniature marshmallows; attach with straight pins. Reserve 2 apricot halves. Cut the remaining halves into two pieces each. Working from marshmallow row, arrange apricot semi-circles in circular fashion, with straight cut side against marshmallows. Be sure to place apricot pieces end to end. Repeat with two more rows. Make an apricot flower in center by arranging three apricot pieces in a circle, ends touching, forming a triangular space in center. Secure each petal with a straight pin. Make center of flower by placing one dried apricot half on top of petals; place raisin in center of apricot and attach both with straight pin. Decorate other side of ball in same way. Tie ribbon into 4-inch bow; attach with pins near hanging loop. Makes a festive tree hanging!

AN OLD-FASHIONED BELL

See color photo opposite

1 Styrofoam bell, about 3 inches in diameter
  Round toothpicks
  White glue
  Orange tassel, about 3 inches long
  Straight pins
7 inches orange cord for hanging loop
  Orange beads, about ¼ inch long
  Orange spray paint (optional)
  Round orange sequins, about ⅝ inch in diameter
1 8-oz. package California dried apricot halves

Make tiny hole in the center of both top and bottom of bell with toothpick; fill with glue. Fasten tassel by pushing straight pin through tassel, then into bottom of bell with toothpick half; leave pick in bell to secure tassel. Attach hanging loop by tying cord to make 3½-inch loop; push straight pin through knot and into hole in top of bell with toothpick half. Leave toothpick in bell to secure loop. Let dry thoroughly. Spray bell with orange paint, if desired; hang on nail until completely dry. (Paint avoids white Styrofoam showing through.) Decorate the top of bell with two circular rows of sequins as follows: Thread straight pin through one orange bead, then through sequin; attach in circular pattern, covering top 2-inch area of bell around cord loop. Cover remaining surface of bell with dried apricot halves arranged in circular pattern; secure apricot halves in place with pins, inserted at top of each apricot half. Hang in window or on the Christmas tree. Or, turn it into a "Kissin' Bell": Using straight pins, fasten a spring of mistletoe near tassel of bell. Hang with thumbtack in doorway.

Photo opposite
An Old-Fashioned Bell
Festive Apricot Ornament

When mailing decorations made of food, use a sturdy cardboard box and plenty of filler. Be sure to mark the package FRAGILE.

Trim-A-Tree Cookies don't have to be restricted to use on the tree itself. To give your home a festive holiday look, try hanging them from a stairway banister along with sprigs of artificial holly.

For a last-minute gift with a personal touch, tie pieces of candy to an inexpensive artificial wreath. Children will love it!

Decorations made of perishable food can be used for only one season—be sure to explain this when giving them to friends. You can preserve some decorations by shellacking them.

If you give Trim-A-Tree Cookies, include an airtight container for storing them between holiday seasons. Otherwise they will become soft or soggy.

POPCORN TREE

½ c. water
½ c. light corn syrup
1 c. sugar
8 c. popped corn
1 Styrofoam cone, 12 inches high
  Wooden toothpicks
  Gumdrops

Combine water, corn syrup and sugar in saucepan. Cook without stirring over medium heat until syrup reaches soft ball stage (240°). Pour syrup over popcorn, mixing with hands until popcorn is coated. Quickly form small amounts of mixture into balls of various sizes. To assemble tree, place a toothpick in each ball and stick into cone to form tree. Use smaller balls for the top of the tree. Insert gumdrops for ornaments.

SPICE BALL

1 Styrofoam ball, 3-4 inches in diameter
  White glue
  Whole cloves
  Whole anise seeds
  Whole poppy seeds
  Whole celery seeds
  Whole caraway seeds
  Ground cinnamon
  Ground paprika
  Ground mustard
  Curry powder
1 sprig plastic holly or pine
7½ inches red velvet ribbon

With a pencil or crayon, mark Styrofoam ball into 8 equal sections. Along these lines, insert whole cloves to outline the sections. Cover one section at a time with white glue, then sprinkle with one of the spices until Styrofoam is completely covered. Alternate sections of whole and ground spices. Let the ball dry, then decorate with a sprig of holly or pine. Make a loop of the ribbon and pin it to the ball so it can be hung. *Note:* Different spices can be substituted for those listed. Experiment until you find a combination with the fragrance and appearance you like best.

GINGHAM WREATH

1 Styrofoam wreath, about 4 inches in diameter
  Round toothpicks
  White glue
7 inches orange cord, for hanging-loop
  Straight pins
1 8-oz. package California dried apricot halves
  Gold foil decorator leaves
1 yard 1½-inch gingham ribbon (green or gold check)
  Staples for bow

Make tiny hole in top of wreath with toothpick; fill with glue. Tie cord to make 3½-inch loop; push straight pin through knot and into hole in top of wreath with toothpick half. Leave toothpick in wreath to secure loop; let dry thoroughly. Cut 12 apricot halves into 2 pieces each. Attach 2 semi-circle pieces with straight pins, directly across from each other on outside edge of wreath, giving scalloped edge to wreath. Some Styrofoam area will show between the 2 apricot pieces. Place apricot half on top of these 2 pieces, covering this white area and forming a cluster of apricots. Repeat to make 11 or 12 more clusters, attached end to end. Entire outside surface of wreath will be covered. Attach gold foil leaves between each cluster of apricots. To make bow, cut 3 pieces of ribbon one 8 inches, one 10 inches and one 15 inches long. Using 8-inch piece, make a loop 3½ inches in length, allowing ends of ribbon to meet in center of loop overlapping about 1 inch. Secure with staple. Repeat with 10-inch piece, making a loop about 4½ inches long. To form bow, place 3½-inch loop on top of 4½-inch loop. Pinch loops together in center, then tie with the 15-inch piece of ribbon around loops. Secure bow to bottom of wreath with straight pins.

TRIM-A-TREE COOKIES

See color photo, page 62

4 c. unsifted flour
1 c. salt
1½ c. water
  Wire for hooks
  Water colors, Tempera or Acrylic paints
  Clear fixative

Combine flour, salt and water in a large mixing bowl. Mix thoroughly with hands. Add more water if dough is too stiff. Shape into a ball. Knead dough about 5 minutes or until smooth. Keep covered with foil or plastic wrap as dough dries out quickly. Roll dough about ¼ inch thick on lightly floured surface. Cut into desired shapes with sharp knife or cookie cutter. Place on ungreased cookie sheets. Insert wire into cookie. A paper clip or hair pin will also work. This will serve as a hook for hanging on tree. Bake in oven 350° until thoroughly dried and hard, about 1 hour depending on thickness. Cool. Paint as desired. Allow to dry. Spray completely with fixative. *Note:* This recipe must not be doubled or halved. Cookies often puff up during baking. **These cookies are not edible.**

WAGON BREAD LOAF

1 loaf frozen bread dough
4 cooked doughnuts
  High gloss varnish
  White glue
  Wooden picks
  Long pretzel
  Small plastic flowers

Follow instructions for thawing bread. Bake in 150° oven 6 hours. Bake the cooked doughnuts in 150° oven 3 hours. Let both set out 3 days to dry. Brush with 1 coat of varnish, letting dry 24 hours; repeat varnish step two more times. For wheels, bore a hole with a skewer into doughnuts and sides of bread. Place wooden picks in bored hole; attach and glue. Make another hole in center front of bread for handle and attach pretzel with glue. Glue flowers into holes of doughnut. Pour glue down top center of bread and lay 10 or 12 flowers (stems cut off) on top of the glue.

61

Trim-A-Tree Cookies, page 61

Yuletime brings to you and me
The season for a cookie tree
Bedecked with goodies to bring surprise
And a wishful shine to childrens' eyes.

On a low table our cookie tree stands
Within the reach of eager hands,
A glimmering, shimmering treasury
Of Christmas hospitality.

Mary A. Selden

INDEX